The anti-Poor Law movement
1834-44

To my parents

Nicholas C Edsall

Assistant Professor of History
University of Virginia

The anti-Poor Law movement
1834–44

Manchester University Press

Rowman & Littlefield, Inc., New Jersey

Published by
Manchester University Press
316–324 Oxford Road
Manchester M13 9NR

ISBN 0 7190 0430 6

U.S.A
Rowman & Littlefield, Inc.
81 Adams Drive
Totowa
New Jersey, 07512

U.S.A. ISBN 0 87471 026 X

*Printed by Butler and Tanner Ltd
Frome and London*

Contents

Acknowledgments

First on any list of acknowledgments must come the staffs of the Public Records Office and the British Museum Newspaper Library at Colindale, the two institutions where the greater part of the research for this book was done. Less frequent but no less valuable assistance was given by the staffs of the library of the London School of Economics, the Goldsmith's Library and the Lancashire County Records Office. My thanks are also due to research librarians and town clerks throughout southern Lancashire and the central West Riding of Yorkshire who more than lived up to the reputation of the North for friendly helpfulness.

Financial assistance without which it would have been exceedingly difficult to complete this work was provided on more than one occasion by the Research Grants Committee of the University of Virginia.

The advice and counsel of Prof. A. H. John of the London School of Economics and of Prof. J. D. Chambers of Nottingham University were enormously helpful in the difficult formative stages of the work. And finally I should like to record the great debt I owe to the late Prof. David Owen of Harvard University. The affection and respect which he inspired in all of those lucky enough to work with him are, I hope, reflected in some measure in what follows.

Abbreviations

B.P.P.	*British Parliamentary Papers*
L.I.	*Leeds Intelligencer*
L.T.	*Leeds Times*
M.G.	*Manchester Guardian*
M.S.A.	*Manchester and Salford Advertiser*
N.S.	*Northern Star*
P.L.C.	Poor Law Commissioners

I The debate on the New Poor Law

Prior to the creation of the modern welfare state, no body of legislation was of greater importance to the average Englishman than the laws for the maintenance and relief of the poor. For the bulk of the population they represented a constant and often considerable burden in local taxes; for the poor they were, apart from private charity, the sole source of relief from distress, whether due to unemployment, illness, old age or numberless other causes. The very scope of these laws insured that they would be under constant scrutiny and subject to constant change, but of all the changes during their three-hundred-year history none was more important than that made by the Poor Law Amendment Act of 1834. Yet, great as its impact on the administration of public welfare was and was intended to be, this was not, by any means, the only source of its importance. It had, or was thought to have had, yet another significance. Many have seen it as a symbol of the ascendancy of the middle class and of middle-class views in British public life, as a sort of incarnation in legislative form of the ideas of the Philosophical Radicals, and, specifically, as 'the first victory of the Benthamites'.[1]

This is in large measure true, and true not only in the sense that later historians have so judged it, but also in the sense that men at that time believed it to be the case. Nonetheless, even had Bentham and the classical economists never lived, and even if there had been no sudden addition to middle-class influence in politics through Parliamentary reform, some major alteration in the Poor Laws would almost certainly have been enacted at this time, for there was, undeniably, a Poor Law problem. The cost of relief had been rising for between thirty and forty years; yet the results which might have made increased costs palatable—declining pauperism and social peace—had not been achieved. It appeared indeed that just the opposite was true. What few statistics were available pointed, though inconclusively, to an increase in pauperism; and, as for any hopes for social peace, they were shattered by the rural

---

[1] E. Halevy, *A History of the English People in the Nineteenth Century* (New York 1961), III, 210.

unrest of 1830. Thus at no time since the 1790s had poor relief been dead as an issue, and in 1831 and 1832 it was very much alive. It is therefore not surprising that, some time before the reform bill was passed, the government appointed a Royal Commission to investigate the Poor Laws. What would have resulted had there been no reform of Parliament is, of course, impossible to say. Parliament might well have settled for yet another measure of partial reform as it did in 1818. And certainly the Poor Law Amendment Act was no partial measure, no mere bit of tinkering with the system; it was, despite its title, not an amendment act at all, but what it was popularly called, a New Poor Law, and for that we may well hold the Benthamites responsible.

The story of the Poor Law Inquiry Commission and the means by which its recommendations were translated, more or less intact, into law do not fall within the scope of this work—such matters have in any case been dealt with elsewhere at length[1]—but the philosophy embodied, or thought to be embodied, within the law is relevant. Four men were particularly responsible for the essentials of the New Poor Law. Two, Bentham and Malthus, can be called the spiritual fathers of the act and were, along with others in the first generation of Philosophical Radicals, the teachers of the other two, Nassau Senior and Edwin Chadwick, who were most directly responsible for the contents of the Commissioners' report and for the law itself. This ideological pedigree is of no small importance, since both Senior and Chadwick felt obliged, in dealing with an issue of such magnitude, to reach back to fundamental principles in the hope of reconstructing the Poor Laws on a firm and lasting base. Their most likely guide in such a task was Malthus, who more than anyone else had attempted to re-interpret the Poor Laws in terms of the new science of political economy. And for this reason alone, his views, whether agreed to or not, had to be taken seriously. Malthus had adopted what would certainly be called an extreme view; he advocated nothing less than the total abolition of all statutory relief to the poor. Yet this position was not, as the establishment of the Royal Commission was, the result of a reaction against the abuses of the Old Poor Law in the early

[1] Perhaps the best accounts are to be found in: S. and B. Webb, *English Poor Law History* (London 1963), Part II, Vol. I, Ch. I; Sir G. Nicholls, *A History of the English Poor Law* (London 1898), Vol. II, Chs. XIV–XV; T. McKay, *A History of the English Poor Law From 1834 to the Present Time* (London 1899), Ch. I; S. E. Finer, *The Life and Times of Edwin Chadwick* (London 1952), Book II.

years of the century. He had come to this conclusion as early as 1798 and it was based largely, though not entirely, on his theory of population.

A guarantee of relief, he argued, tended to increase population by encouraging improvident marriages and the begetting of children without thought to their future support. Since, in Malthus' view, the supply of food ordinarily increased at a rate far slower than that of the increase of population, a policy which actually encouraged such growth was sheer madness. What is more, he noted, such a policy was cruel for it was precisely those whom the Poor Law sought to help who suffered most from its workings. According to Malthus:

> The poor-laws of England tend to depress the general condition of the poor in these two ways. Their first obvious tendency is to increase population without increasing the food for its support . . . and as the provisions of the country must in consequence of the increased population be distributed to every man in smaller proportions, it is evident that the labor of those who are not supported by parish assistance will purchase a smaller quantity of provisions than before, and consequently more of them must be driven to apply for assistance.
>
> Secondly, the quantity of provisions consumed in the workhouse . . . diminishes the shares that would otherwise belong to more industrious and more worthy members [of society], and this in the same manner forces more to become dependent.
>
> The poor-laws of England appear to have contributed to raise the price of provisions and to lower the real price of labor. They have therefore contributed to impoverish that class of people whose only possession is their labor. It is also difficult to suppose that they have not powerfully contributed to generate that carelessness and want of frugality observable among the poor . . . [who], even when they have an opportunity of saving . . . seldom exercise it . . . The poor-laws may therefore be said to diminish both the power and the will to save among the common people, and thus to weaken one of the strongest incentives to sobriety and industry, and consequently to happiness.[1]

The influence on the New Poor Law of that part of Malthus' argument which was based on his theory of population has often been overestimated. Senior belonged to a later generation of political economists which was rarely unreservedly Malthusian. He believed that Malthus was unnecessarily fatalistic and that there were a number of social checks on population which Malthus

[1] T. R. Malthus, *An Essay on the Principles of Population*, 9th ed. (London 1885), 303.

had overlooked, the most important perhaps being personal ambition. 'I consider', Senior said, 'the desire of bettering our condition as natural a wish as the desire for marriage.'[1] But the argument against the Poor Laws from population was only one part of Malthus' thesis; beyond that, and independent of it, was the problem of the impact of relief on the prices of necessities and the price of labor, in short on the basic price and wage structure of the national economy. Clearly, since that impact could well be considerable, any system of compulsory relief was, from a strictly *laisser faire* point of view, questionable at best.

The effects of the Old Poor Law, as represented in the Royal Commission report, certainly appeared to support such doubts. In parts of southern England the poor rates had, since 1795, been used extensively not merely to relieve destitution among the sick, the aged, or the totally unemployed, but to supplement the wages of the able-bodied worker in full or partial employ. There were a number of variations on this practice—the roundsman system, the labor rate, and so on—but the primary evil in the view of the Commissioners was the direct allowance system. Its workings were comparatively simple. Local authorities, using the price of bread as a basis, estimated minimum standards for the support of laborers and their families. Should the wages of a laborer not come up to this level, the difference was paid out of the parish rates. Thus, automatically, wages and relief were confused and wages ceased to be determined by the laws of supply and demand.

Moreover, the Commission report was careful to point out, the laborers, for whose benefit the allowance system had theoretically been devised, were in fact the chief sufferers from it. Naturally enough the local authorities and ratepayers desired to keep the cost of relief as low as possible, and clearly it was less expensive to give a man a small sum in addition to his wages than to support him, let alone his family, entirely from the rates. As a result it was the number of mouths a laborer had to feed together with the possibility of their having to be fed by the parish which often determined a laborer's priority in getting employment. A single man, however industrious, or a man with small savings could well be penalized. Idleness and profligacy, two of the Commissioners' favorite words, were benefited. Other evils were identified as well, including some aspects of relief in workhouses, the laws

[1] M. Bowley, *Nassau Senior and Classical Economics* (London 1937), 120.

relating to bastardy, and the whole confused problem of legal residence and settlement. But the attack on the allowance system was the meat of the report, and for all their supposed objectivity, the Commissioners could not refrain from painting their dark picture in lurid colors.

All other classes of society are exposed to the vicissitudes of hope and fear; he [the able bodied laborer receiving an allowance] alone has nothing to lose or gain . . . It appears to the pauper that the Government has undertaken to repeal the ordinary laws of nature: to enact, in short, that the penalty which after all must be paid by someone for idleness and improvidence, is to fall, not on the guilty person or on his family, but on the proprietors of lands and houses incumbered by his settlement. Can we wonder if the uneducated are seduced by a system which offers marriage to the young, security to the anxious, ease to the lazy, and impunity to the profligate?[1]

Senior, who, in the years preceding his appointment to the Royal Commission, had studied the question in detail, was also concerned with the preservation in force of the 'ordinary laws of nature', and it was clear to him that, both in its effects on the labor market and on the moral condition of the poor, the Old Poor Law violated these laws. The scope of governmental interference, he believed, must be limited to activities which would not diminish 'industry, forethought, and charity'. Strictly interpreted such views could well have led to a severe limitation if not the outright abolition of poor relief, at least to the able-bodied; but Senior was not a doctrinaire *laisser faire* economist and his studies of the Poor Laws led him to the conclusion that in certain areas where there were social 'evils too great to allow individuals to make a sufficient provision against them'[2] government had a clear responsibility to intervene. Thus Senior's problem in confronting the reform of the Poor Laws was not that of overcoming his own *laisser faire* views, but that of translating possibly conflicting views about the role of government in public welfare into practical institutional terms.

Having arrived at this view of the situation, Senior found a valuable ally in Edwin Chadwick. Chadwick, it seems, unlike Senior, had never felt the need to wrestle with the *laisser faire* arguments against poor relief. He had long since accepted the

[1] Poor Law Commissioners, Report of H.M. Commissioners for Inquiring into the Administration and Practical Operation of the Poor Laws, *B.P.P.*, 1834, XXVII, 34.

[2] Bowley, *Senior*, 244.

Poor Laws as necessary and turned his attention to the problem of administering them efficiently. From Bentham, in whose circle he had received much of his training, Chadwick derived most of his attitudes towards the problem of Poor Law administration. Bentham himself had written a good deal on the subject of poor relief, though his various proposals were far from being consistent. In the 1790s he had advocated turning over the entire administration of relief to a private joint stock company which would run it as a business for profit.[1] This scheme was never taken seriously, except perhaps by Bentham himself, but there were embedded within it a number of principles which Chadwick was to draw on a third of a century later. The factory workhouses which Bentham hoped to establish all over the country were to be elaborately classified within so that each category of pauper—orphans, the aged, the sick, the able-bodied, and so on—would be able to receive the sort of care or perform the sort of task best suited to its condition and abilities.

Of no less importance than their internal arrangement was the relationship these workhouses were to have with the world outside. Making poor relief pay was subsidiary in Bentham's view to the larger aims of diminishing the effect of pauperism on the economy as a whole and, if possible, of decreasing the extent of pauperism itself. To these ends he proposed that there be 'no relief but upon the terms of coming into the house and working out the expense' and that, by workhouse discipline and other means, 'maintenance at the expense of others should not be made more desirable than self maintenance'.[2] Thirty years later Bentham's ideas, at least as regards the executive machinery of poor relief, had changed considerably. In his Constitutional Code he advocated not a joint stock company but a government department under an Indigence Relief Minister of cabinet rank as the central agency for the efficient administration of a reformed Poor Law.[3]

Within Bentham's writings these ideas lay scattered or buried among a host of others so that in picking them up Chadwick cannot be accused of blindly adopting his master's views. In any case, he was not, as Bentham was, dealing with a theoretical problem. As an Assistant to the Poor Law Inquiry Commission and later on

[1] J. Bentham, 'Tracts on Poor Laws and Pauper Management: Outline of a Work Entitled Pauper Management Improved', *The Works of Jeremy Bentham* (Edinburgh 1843), Vol. VIII.

[2] *Ibid.*, 383–4.

[3] Bentham, 'The Constitutional Code', *Works*, IX, 441.

as a member of that Commission he had set himself the task of devising a workable system of poor relief and of getting his proposals enacted into law. His suggestions had, therefore, to be both practical and politically acceptable. The abolition of relief to the able-bodied was politically out of the question, but its control, indeed its very strict control, was not. The means of control which Chadwick proposed was based on what came to be called the less eligibility principle, which required that the pauper's 'situation on the whole shall not be made really or apparently so eligible as the situation of the independent laborer of the lowest class'.[1] But how could it be assured that in practice less eligibility would apply? To this as well Chadwick believed he had the answer: by decreeing that 'all relief whatever to able-bodied persons or to their families otherwise than in a well regulated workhouse shall be declared unlawful'.[2]

By this relatively simple expedient, so the report asserted, most of the evils then associated with poor relief could be abolished. The allowance system would go with all its disastrous effects on employed and employer alike. The employer would be forced to hire his laborers for long periods at reasonable wages or see these workers removed entirely from the labor market into the workhouse. Laborers would be hired according to their worth, not the size of their families, and thereby every incentive would be given to self-improvement and forethought. Thus the Poor Laws, the Commissioners' report concluded, instead of being a source of the moral degradation of the poor and a distorter of the free economy, could be a means of ensuring the status of the independent laborer and the smooth functioning of the labor market.

But the reform of Poor Law policy, however firmly based on principle, was not considered sufficient guarantee that the needed changes would take place. Similar reforms had been enacted before, had worked well for a time, and then been once again submerged in abuses. The blame for this, the Commissioners felt, rested squarely with the administrative machinery of the Old Poor Law. Each parish under the old law was responsible for the relief of its own poor and the parish officials in charge, the vestrymen

---

[1] P.L.C., 1834 Report, 127. S. E. Finer suggests that the concept of less eligibility came from Bentham's Panopticon rather than from his writings on the poor laws (Finer, *Chadwick*, 43–4, 73–5). While it is true that the exact wording is to be found only in the Panopticon, the concept was clearly put forward in the works on pauper management.

[2] P.L.C., 1834 Report, 146.

and overseers, were all too often ill-equipped for their offices and
not effectively under the control of the ratepayers they theoretically represented. Also, and perhaps even more important, there
existed under the Old Poor Law no central authority with powers
to direct and systematize the administration of relief. To rectify
these evils the Commissioners recommended three major changes.
In the first place they proposed the creation of fewer units of
greater size by placing groups of parishes together in Poor Law
Unions. Secondly, in each of these Unions, there was to be a Board
of Guardians elected by the ratepayers and, under the control of
the Board, a number of paid full-time officers. And, finally, over-
seeing the whole administrative structure, there was to be a Poor
Law Commission whose job it would be to ensure a degree of
efficiency and uniformity hitherto unknown in Poor Law history.[1]

There were other recommendations as well—the report contained no less than twenty-two—but they dealt primarily with administrative details or specific limited abuses. Compared with the
crucial half-dozen recommendations relating to the relief of the
able-bodied and overall administrative reorganization, these others
were of marginal importance. Certainly it was these major recommendations which the Commissioners most anxiously hoped
would be adopted by the government. This was in fact achieved
with remarkable ease. A few days of discussion within the cabinet
led to a virtually unanimous decision to adopt the Poor Law report
in full. There were as a result very few differences between the
report and the Poor Law Amendment Bill as presented to Parliament. Of these by far the most important was the omission in the
bill of any specific endorsement of workhouse relief for the able-
bodied. But allowances in aid of wages were outlawed in the bill
and a rigorous workhouse system was strongly implied as well, so
that, even without the inclusion of a workhouse test, the bill was
expected by the government to have a stormy passage. It was, after
all, a major break with long-established practices, the most important move in more than a century to restrict relief severely, and
an attempt to re-establish the Poor Laws on a new theoretical
base which was in itself controversial. Small wonder then that its
passage into law, both quietly and quickly, surprised both the
government which sponsored it and the men who were its main
architects.

[1] P.L.C. 1834 Report, 159 ff.

That the opposition proved ineffective in the end did not mean that it did not exist; indeed very nearly every one of the bill's 109 sections was bitterly opposed by some group in Parliament. The main attack, however, was concentrated on two areas of the bill: the clauses defining the powers of the Poor Law Commission and those relating to relief itself, and of these issues the former was perhaps the more important. Both government and opposition agreed that the creation of the Commission was the heart of the bill, for without it there was no guarantee that any of the other proposed changes would take place. Certainly the powers of the new Commissioners as outlined in the bill were to be immense:

the administration of Relief to the Poor throughout England and Wales . . . shall be subject to the direction and control of the said Commissioners, and . . . [they] shall, and are hereby authorized and required, from time to time as they shall see occasion, to make and issue all such Rules, Orders and Regulations for the management of the Poor, for the Government of Workhouses, and the education of the children therein, . . . and for the apprenticing of the children of poor Persons, and for the guidance and control of all Guardians, Vestries, and Parish Officers, so far as relates to the management or relief of the Poor, and the keeping, examining, auditing, and allowing of Accounts, and the making and entering into Contracts in all matters relating to such Management of Relief, . . . and for carrying the Act into execution in all other respects, as they shall think proper.[1]

What is more, the Commissioners were to have the power of calling witnesses and taking testimony on oath, of appointing Assistant Commissioners to act for them in dealings with local authorities and numerous other powers which together amounted, in the opposition's view, to powers of virtual legislation. Indeed, about the only thing which the Commission was not allowed to do was compel a local authority to build a new workhouse against its will. Yet, as far as the opponents could see, there were to be remarkably few checks on this exceedingly powerful body, which was not to be under a minister responsible to Parliament, but a separate statutory board subject to control only in so far as it had to make annual reports and submit all General Rules (rules applying to more than one local administrative unit) to a Secretary of State.

---

[1] Poor Law Amendment Act, Clause 15. The text of the Amendment Act can be found in any number of books, but the best footnoted and most informative edition is: W. G. Lumley, *A Collection of Statutes of General Use Relating to the Relief of the Poor* (London 1843).

B

A large number of M.P.s, perhaps even a majority, were distinctly uneasy about the creation of a body which would have such wide powers to interfere in local affairs as well as apparent freedom from close ministerial and Parliamentary oversight. The money for relief, it was argued, came from locally raised rates and therefore should be locally administered. The poor themselves were local men and women; their character and material condition were best known by other local men. Where, the opponents asked, into this situation, could a London-based Poor Law Commission fit? Either it would not interfere, in which case it was pointless, or it would, in which case it was dangerous. The best traditions of English local government, of initiative on the part of leading local citizens, would be sapped by a body which was designed to check all local deviation from a uniform national system. Different areas of England had different traditions, a situation which had always been respected, even cherished, by England's rulers; yet now it seemed England was about to take the first steps on the road to a French or Prussian (at any rate continental) despotism.

Among those who argued along these lines there were some who saw no need for change of any kind. But they were few—it was after all virtually impossible to overlook all the abuses that had been uncovered—and the more realistic opponents of centralization recognized and tried to deal with the problems of administrative reform. It was suggested that all vestries be open (i.e. elected by the ratepayers), and that the often-abused powers of magistrates to order relief and fix its amount be curtailed. But the proponents of a Commission replied that open vestries were not immune to corruption or laxity and, moreover, that without a powerful central authority there was no guarantee that good procedures in one area would be adopted in other areas. These were difficult, perhaps impossible, arguments to answer and at no time did the opponents really come to grips with them. Partly as a result of this they were never able to mobilize Parliamentary distrust of centralization, and it is significant that the powers granted to the Poor Law Commissioners over local authorities were in no way diminished during the passage of the bill through Parliament.[1]

[1] Hansard, *Parliamentary Debates*, Third Series, 1834. These and related issues occupied more time in both houses of Parliament than any others. Nearly every speech in the debate on the second reading touched on them (see in particular the speech of Sir Samuel Whalley, XXIII, 807 ff). And in the committee stage they tended to dominate the discussion of the early clauses (XXIII, 971–1002, 1276–1304, 1320–49;

Realizing that their attacks on centralization were without effect, the opponents fell back on the argument that the Poor Law Commission was irresponsible, and in the battle along these lines they won a couple of minor victories. A five-year term was imposed on the Commission and it was required to submit to a somewhat closer form of inspection and review than had been envisaged in the original bill.[1] But, however many restrictions might be placed upon its unsupervised freedom of action, the Poor Law Commission remained a non-departmental body with wide discretionary powers, and as such, in the view of many of the bill's opponents including Lord Eldon, an unconstitutional one. With this argument, however, the opponents made no headway at all. Lord Brougham, the Lord Chancellor, answered the objections of the opponents by citing precedents for the creation of such a Commission, but he never took the constitutional issue very seriously, nor, considering the number of votes the opposition was able to muster, need he have done so.[2]

With the existence of the Poor Law Commission decided, relief itself became the major issue, and, as it turned out, an even more difficult one for the opposition to deal with. This was true largely because the bill itself was vague. As we have seen, no mention was made of a workhouse test for able bodied laborers; indeed the only specific injunction in the bill was that allowances in aid of wages were to cease on June 1, 1835. Yet even this clause was dropped by the government during the progress of the bill as being too great a restriction on the flexibility of the Poor Law Commissioners. As a result the opponents were left with little to dig their teeth into. All that was clear was that the local Boards of Guardians were to have the sole power of granting relief subject to the rules and orders of

---

XXIV, 309–18; XXV, 440–56, 469–73). Prominent among those who opposed the bill on these grounds, in addition to Whalley, were Torrens and Colonel Evans in the Commons and Wynford and Alvanley in the Lords. Of those who supported the bill, but only with strong misgivings concerning the powers it gave to the P.L.C., perhaps the best examples are Edward Buller and George Grote. Althorp in the Commons and Brougham in the Lords acted in this, as in all matters, as spokesmen for the bill.

[1] Clauses 4 and 10.

[2] Hansard, *op. cit.* It is difficult to separate the debate on constitutionality from that on the powers of the P.L.C. as the two were usually linked. However, both Colonel Evans (XXIII, 806) and Lord Wynford (XXV, 259–61) addressed themselves particularly to this issue, as, among the supporters of the bill, did Joseph Hume (XXIII, 834).

the Poor Law Commissioners. Only the barest hints were given of what this would mean in practice; indeed, apart from clauses placing workhouses under the management of the Boards of Guardians, empowering the Poor Law Commission to order repairs to old workhouses, and specifically excluding magistrates and overseers from giving relief, very little was spelt out in detail. Fundamental questions involving the sort of relief to be given to different classes of paupers and the arrangement and management of workhouses were left entirely at the discretion of the Commissioners. Superficially this lack of specifics appeared to favor the opponents of the New Poor Law, for, while it is true that they had not been able to mobilize distaste for centralization to defeat the creation of the Poor Law Commission, such distaste was still a factor to be reckoned with, and could be used to restrict and define the powers of that Commission. Thus they were fairly optimistic and made all the more so by the fact that there was in Parliament a widely shared fear that any sudden change towards severity in Poor Law policy would lead to rural unrest and violence.

Yet, time after time, when it was pointed out that this or that particular clause opened the way to Poor Law Commission dictation or undue harshness to the poor, the government assured the House that no such things were intended or would be allowed. In any case, the government argued, having created the Commission, Parliament could not sensibly refuse it extensive powers over local authorities or a large degree of discretion in determining policy.[1] In the event, these latter arguments prevailed, and the hopes of the opposition were bitterly disappointed. An attempt to exclude areas where rates were low and abuses few from the authority of the Poor Law Commissioners failed as did a motion to leave the administration of relief to all but the able-bodied entirely in local hands.[2]

In fact, only two changes of any significance were made, both designed to restore to traditional local authorities some of the powers which the bill as originally conceived had taken away from them. The magistrates were given the power of ordering outdoor relief (though not its amount, that was to remain a matter for the

[1] Hansard, *op. cit.* Relief was the major subject of debate during much of the committee stage (XXIV, 344–52, 385–92, 427–33). Perhaps the most interesting and important opposition speeches were made by William Cobbett (XXIII, 1335–7; XXIV, 386–7) and Poulett Scrope (XXIII, 1321–3; XXIV, 345–6).

[2] Hansard, *op. cit.*, XXIII, 1291; XXIV, 346.

Boards of Guardians) for the aged and infirm, and the overseers were given the right of granting relief in cases of sudden and urgent necessity.[1] But that was the extent of the changes made. In all other respects, and certainly as regards fundamentals, the proponents of the Poor Law Amendment Act had it all their own way.

The clauses creating the Poor Law Commission and granting to it wide powers over relief were, though the most important sections of the bill, by no means the whole of it. New local authorities, the Boards of Guardians elected by the ratepayers, were to be created, and on this issue as well the opposition, though badly disunited, put up a fight. Conservative anti-New Poor Law M.P.s disliked the whole idea of replacing the traditional vestries and overseers, while radical opponents concentrated their fire on the multiple votes to be given to wealthy ratepayers. In any case, both attacks, as usual, failed completely.[2] There was in fact one area, and only one, in which the opponents were able to make their mark: the clauses relating to bastardy. This was, as it turned out, a very sensitive issue and the government, which had been unemotionally practical in dealing with it, was taken completely unaware by the storm that its proposals created. The major abuse of the old bastardy laws was that, by making it exceedingly easy for an unmarried mother to charge a man with being the father of a child, the law encouraged both litigation and, so it was thought, licentiousness. It was, therefore, proposed that the mother be made responsible for the support of illegitimate children and that the laws for the punishment of putative fathers be repealed. This seemed no more than common sense to the government, but to many, in fact a majority, in Parliament, particularly in the House of Lords, it appeared as an insult to womanhood, a license for male licentiousness and an encouragement to infanticide on the part of unwed mothers. Many days were spent debating these clauses and in the Lords no less than five amendments were made to the Bill giving the overseers and magistrates power to seek out putative fathers and charge them with the support of bastard children. These changes constituted the one important victory for the opponents; yet even this was only a partial victory since, unless paternity could be proved in the courts, the care of the child remained, as the bill had originally proposed, entirely the mother's responsibility.[3]

[1] Clauses 27 and 54.   [2] Hansard, *op. cit.*, XXIV, 330–7.
[3] Hansard, *op. cit.* Clauses 72–6 were added in the Lords and the

Thus, even in the bastardy clauses, as in all other sections of the act, only details and nothing touching the principles of the Royal Commission Report had been altered. The serious opposition which was expected had never materialized and the victory of the proponents of the New Poor Law was complete. Yet that this was the case should in fact have surprised no one. The generally held belief that something must be done worked against the opponents, as did the unwillingness of the Tory front bench to make it a partisan issue. In such circumstances it was nearly impossible to mount a numerically formidable opposition; nor—perhaps more important—did it prove possible to mount a coherent one. The report was published in February 1834 and the bill was introduced in April; there simply was not enough time in these two months to work out arguments against a bill resting on a report which was the result of two years' investigation and research. Because of the sense of urgency, many who might otherwise have opposed the act were silent or only mild in their criticism. Because of the lack of any official opposition, the number voting against even the most controversial clauses was never large enough to pose any serious threat to the government, and, because of the time factor, many opponents, often it seems simply because they had not had the opportunity to study the bill sufficiently, or perhaps because they were intimidated by the mass of evidence presented by the report, were reduced to expressing vague doubts about the general tendency of the legislation. In any case they were never able to muster more than fifty votes against the bill, and even these fifty, far from being a united opposition, represented a curious coalition of dissident Tories, extreme radicals and a scattering of Irish M.P.s.

Among these opponents some were against any major changes in social legislation, others felt that this was the wrong sort of change, and a few believed that it did not even touch the real causes of social distress. The first group, of course, had the easiest time of it; they ignored the abuses of the Old Poor Law and opposed the new for its centralization, its harshness and its tampering with the machinery of local government. But the more responsible critics were placed in a very difficult position. While they admitted that the Old Poor Law had been subject to great abuses

---

major debates on bastardy were also held there (XXV, 586–612, 777–82, 1061–96). See in particular the speeches of the Bishop of Exeter.

and agreed that the evils associated with its administration had to be removed, they could not accept what the Royal Commissioners' report had claimed to prove, that the Old Poor Law and these evils were inseparable. They maintained that the Poor Law was fundamentally sound, that it was the recently introduced system of allowances in aid of wages that had caused the existing abuses, and that, with the abolition of such allowances and perhaps a few other minor alterations and safeguards, the Old Poor Law would be found to work quite well again. A few went even further and dismissed the new law as not only unnecessarily drastic but essentially irrelevant. Rural distress, they believed, was not a result of Poor Law abuses; on the contrary, both this distress and these abuses were symptoms of a general dislocation in the economy caused by, among other things, high taxes, the corn laws, the national debt, and enclosures.[1]

By no stretch of the imagination could those who argued for sweeping social reform as the only solution to the Poor Law problem be put in the same category as the ultra-Tory opponents. They were agreed only in a negative sense, which was in itself perhaps one of the causes of the opposition's dismal failure. But more important was the feeling they must have had that they were hopelessly outnumbered and bound to fail. How else is it possible to explain the unimpressive Parliamentary performance of men like Thomas Attwood, John Walter and William Cobbett who knew the Old Poor Law and knew as well the grounds on which they opposed the Amendment Act? Throughout the debates it was clear that the great majority of M.P.s accepted both the general conclusions and specific recommendations of the Royal Commissioners. To criticize them adequately would have consumed more than the time allotted in debate to these opposition leaders; to be able in addition to do justice to their own case in such circumstances was impossible. They had so many objections to the bill and so many alternative ideas that they found themselves able only to list them, not elucidate them. So far in fact were their ideas from those of the majority in Parliament, that they were simply dismissed as being irrelevant or obstructionist or both. As a result

---

[1] Hansard, *op. cit.* This argument was put forward by, among others, Colonel Evans (XXIII, 805–6), Thomas Attwood (XXIII, 1337–8), G. R. Robinson (XXIII, 964–9) and William Cobbett (XXIV, 309–10). The view that only minor reforms were needed was best presented by Sir Francis Burdett (XXIII, 322–3).

it is as frustrating to read these speeches as it must have been to make them. What comes across now, and what must have come across then, are only the fragments of an argument; for the whole argument it is necessary to turn to the writings of these men.

The publication of the Royal Commission's Report was followed by a deluge of pamphlets, lectures and articles on the subject. Most of these were, and are, of little interest or importance; panaceas were proposed, matters of marginal interest were end-lessly rehashed, or the Old Poor Law was simply upheld as sacro-sanct. Much of this sort of thing, and particularly of the last atti-tude, had been heard in Parliament and gained nothing from publication, but a few among the many who felt compelled to rush into print knew their subject well and had something valuable to say. What chiefly distinguished them from the mass of pamph-leteers was that they took exception not merely to details in the report or the bill but to the whole body of assumptions which underpinned them. Their first complaint was that the Royal Com-mission had doctored the evidence by concentrating their atten-tion on areas where abuses were most flagrant or remedies most stringent, to the exclusion of areas where neither abuses nor severity were the rule. Up to a point, the opponents would perhaps have agreed, this might have been acceptable as a legitimate means of putting in its most favorable light the case which the Commis-sioners wished to present. But, it was argued, not only had the Commission been tendentious in its selection, it had been misleading, perhaps even dishonest, in the gathering of the evi-dence. The Commissioners had relied almost entirely on two major sources of information: reports from Assistant Commis-sioners sent out to investigate local conditions, and questionnaires filled in by overseers, churchwardens, landowners, farmers and other leading citizens from all over England and Wales.

Both of these sources were severely censured by the New Poor Law's opponents. J. R. McCulloch, an exceptional figure among important economists because of his criticisms of the New Poor Law, assailed the Commissioners and their Assistants, who, he claimed, 'with very few exceptions, appear to have set out with a determination to find nothing but abuses in the Old Poor Law, and to make the most of them'.[1] John Walter, M.P. for Berkshire and

[1] J. R. McCulloch, *The Literature of Political Economy* (London 1845), 290.

proprietor of *The Times*, attacked the Commissioners for framing
the questionnaires 'with a view to draw out answers corresponding
with . . . [their] preconceived opinions'.[1] Such accusations were
not without foundation. The Assistant Commissioners' reports
piled up examples of abuses, corruption and mismanagement
while the wording of questionnaires managed subtly to suggest a
link between the Poor Laws and the agricultural riots of 1830, a
possible decline in the efficiency of laborers, and a diminishing of
agricultural capital. But, annoying as such things were to men like
Walter, what perhaps angered them even more was that at no
point had the Commissioners sought information concerning any
positive role which the Poor Laws might play. This was certainly
no accident. The Commissioners conceived of the Poor Laws as
playing a positive role only in relation to the pauper and not in
relation to the economy as a whole. Thus, relief could be afforded
where it was clearly called for but it should never be given in such
a way as to alter the level of employment and wages as determined
by an open market. It was, as a result, one of the Commissioners'
primary tasks to decide whether or not a system of statutory poor
relief was compatible with a free market in labor. Eventually, as
we have seen, the Commissioners decided that they were compatible, but only on condition that relief be given in accordance
with the principle of less eligibility and, where possible, in a
workhouse.

Such views were totally alien to those of most opponents of the
New Poor Law, whether Conservative or Radical. The Poor Law
was to them not merely the last resort of desperate men or the first
resort of the idle, but a tool of economic policy. That it interfered
in the labor market was not in itself at all a bad thing, though particular forms of interference might well be. Thus, to fundamental
propositions of the New Poor Law's proponents such as that relief
should be granted to the able-bodied only in return for labor,
Walter, for example, replied that, indeed, 'Able-bodied paupers
ought not to receive relief except in return for labor: but, then,
labor ought to be provided for them, when they are not able to
procure it for themselves. Most of those who come under the
description of able-bodied paupers, would not be so if they could
procure work.'[2] That the machinery of the Poor Law should be
used as a kind of employment agency was not, however, the only

---

[1] J. Walter, *A Letter to the Electors of Berkshire* (London 1834), 20.
[2] *Ibid.*, 35.

positive function that Walter, along with a good many others, believed it should assume. Both he and the conservative *Quarterly Review* insisted that one of the objects of poor relief was to raise the wages of laborers, or, at the very least, secure them from falling. To a great extent, asserted the *Quarterly*, 'it is the parish rate of pay . . . which determines the rate of wages'. Thus, to apply the principle of less eligibility and make relief payments always lower than wages, would, in effect, prevent wages from rising and perhaps lead to their falling. Clearly, then, the less eligibility principle ran directly counter to what the *Quarterly* believed to be 'the true and only principle by which parish relief . . . must be determined . . . [namely] the natural wants of the pauper, taking into consideration the habitual standard of necessaries among the population of the country'. To abandon this conception of poor relief, as the *Quarterly* believed the Commissioners had done, was to ignore completely the fact that 'one great benefit which the poor law has conferred upon this country is, that it has established a fixed standard of adequate maintenance, and declared that no one should be forced below that level by any circumstances'.[1]

No more direct challenge to the fundamentals of the New Poor Law can be imagined than this denial of the validity of the principle of less eligibility, and it is hardly surprising that the proponents of the Amendment Act dismissed it as laxity born of misguided sentimentality. But neither Walter, nor the *Quarterly Review*, nor those who shared their views, felt that they were in any way open to such a charge. To include aid in finding employment and a degree of wage support among the objects of a system of poor relief did not mean advocating the allowance system or any other form of unrestricted benevolence. The opponents of the New Law agreed that relief in aid of wages was degrading in its effects on the recipients of such relief and that, in the long run, it tended to depress wages. But they could not accept the conclusion of the Commissioners that workhouse relief was the only sure way of eradicating the allowance system. Surely, they argued, this was only replacing one form of abuse by another, substituting degradation through allowances with degradation by incarceration in a prison-like workhouse. The government, in short, was overcorrecting, and, in so doing, dealing a terrible and unnecessary blow to the standard of life and dignity of the poor. That it was unnecessary the opponents had no doubt, for there was, they be-

[1] *Quarterly Review*, August 1834, 241–2.

lieved, an alternative. The allowance system may best be extinguished, Walter asserted,

by adhering strictly to the provisions of the 43rd Elizabeth [the Old Poor Law]: that is by setting them on work; such employment to be entire not partial; and whilst, perhaps, in a degree, inferior to agricultural labor, and the wages somewhat below the average, may neither degrade the party receiving it, nor change his domestic habits, nor be wholly unprofitable to the parish providing it. Thus the indolence which corrupts, and the dependence on parochial funds which enervates and destroys the character of an independent laborer, would be removed. . . . If, too, this provision were made for surplus or inferior labor, the remuneration of the more able and industrious would be more adequate and secure. I conceive that abundant sources of parochial labor might be found . . . and that with proper superintendence this might be done, without immuring all persons, without discrimination, within the walls of a workhouse.[1]

The *Quarterly* agreed, and, in doing so, singled out what was perhaps the weakest link in the argument of the New Poor Law's supporters. In the Royal Commission report, in the paragraph immediately following that in which the workhouse test was recommended, it was admitted that 'nothing is necessary to arrest the progress of pauperism, except that all who receive relief from the parish should work for the parish exclusively, as hard as and for less wages than independent laborers work for individual employers, and we believe that in most districts useful work which will not interfere with the ordinary demand for labor may be obtained in greater quantity than is usually conceived'.

Why then, the *Quarterly* asked, did the Commissioners insist so passionately on a workhouse test? Because, the Poor Law report said, 'cases . . . will occur where such work cannot be obtained in sufficient quantity to meet an immediate demand; and when obtained, the labor, by negligence, connivance, or otherwise, may be made merely formal, and thus the provisions of the legislature may be evaded more easily than in a workhouse. A well regulated workhouse', they concluded, 'meets all cases.'[2]

This answer the opponents could not accept. The remedy, they felt, was too extreme, the difference between a labor test and a workhouse test too great. Therefore, they concluded, there had to be other motives. One certainly was the Commissioners' fetish of simplicity and uniformity; but the most important was the

[1] Walter, *Letter*, 36–7.   [2] P.L.C., 1834 Report, 143.

ambivalent overall attitude of both the government and the Royal Commissioners towards poor relief in general. Overzealousness combined with a misreading of Poor Law history, the opponents believed, had led the Commissioners to allow their detestation for the allowance system to overflow into a general attack on the Poor Laws as a whole. 'Throughout [the report]', the *Quarterly* noted, 'there is an unworthy attempt to fasten upon the poor law of Elizabeth, or upon the powers conferred in the succeeding century upon justices, the discredit of having occasioned evils, which notoriously did not exhibit themselves till after . . . the introduction of the allowance system by the magistracy of the south of England, in direct opposition to the letter and previous practice of the law . . . All experience is . . . in favor of the law as it stood between 1600 and 1796; and yet it is insinuated [by the Commissioners] that such a law is wrong "in principle" and ought to have been productive of mischief.'[1]

This could perhaps be ascribed to carelessness or inadequate investigation, but the opponents felt that there was a far more sinister explanation; they believed that the New Poor Law was meant to be the prelude to no Poor Law at all. Only in such a context could they make sense of the Commissioners' insistence on workhouse relief, which then appeared in its true colors, not as a test of pauperism, or even as a deterrent to paupers, but as a tool later to be used for the destruction of all kinds of poor relief. In support of such a view more than a little evidence was provided by the often overzealous friends of the New Poor Law. In particular, Lord Brougham, who was never at a loss for the picturesque and sometimes incautious phrase, supplied the opposition with a fund of ammunition. He attacked the principle of statutory poor relief with an outspokenness which few dared emulate. 'Anything more mischievous, anything more fatal to the country, anything more calculated to multiply indefinitely the numbers of the poor, cannot be conceived than the applying to them of any regular and fixed provision.'[2] He hinted that the Amendment Act was only a cautious first step towards abolition. 'It is the evil of all bad laws worse administered, that we must continue to bear them, on account of the danger which may spring from their sudden repeal.'[3]

[1] *Quarterly Review*, August 1834, 236-7.
[2] H. P. Brougham, *Corrected Report of the Speech of the Lord Chancellor in the House of Lords* (London 1834), 8.
[3] *Ibid.*, 34.

He even went so far as to praise the *bête noire* of the opposition, Malthus, and link his name indissolubly with the provisions of the New Poor Law. 'Those who framed the statute of Elizabeth were not adepts in political science—they were not acquainted with the true principles of population—they could not foresee that a Malthus would arise to enlighten mankind . . . ,—they knew not the true principles upon which to frame a preventive check, or favor the prudential check to the unlimited increase of the people.'[1]

Actually, this emphasis on Malthus was a distortion of the Commissioners' report and the Poor Law Amendment Bill, in both of which the influence of Malthusian population theory, though discernible, was only of secondary importance. Still, some parts of the report, and at least one clause of the bill, were explicitly Malthusian, and the opposition, quoting Brougham in support, were able to present such things not as minor points but as craftily hidden keys to the true nature of the bill and the intentions of its framers. The report, for example, held out the promise that one of the effects of its adoption would be to arrest 'the increase of population which the evidence shows to be produced by the present state of the law and of its administration'.[2] And in the bill itself there was a clause empowering local authorities to finance emigration from the rates.[3] Apart from this, however, the bill and the report tended to ignore, and up to a point even contradict, the fears of unduly rapid population growth. Indeed, one of the basic premises of the report was that the much complained of surplus of population was more apparent than real. The Commissioners confidently asserted that, in those few areas where there was overpopulation, a free labor market together with a little internal migration and perhaps a bit of emigration would solve the problem.[4] But the opponents refused to believe that the government was being honest in this matter. The report had traces of a Malthusian interpretation and Brougham's speeches were laced with far stronger doses of the same stuff; thus the most vocal of the opponents, including Walter and most especially Cobbett, never doubted that the Amendment Act was what its proponents assured Parliament and the public it was not, a Malthusian bill designed to force the poor to emigrate, to work for lower wages, to live on a coarser sort of food.

[1] *Ibid.*, 29–30.   [2] P.L.C., 1834 Report, 134.
[3] Clause 62. See also Hansard, *op. cit.*, XXIV, 451–77.
[4] P.L.C., 1834 Report, 199–200.

Only if it is realized that the opposition leaders sincerely believed that the New Poor Law was designed, in accordance with the strictest dictates of Malthusian and *laisser faire* philosophy, as the first step towards the abolition of statutory relief for the poor, is much of what they said intelligible. For, not only did they oppose to it a view of relief as a protector of wages and employment, they also saw the New Poor Law as a violation of the Constitution and of the laws of God. Much of what was written now seems unduly alarmist. The Poor Laws were not abolished and it is clear that their abolition was never seriously considered. But at the time this could not have been clear, and, to those who eyed the legislation with suspicion, not only the words of Lord Brougham, but one or two provisions of the law itself, hinted at harsher things to come. For example, the provision that relief could be given as a loan seemed to point towards the end of the principle, which the opponents asserted lay at the heart of the English Poor Laws, that the destitute had a right to relief. Indeed the whole bill appeared to question this long-held assumption, a fact which was quickly recognized by the opponents and soon became the center and basis of their attack upon it.

Cobbett put the case in its classic form in a pamphlet, *The Legacy to Laborers*, which was to be used as the basis for anti-Poor Law speeches for the next decade.[1] Relief of the poor, he argued, had been considered by the medieval church as one of its primary duties, and much of the wealth of the abbeys, as well as a fixed percentage of the tithes, had traditionally been allocated to this purpose. With the spoliation of the abbeys by Henry VIII, this function of the church had for the most part come to an end, and the new owners of the church lands had failed to assume this responsibility. As a result the state had been compelled to assume the burden, and, in 1601, as the culmination of a series of statutes, had passed the Poor Law of Elizabeth which, until the bill of 1834, had remained the basis of all poor relief. That it had been added to many times was, in Cobbett's view, not material, since, he asserted, none of these amendments had altered its fundamental character as a sort of bill of rights for the poor. Relief was guaranteed and provision made 'for setting to work all ... persons ... having no means to maintain them, and no ordinary and daily trade of life';[2]

---

[1] W. Cobbett, *Legacy to Laborers* (London 1835), passim.
[2] The text of the Elizabethan poor law can be found in P.L.C. 1834 Report, Appendix; or in Lumley, *Statutes*.

no mention was made of workhouses or of giving relief as a loan.

That the receipt of such relief was a right Cobbett did not for a moment doubt; tradition sanctified it and, so he claimed, all the great legal thinkers confirmed it as such. Therefore, to undermine that right by making relief a loan or conditional upon coming into a workhouse was not only to be inhuman, but to endanger the fabric of society and the constitutionality of government. For what was the New Poor Law but an abdication of responsibility both by those who held land and by the government? Those who held the land, argued Cobbett, did not do so absolutely, for the land itself was created by nature and its social value by labor. Thus no owner of land, however old his title, could be said to have exclusive rights in it; the men who worked it and their descendants had as much of a claim to a portion of its produce, whether through wages or relief, as those who had inherited the land. The pre-reformation tithes and the post-reformation rates were proof, if proof were needed, of the general acceptance of this, at least until 1834. This apparent abdication of responsibility by the holders of land distressed Cobbett, though it did not particularly surprise him. But the abdication of responsibility on the part of the government was another matter. To restrict relief, to hedge it round with conditions, to humiliate its recipients was to make a mockery of decent government, the basis of which was that 'constant protection is due from the state to every man'. To withdraw that protection from any man was not only cruel but self destructive, for that 'constant protection' was in fact 'the sole foundation of its [the state's] claim to his allegiance'.[1]

The proponents of the new law might well have replied, if they had bothered to reply, that all this was hysterical nonsense. Relief was still to be given, and surely society had the right to place conditions on the giving of such relief. It was a matter of expediency and to talk of rights and hazy constitutional theory only clouded the issues. But the opponents would have none of these arguments. If expediency called for the workhouse in 1834, might it not demand the end of poor relief in another generation? In fact, had not the Commissioners said,

If we believed that the evils [associated with the Old Poor Law] or evils resembling or even approaching them, to be necessarily incidental

[1] Cobbett, *Legacy*, 98.

to the compulsory relief of the able bodied, we should not hesitate in recommending its entire abolition.[1]

This, to the opponents, was the real issue, and not to talk of rights was to risk the future of poor relief, indeed, perhaps, of far more than that. For, said Cobbett, 'if you maintain that the poor have no right, no legal right, to relief, you loosen all the ligaments of property; . . . you do all in your power to break up the social compact'.[2]

[1] P.L.C., 1834 Report, 127.
[2] Cobbett, *Legacy*, 124.

II The New Poor Law in rural England

In spite of the almost pitiful weakness of the opposition to the New Poor Law in Parliament, it still seemed possible that effective opposition might arise when the time came to implement the law. Parliament was not, after all, the country, and the government harbored considerable doubts concerning the state of extra-Parliamentary opinion. A degree of hostility was to be expected from magistrates and overseers whose powers were to be curtailed and it was not inconceivable that they could, by determined opposition, make the law unworkable in many areas. An additional source of misgivings was the press. Many local papers, as well as a mixed group of national publications ranging from Cobbett's *Political Register* to the *Quarterly Review* and *The Times*, were either openly unfavorable, or at best had suspended judgment. Early mistakes on the part of the Commissioners, or the appearance of effective opposition in areas where the law was first to be put into practice, could well turn initially neutral papers, and perhaps their readers, into active opponents. Since ultimately the Commissioners could only be successful with the co-operation or at least the acquiescence of local authorities, these were considerations of no small importance.

Yet they were no more than conjecture and speculation, and the hard facts revealed a very different prospect. The main advantage of the opponents, their control of many influential papers, gave an impression of strength which was in no way borne out by other factors. There was no national anti-Poor Law organization, nor any attempt to create one. And, so far as we know, there were no well-organized local opposition groups. Nor did the self-appointed opposition leaders—Walter, Cobbett, *et al.*—furnish their followers or likely followers with any specific recommendations for local action when the time came for the machinery of the law to be set in motion. Instead, what they seem to have hoped for and expected, was that some sort of spontaneous revulsion against the New Poor Law would arise, or that, at the very least, a climate of opinion could be created which would allow the overseers, magistrates, Boards of Guardians and laborers to combine to defeat the law by demanding its amelioration. Certainly this, or something like it, was confidently predicted by a number of pamphleteers. Some trusted in the kindheartedness and good sense of the English landowner. Others, who did not, warned that unless the rural middle class was willing in practice to mitigate the severities of the new law, they would be faced with a laborers' revolt. But, in either case, they waited upon events, and neither planned nor organized in anticipation of them.[1]

The Poor Law Commissioners, by contrast, did both. The last few months of 1834 were spent in setting up their London office in Somerset House and above all in planning the administrative revolution in the parishes. Assistant Commissioners were appointed and districts allotted to them, and by the end of the year some of them were already in the field. They quickly established a pattern of procedure which proved highly successful and was used with little variation throughout England. An Assistant Commissioner, on arriving in his district, met with what were usually described as the 'respectable inhabitants' in order to test local feeling and explain what was intended. At the same time he found out which towns acted as market centers and judicial centers, investigated existing workhouse accommodation, and, on the basis of all this information, divided up his district into Poor Law Unions. This preparatory work often took some time, for speed, though desirable, was not as important as being sure of the future of a Union. The Assistant Commissioners tried to find out who were likely to be elected to the Boards of Guardians, who were likely to be made chairmen of the Boards, and who were most likely to be appointed as paid officials. If local opposition existed, its importance had to be gauged, and its leaders had, if possible, to be won over or at least neutralized. All of this could often take some months and it was not until early 1835 that the first Poor Law Unions were declared and put into operation. It was a cautious policy, designed, so the Commissioners believed, to take into account almost any eventuality.[2]

[1] Quite apart from newspapers, there was a flood of anti-Poor Law commentary, mostly in the form of pamphlets. The following are typical or especially interesting: R. Bligh, *Bellum Agrarium: A Foreview of the Winter of 1835* (London 1835); J. Bowan, *A Refutation of Some of the Charges Preferred Against the Poor* (London 1837); J. Wade, *Appendix to the Black Book* (London 1835); Wilmot, *Disinherited* (London 1835).

[2] On the procedure of the Commissioners in southern England, see P.L.C., First Annual Report, *B.P.P.*, 1835, XXV, 8–12 and Appendix B. There is a wealth of information in the Commission's files on individual

The first tests were not long in coming. The first Unions under the Poor Law Amendment Act were declared in February 1835, and it was not until March that the Commissioners began local reorganization on a large scale. Yet by the end of May the Poor Law authorities had had to contend with serious riots or near riots in at least half a dozen Unions widely scattered through the Home Counties. In no case was this primarily the result of opposition from the newly elected Boards of Guardians or by disaffected Old Poor Law authorities. Indeed the whole process of changing over to the new machinery was carried out smoothly everywhere. There were, for example, few cases of the overseers refusing to co-operate in arranging for the election of Guardians, the elections themselves were rarely contested and there appear to have been virtually no cases of ratepayers refusing to appoint Guardians. The functioning of the newly elected Boards was usually equally uneventful. At the first meetings, with the Assistant Commissioner almost always present, officers were elected, relief and workhouse committees were appointed, and the Unions were divided into relief and medical districts with little or no difficulty. Trouble, if there was any, came at a later stage, most often when relief in money was replaced by relief in kind.

One of the earliest and most serious examples of disturbances touched off by this change was the series of riots which took place in the Milton Union near Rochester in Kent.[1] The Union was declared by the Poor Law Commissioners late in March and the Board of Guardians, after their first meeting, received the highest praise from the Assistant Commissioner for East Kent, Sir Francis Bond Head. Its progress was therefore rapid, and by the end of April the granting of relief had been handed over to the newly appointed relieving officers by the old parish overseers. What is more, it had been decided that the change of machinery was to be accompanied by a change in policy. Direct allowances for children were to be reduced and, where possible, relief was to be

Unions. Particularly interesting reports on individual unions are: Uckfield Union, Sussex: MH 12.13157 Hawley to P.L.C. 11 and 23 Jan. 1835; Bishop's Stortford Union, Hertfordshire: MH 12.4536 Power to P.L.C. 16 Nov. and 1 Dec. 1834. Unusually good reports on a whole district (North Devon) are: MH 12.2493 Gilbert to P.L.C. 29 Oct. 1835; MH 12.2124 Gilbert to P.L.C. 30 Oct. 1835; MH 12.2636 Gilbert to P.L.C. 30 Oct. 1835.
[1] Milton Union, Kent: MH 12.5279 30 April–8 May correspondence; *The Times*, 14 May and 5 June 1835.

given in tickets redeemable for goods rather than in cash. On the very first day of granting relief under this new dispensation there was a riot at Bapchild, a village just east of Sittingbourne on the Faversham road, in which the Relieving Officer was mobbed and his books and papers destroyed. But he himself was not hurt and what damage there was was not serious. Moreover, it appeared that the riot might not have resulted from anti-Poor Law feelings at all, but rather from the fact that paupers from many villages were being relieved at one place and that, as a result, many had been forced to wait a long time. The Poor Law Commissioners therefore sent down orders that relief was to be given in each village separately and that under all circumstances the bringing together of large groups of paupers was to be avoided.

But new difficulties a few days later, including another minor riot and the stoning by paupers of the Guardians as they rode away from their weekly meeting, convinced everyone involved of the depth of popular feeling against the new law. This time, un-questionably, the disturbances had been occasioned by the offer of relief in kind rather than money and the Poor Law Commissioners, realizing this, made a few important concessions. It was agreed between the Guardians and Assistant Commissioner Head that laborers in full employment would continue to be given relief in kind only, but that all other classes of paupers should receive relief on the old scale, half of it in money. By this time, however, it was too late; the agricultural laborers were aroused, and on May 7 at Rodmersham, a small village near the center of the Union, a serious breach of the peace took place. The Relieving Officer, with the aid of the overseers of Rodmersham, was interviewing applicants for relief in the village church, but a crowd of laborers outside took the relief tickets from the paupers as fast as they were being handed out. When one of the overseers intervened to stop this, he was assaulted and forced back into the church which was then sur-rounded by the mob. After four hours, the men in the church, who had by this time been joined by the chairman and other Guardians, decided to make a break for it. They were chased by the mob for some distance, pelted with stones and probably saved from more direct physical attack by the opportune arrival of a detachment of soldiers who quickly dispersed the angry laborers. This affair marked the end of concessions by the Board of Guardians. Special constables were sworn in, policemen were brought down from London and within a few days twenty arrests had been made. This did not quite end the matter—some of the arrests were made in near riot conditions and when the prisoners were taken off to jail in Canterbury the yeomanry who accompanied them were stoned—but these minor clashes which followed the Rodmersham affair proved to be merely the backwash from it, and within a week or so the area had returned to normal.

The disturbances in the Milton Union had related almost entirely to the transition from money payments to payments in kind. But, as far as the Commissioners were concerned, this was only a secondary matter, a step in the right direction. Their object in insisting on payments in kind, aside from making sure that relief was really relief and not a free handout of spending money, was to pave the way for the eventual end of outdoor relief for the able-bodied and the imposition of a workhouse test. Resistance to any one of the preparatory stages as in the Milton Union could throw the timetable off a bit; it did not, however, alter the goal, nor did it mean that other preparations and changes had necessarily to be delayed. Thus even at the height of the troubles in the Milton Union plans were quietly being made for the erection of a new workhouse. Because it was still in the discussion stage and unknown to the general public, the resolve to build a new workhouse was not, so far as we know, a cause of the riots in Rodmersham, Doddington or Bapchild. But in other Unions the Guardians, rather than build a new workhouse, decided to renovate and reform the old ones, and this could hardly escape public notice. Indeed, as immediate causes of anti-Poor Law disturbances, such changes in workhouse management were of scarcely less importance than changes in out relief.

Here again a number of Poor Law Unions could serve equally well as examples, but of these the Amersham Union on the eastern slopes of the Chilterns in Buckinghamshire is perhaps the most instructive.[1] One of the major problems facing this Union was that far from there being an insufficiency of workhouse space, there was too much, or at least there were too many workhouses. The Board of Guardians therefore decided, on the advice of Assistant Commissioner Gilbert, to reduce the number of workhouses in use, move all the paupers into the few workhouses to be kept and in the process classify them, house by house, according to age, sex and type. Thus two processes, the removal of paupers from one

[1] Amersham Union, Buckinghamshire: MH 12.380 May 1835 correspondence and transcript of evidence at trial in August.

parish to another and reclassification within the remaining work-houses, were involved, and there is some evidence to suggest that both were felt as grievances by the working population. Be that as it may, it was the transfer of paupers out of the smaller parish work-houses that proved to be the immediate cause of a series of riots.

The first indication that trouble might be expected was a memorial from a group of ratepayers in the parish of Chalfont St. Giles protesting against the closing of their workhouse and the removal of its inmates. A few days later, near the end of May, the first incident took place; as the inmates were being taken from the Beaconsfield workhouse, a crowd, largely made up of women, gathered and started throwing stones. It was not a very important affair, but it did accurately reflect the state of local feeling and should perhaps have made the Guardians put off for the time being any further changes. But no such decision was taken, nor, it seems, was any adequate provision made for ensuring the safe transfer, only two days later, of a group of paupers from Chesham to Amersham. Thus, by the time the paupers were loaded into a cart in the courtyard of the workhouse, a large crowd had massed in front of the courtyard gates and refused to let them be opened. One of the magistrates read the Riot Act and for a moment the crowd fell back. The gates were opened and the cart, accompanied by this one magistrate, started off towards Amersham. There was not much distance to cover—two miles at most—but a spur of the Chilterns had to be crossed and it was uphill all the way to the village of Chesham Bois. The crowd followed, closing in gradually as the cart worked its way slowly along. One by one the paupers were lifted out of the cart, until at Chesham Bois it was empty. Then the crowd turned on the magistrate, first pelting him with stones and finally directly assaulting him. He managed to escape by hiding in a hedge and the crowd, having nothing else to do, dispersed. As for the paupers, once they had been liberated by the crowd, they simply returned to the workhouse at Chesham. The next day police arrived from London and on the day after that the yeomanry were brought in. Arrests were made and soon thereafter the paupers were moved, this time under guard and without incident, to the Amersham workhouse. That, as it turned out, was the end of the affair; there were no further disturbances and, as in the Milton Union, the business of the Board of Guardians went along very much as if nothing had happened.

The series of riots in these two Unions was as typical as any individual events can be of the sort of opposition faced by the Poor Law Commissioners in the south of England in 1835. At Ampthill in Bedfordshire there were 'money or blood' riots very like those in East Kent except that in Ampthill the rioters anticipated the changes to be made and attacked the relieving officer even before he had officially supplanted the overseers.[1] In Sussex, on the other hand, it was, as in Amersham, the workhouse which was the object of hatred and attack.[2] In Eastbourne mass meetings and a near riot were caused by the proposal to separate married couples in workhouses. And in the Uckfield Union one of the workhouses was broken into, evidently with the intention of taking the paupers who belonged to other parishes back to their own workhouses.

All of these disturbances, whatever their individual peculiarities, had much in common. In no case, it appears, was there what could be called proper or co-ordinated leadership. Eastbourne came nearest to having it. There an Agricultural Labourers Benefit Society was established, organizational meetings were held in a number of parishes, a system of communications between the laborers in various parishes was set up, and protest marches and rallies were staged on the days of meeting of the Board of Guardians. But nothing came of it. The presence of troops and London policemen prevented not only violence but even peaceful rallies of any size and the organization, thwarted in everything, collapsed within little more than a fortnight of its establishment. Even so, for all its weaknesses, there was the semblance of organized resistance in the Eastbourne Union.

In the other unruly Unions there does not seem to have been anything even remotely approaching this; indeed if there ever was such a thing as spontaneous rioting, these anti-Poor Law riots were examples of it. Troublemakers existed of course. Certain men tended to turn up at every disturbance and self-appointed carriers of news and haranguers of the crowd sprang up in all these trouble spots. Of the Milton Union, for example, it was reported that agricultural laborers were roaming the countryside with clubs, 'forcing the peaceable labourers to quit their work, menacing the

---

[1] Ampthill Union, Bedfordshire: MH. 12.1 May 1835 correspondence; *The Times*, 19 May 1835.
[2] Eastbourne Union, Sussex: MH 12.12854 April and May 1835 correspondence; Uckfield Union, Sussex: MH 12.13157 May 1835 correspondence.

civil authorities, extorting money, and committing violent assaults on persons who refused to comply with their unlawful demands'.[1] But this sort of thing was hardly organization; it was far nearer to the kind of rural anarchy that had swept England in 1830. For the most part it seems that the crowds simply gathered out of curiosity, because something had happened or seemed likely to happen, or as a result of rumors. Rumors indeed played a very large role. In Amersham, for example, it was believed by many paupers that terrible cruelties were to be practiced on the inmates of work-houses and that all who had ever received relief were to have their children taken away from them.[2] Similar stories about the breaking up of families and the starving of the poor appear to have been circulated in most of the districts where trouble arose.

Largely because of such factors as the influence of false rumors and the spontaneous character of the riots, the laborers involved gained a good deal of public sympathy. One Assistant Com-missioner characterized them as 'misguided men who have risen to oppose they know not what',[3] and it was therefore to leniency, the gradual introduction of new policies and long-term experience of the new dispensation that the authorities looked as the means of overcoming distrust and fear. In practical terms such a policy could mean putting off major changes for a time until resistance had died down; but it most certainly did not mean any basic change in Poor Law Commission policy. Thus, for example, the Commissioners suggested to the Eastbourne Board of Guardians that instead of rousing local opposition by taking married paupers into the workhouse and separating them, it should, at least 'in the first instance', relieve them out of the house in return for work performed for the parish. Only, the Commissioners concluded, when this and 'other cautious and preliminary measures shall have been tried should the workhouse . . . be brought into more exten-sive use than under present circumstances it may be desirable to attempt'.[4] But that the workhouse test should be applied eventually there was no question, and luckily for the Commissioners the Boards of Guardians almost without exception agreed. To feel sympathy for the rioters did not necessarily imply sympathy for their objections to the New Poor Law, and though the first form

[1] *The Times*, 14 May 1835.
[2] MH 12.380 Evidence of Fuller, a magistrate, given at a trial in Aug. 1835.
[3] MH 12.5279 Head to P.L.C. 7 May 1835.
[4] MH 12.12854 P.L.C. to Thomas 29 April 1835.

of fellow feeling was common, the second proved to be almost non-existent.

The Guardians of rural unions, largely because there was a property qualification for the office, were drawn almost exclusively, as one Assistant Commissioner put it, from the classes of substantial farmers, local professional men and the better sort of shopkeepers.[1] Between them and the 'lower orders' there was a gap in understanding and sympathy which, though difficult to define, was nonetheless real and came out very strongly in almost all the reports of anti-Poor Law disturbances. Men of substance and agricultural laborers did not of course constitute the entire population of the rural unions, still less of partially urban districts such as Eastbourne. There was in addition a class of small ratepayers including the lesser landholders, most shopkeepers, tradesmen and the like. From such people greater sympathy with the aims of the rioters might have been expected; the small farmers might, in bad years, find themselves applying for relief and the little shopkeepers, particularly the tavernkeepers, were said to have done well out of the cash payments given under the allowance system. Very often the blame for instigating the riots was placed on the heads of such people and the rioters themselves were seen as the ignorant tools of self-seeking shopkeepers and disgruntled parish officials turned out of office by the machinery of the New Poor Law.[2] Even so, important as their role in fomenting discontent may have been, such men were not, in the long run, in a position to control local policy. The men who did, the magistrates and, because of plural votes as well as property qualifications, the Guardians were men of means and, for the time being at least, active supporters of the New Poor Law.

The riots, far from intimidating them, spurred them on to greater exertions. In no case was the decision to institute relief payments in kind reversed; delays, if any, were measured in days not weeks. As regards workhouses, the same determination to press on, if anything with greater speed, was shown at the time of the riots and immediately thereafter. Up to a point it may even be said that these disturbances worked to the advantage of the Poor Law Commissioners. Their hand was strengthened and the powerlessness of their opponents was demonstrated beyond doubt.

[1] MH 12.13157 Hawley to P.L.C. 30 March 1835.
[2] See, for example: MH 12.13157 Hawley to P.L.C. 8 May 1835; MH 12.380 Gilbert to P.L.C. 24 May 1835.

Admittedly the ease with which the Poor Law Commissioners and local authorities had overcome and, to a degree, been able to ignore these disturbances was in part due to the fact that they were widely scattered. No large area, no cluster of Unions had as yet risen to oppose the law and it was at least possible that should this happen the Commissioners would not be able to pass it off so easily. But there was not much comfort for the opponents in such reflections; indeed the lack of resistance over a wide area was as much a sign of weakness as any of the other failures revealed by the events of April and May 1835.

Nothing happened in the summer of 1835 that was calculated to raise the opponents' hopes.[1] Unions by the dozen were put into operation; yet even the sporadic resistance which had shown itself in the spring seemed to have died away. But in the winter months of 1835-6 the New Poor Law was again put to the test, and this time by resistance of a ferocity and on a scale far beyond that of May. Two widely separated areas were involved: East Suffolk and North Devon. The Suffolk disturbances differed from all others in South England in a number of ways, one of the most important being that the final explosion was preceded by many months of discontent. In the rural Hoxne Union, centered on the village of Stradbroke some ten miles north-west of Framlingham, the Assistant Commissioner encountered far more than the usual degree of opposition when he made his preliminary enquiries. A number of the local Church of England ministers were vociferously anti-New Poor Law (a common thing in East Anglia) and a Stradbroke shoemaker, who fancied himself a disciple of Cobbett, spent much of his spare time rousing the local laborers. At about the same time, in the Cosford Union, just west of Ipswich, the governor of the workhouse was assaulted by eight of the inmates.[2]

Such events should certainly have been understood as warnings of possible future trouble, and perhaps they would have been but for two decisions by the Poor Law Commissioners. The first was to change Assistant Commissioners in the middle of the summer

---

[1] There were a few disturbances during the summer, but they were scattered geographically and of only minor importance. Hungerford Union, Berkshire: MH 12.234 Sept. 1835 correspondence; Docking Union, Norfolk: July 1835 correspondence; HO 73.51 Chadwick to Russell 7 July 1835.

[2] Hoxne Union, Suffolk: MH 12.11837 Jan. and May 1835 correspondence; Cosford Union, Suffolk: MH 12.11793 Jan., March and April 1835 correspondence.

and the second was to appoint Kay as the new Assistant Commissioner. Kay was ambitious, impatient and vain; he liked to be everywhere at once and he pushed his Boards of Guardians hard. Had this not been true, he might, despite his having come fresh to the area in August, have been able to see what was coming. There were certainly plenty of warning signs. The Hoxne Union never really quieted down. For months the Relieving Officers had been harassed and tormented by the paupers and in late November Kay himself was stoned by a small mob during one of his periodic visits to the district. Nor was the opposition confined to the primarily rural Unions in East Suffolk. In Ipswich, by far the largest town in the area, the New Poor Law had become the subject of political controversy in a way rare in southern England. Local feeling was in fact so strong that Kay decided not to hold the open meeting which usually preceded the declaration of a Union. The Board of Guardians election was bitterly contested and the opponents had the active support not only of the Old Poor Law officials but of one of the prominent local newspapers as well.[1]

Thus, by early December, the position of the Poor Law authorities in East Suffolk was exceedingly precarious and a single event almost anywhere could have touched off a fully fledged crisis. The Hoxne Union, in which the Board of Guardians and the Relieving Officers were constantly under threat of mob action, seemed the most likely danger area, but it was in Ipswich that the first events leading to a crisis actually took place. The Board of Guardians, despite strong opposition, was enthusiastically in favor of the New Law and, rather than waiting for the easier spring months to start imposing the workhouse test on able-bodied paupers, they decided to begin the process immediately. Thus, in December, they made arrangements for classification in the three workhouses to be retained for Union purposes and began the necessary repairs and alterations which proper classification required. Protest meetings were held almost nightly, the *Suffolk Chronicle* whipped up public feeling, and then, on the night of December 16, a crowd assembled at the St. Clement's workhouse 'and commenced the demolition of that house'.[2] The front wall was battered down, one wing was

[1] MH 12.11837 Owen to P.L.C. 26 Nov. 1835; Ipswich Union, Suffolk: MH 12.11855 Mott and Kay to P.L.C. 12 Aug. 1835 and Kay to P.L.C. 20 Sept. 5, 11, 14 Nov. 1835.

[2] MH 12.11855 Kay to P.L.C. 17 Dec. 1835.

totally destroyed and, but for the arrival of soldiers stationed in Ipswich, the entire building would have gone.

This, as it turned out, was the start of a general rising against the New Poor Law in East Suffolk. In the smaller villages of the Plomesgate Union, to the north-east of Ipswich near Framlingham and Orford, the Relieving Officers were attacked and the Guardians threatened.[1] The agricultural laborers of the Hoxne Union organized a march on Stradbroke where the Guardians were meeting, and only the coolness of the chairman of the Board prevented serious fighting and the destruction of property.[2] In the Cosford Union, as at Ipswich, the workhouse was the object of attack and once again only the courage of a handful of local Guardians and magistrates prevented its demolition.[3] All of these outbreaks, as well as many others of only slightly less importance, took place within a week of the attack on the St. Clement's workhouse at Ipswich. Together they constituted a kind of sustained assault on the New Poor Law which was without precedent, and the machinery not only of the Poor Law but of law enforcement in general broke down under the strain. Local constables and special constables were ineffectual objects of derision by the crowd and, though the magistrates, by and large, had the will to act, they lacked the means. Thus, as in May 1835, both the army and the London police had to be brought in. Yet they too were dangerously inadequate. Kay felt, quite correctly as it turned out, since at one time or another during that week at least half a dozen workhouses were attacked, that every workhouse would have to be defended. This, however, meant spreading available forces so thinly that no single area was really properly protected. On more than one occasion Kay himself, along with a large body of police or soldiers, went to an area only to find it quiet while violence was erupting elsewhere. 'I am sure', he wrote to London at one point, 'that we have not force enough to preserve the peace of the county.'[4]

But Kay was wrong; the peace was preserved. Indeed, within a few days of this despairing statement relative calm had been restored throughout the area. The riots in East Suffolk had been more dramatic, more widespread and better prepared for than those of the spring of 1835, but they did not differ from them in

[1] Plomesgate Union, Suffolk: MH 12.11932 Kay to P.L.C. 21, 22, 25 Dec. 1835.
[2] MH 12.11837 Ellis to P.L.C. 22 Dec. 1835; Kay to P.L.C. 23 Dec. 1835.
[3] MH 12.11855 Kay to P.L.C. 21, 26 Dec. 1835.
[4] MH 12.11932 Kay to P.L.C. 22 Dec. 1835.

any fundamental way. Reports even of the ugliest incidents pointed out how badly led the mobs were. Of the workhouses attacked, few were taken and even fewer were seriously damaged. The presence of a few policemen, sometimes even of a couple of magistrates, usually deterred the mob; the presence of troops always did so. Much the same can be said of the attempts to intimidate the Guardians, Relieving Officers and magistrates. Now and then a man was roughed up, here and there some property was destroyed, but there does not seem to have been any co-ordination or planning and the rioters were easily dispersed. Perhaps, despite these deficiencies, the rioters would have been successful had the Guardians been either sympathetic or afraid. This was not the case, however; in fact, as in May, the Guardians were, if anything, pushed into intransigence by such resistance. Relieving Officers were sent into villages to carry out their duties accompanied by armed guards, arrests were made in the same way and the building or re-building of workhouses was carried out with vigor and publicity. No chance was missed to display a firm hand and the continuing authority of the Poor Law officials.[1] Thus it may be said that, while the Suffolk riots differed somewhat in their origins and character from those of May, they had, for all practical purposes, the same weaknesses and the same results.

Compared with the December riots in Suffolk, the disturbances two months later in Devon were relatively mild affairs.[2] There was no long build-up and very little property was destroyed. Indeed, except for the fact that they involved a number of Unions rather than scattered isolated areas, they resembled the riots of May 1835 more than those of December. The district involved was the northernmost portion of Devon including the Unions centered on Barnstaple, South Molton and Torrington. It was not an area from which the Poor Law Commissioners expected much trouble. There was little pauperism and the local men of means and influence, though often suspicious of outside interference, were not actively hostile. But the Assistant Commissioner, Gilbert, as was so often the case, did not pay sufficient attention to reports of the feelings of less important citizens. He pressed the Guardians to institute relief in kind immediately throughout the district, thereby

[1] For the aftermath, see in particular: MH 12.11837 and MH 12.11855 Jan. 1836 correspondence.
[2] South Molton Union, Devonshire: MH 12.2493 Feb. 1836 correspondence.

precipitating a series of riots involving towns and villages in every part of North Devon. In character they were very like those which had taken place in Milton, Ampthill and parts of East Suffolk. Relieving Officers were assaulted and driven out of villages, relief in money was demanded and relief in kind refused, and local tradesmen, particularly bakers, were intimidated in the hope that they would refuse to supply the Union with goods for distribution as relief.

In other ways, too, the Devon riots harked back to the disturbances of early 1835. They came and went just as quickly, they lacked leadership of all but the most primitive kind, and they were fed by rumor and misinformation. In this last respect they were particularly interesting and especially pathetic, for rumor seems to have played a larger role in North Devon than almost anywhere else. Stories were spread of mass uprisings in other parts of southern England, the paupers were told that the New Poor Law meant prison for all of the poor and it appears to have been almost universally believed among the laboring population that the new law meant death either in the workhouse or through the distribution of poisoned bread. 'Some of the paupers', Gilbert noted, 'actually believed that if they touched the bread they would drop down dead.'[1] That such pathetic misconceptions had played a large role in bringing about the riots did not however deter the Boards of Guardians in these Unions from reacting with a severity far greater than was usual. Previously the tendency had been simply to enforce and extend the giving of relief in kind, while holding back further changes until the situation had cooled off. But in the North Devon Unions the Guardians went a great deal further. Throughout the area they either imposed the workhouse test immediately on able-bodied paupers in the refractory parishes or they instructed the Relieving Officers to boycott the villages where they had been attacked until the poor of these districts actually applied for them to return.[2]

The remainder of 1836 proved remarkably quiet. A handful of Unions—in South Devon, Huntingdonshire and Norfolk[3]—presented difficulties, but for the most part the transition to the New

[1] MH 12.2493 Gilbert to P.L.C. 20 Feb. 1836. See also his letter to the P.L.C. of 1 Dec. 1835.
[2] MH 12.2493 Feb. and March 1836 correspondence.
[3] Okehampton Union, Devonshire: MH 12.2394 April–June 1836 correspondence; Huntingdon Union: *The Times*, 16 April 1836; Lodden and Clavering Union, Norfolk: MH 12.8455 April 1836 correspondence.

Poor Law was achieved by the Commissioners with comparative ease. By the end of the year very little of southern England remained to be reorganized and only one county, Cornwall, had not yet been touched. Most of the Cornish Unions were put into operation smoothly enough, but two, Stratton and Camelford, in the northeast corner, perhaps influenced by the disturbances of the year before in neighboring North Devon, passed under the new law only after a show of defiance.[1] It was, as compared with some of the other earlier anti-Poor Law riots, not much of an affair. But it was unique in that the trouble came at the time of the first meeting of the new Boards of Guardians, long before relief in kind or workhouse alterations, which had been the main causes or at least occasions of all earlier mob action, were even proposed.

All in all it was a curious affair. A mob assembled at Camelford and later marched to Stratton. The Boards of Guardians at both places, having no means at hand for breaking up the crowd, simply abandoned their meetings and allowed the mob to disperse of its own accord. For the second meeting, a week later, the magistrates brought in troops, police and Assistant Commissioner Gilbert. Elsewhere, such a show of force had been sufficient to prevent further outbreaks, but, despite such precautions, there were riots in both Unions. These were easily put down and peace restored, but this did not have the usual effect on local morale. The long run effects of these disturbances turned out to be as unusual as the disturbances themselves had been. The Boards of Guardians did not react harshly; indeed they hardly reacted at all, for they were, unlike their far more sorely tried counterparts in other places, frightened by the resistance shown. The New Poor Law, as a result, suffered its first setback and Gilbert was forced to report to London that it would be a very long time before he would dare introduce the subject of a workhouse to the Boards of Guardians in this area.[2]

The formation of the Cornish Poor Law Unions between January and May 1837 completed the reorganization of southern England under the Poor Law Amendment Act, and, as it turned out, the disturbances which attended the formation of these Unions also proved to be a final stage. Nothing like it was to happen again and

[1] HO 73.52 Gilbert to P.L.C. 8, 9 Feb. 1837; Stratton Union, Cornwall: MH 12.1299 Gilbert to P.L.C. 18 Feb. 1837.
[2] MH 12.1299 Gilbert to P.L.C. 18 Feb. 1837.

the administration of the new law in rural southern England became very quickly a matter of routine. That this would be the case soon became apparent as the Unions where there had been trouble settled down. For all practical purposes these disturbances might as well have never happened. After a few weeks of caution, the Boards of Guardians returned to their original policies and reimposed and extended payments in kind. Nothing happened. Growing bolder, they added other restrictions on out-relief, began the building or rebuilding of workhouses and even tried out the workhouse test on a selective basis. Still nothing happened, and, as a result, they felt able to take the final decisive step of imposing the workhouse test on all able-bodied paupers and their families. This too was achieved without resistance and what is more it was achieved, in most of the Unions where resistance had been greatest, within a year or less after the riots.

Admittedly the speed and ease with which this was done was probably due in part to luck and exceptionally favorable circumstances. Harvests were good in 1835 and 1836. Abundant employment was offered not only by farmers but by the boom in railway building. These were, all in all, prosperous years, the peak years in fact of a boom. Also the Poor Law Commissioners were cautious and took no chances. The order prohibiting out-relief to the able-bodied was usually issued in the spring or summer months when unemployment in rural areas was low in any case. For all these reasons the change in many areas was probably not even noticed.

But such factors, while they explain a lot, do not explain everything. Prosperity was not universal. Some areas had a surplus of labor even in the best of times. In such districts the change was felt and, while the effect may sometimes have been, as the Commissioners hoped it would be, to press employers into giving better wages and long-term employment, it was by no means always so. Reliable evidence as to the effects of the prohibitory order is exceedingly difficult to get. The Poor Law Commission received its information almost entirely from the employers of labor and, moreover, from men within this class who were biased in favor of the new law. It is hardly surprising therefore that the annual reports of the Commission were filled with glowing accounts of rising wages, of more secure employment and of the general moral betterment of the poor.[1] But the Commissioners did receive other

[1] P.L.C., Second Annual Report, *B.P.P.*, 1836, XXIX (Part I), 23–9 and Appendix B.

information, all of which it tended to suppress, that, at least in some areas, directly contradicted their claims for the New Poor Law. Particularly damaging were the not-so-glowing reports sent to London from some of the Commissioners' most ardent supporters. 'The greater proportion . . . of the single male paupers', reported the chairman of one of the Suffolk Boards, 'are at this time ill off; and such of them as do not subsist by poaching or plunder are very glad to work for any wages, however low, which are sufficient to keep them out of the Work House. The depression of wages, which it is the great object of the Poor Law Amendment to correct, is at this time aggravated by its operation.'[1]

Such a state of affairs confirmed the worst fears and most pessimistic predictions of the New Poor Law's opponents, yet it did not produce the sustained popular resistance which they had also predicted. Part of the explanation lies, it would appear, in the nature and circumstances of those few attempts at popular resistance which were made. As we have seen, two of the primary characteristics of the anti-Poor Law riots in southern England were ignorance of what was being opposed and lack of leadership in the struggle against it. A sort of panic born of wild rumors seems to have swept across whole districts resulting here and there in brief periods of rioting. These were, with few exceptions, both sudden and unplanned. Only in East Suffolk was there a long period of rising discontent and lawlessness before the major outbreak; elsewhere the riots took place within three months or less of the formation of the Union. In such circumstances they could hardly help but die away, leaving behind, in most cases, not the slightest evidence that anything had happened. The void left by the collapse of spontaneous popular opposition was never successfully filled and only a few attempts were made to build up a less dramatic but more effective and lasting form of resistance.

Of the efforts to resurrect and channel the popular energy so pitifully wasted in the early disturbances, by far the most interesting was that made by the Rev. F. H. Maberly, a Cambridgeshire parson. The main field of his operations was in the area to the south of Cambridge where Cambridgeshire, Hertfordshire and Essex meet. Superficially this seemed a very promising district, for three of the Unions there had experienced difficulties in the early months of their operation. In the Royston Union, in August 1835, a mob had attacked the Relieving Officer, while, in

[1] MH 12.11793 Calvert to P.L.C. 9 March 1836.

D

December of the same year, the workhouses of the Bishop's Stortford and Saffron Walden Unions had been set on fire.[1] There had been no further trouble but the local authorities were understandably nervous and fearful of revived opposition. Maberly, on the other hand, was as confident as they were anxious. He believed that the situation was ripe for exploitation and that all that was needed was firm leadership.

He began his campaign in the late spring of 1836.[2] Anti-Poor Law leaflets were distributed throughout the district and a series of eight mass public protest meetings were called to organize pressure on local Boards of Guardians and to raise petitions to be sent to Parliament and the Poor Law Commissioners. The largest of these meetings was scheduled for Royston and timed to coincide with the near completion of the new Union workhouse late in June. The local authorities feared that an attempt might be made to destroy this still unfinished and therefore highly vulnerable symbol of the New Poor Law unless Maberly was restrained, or, if possible, actually prevented from holding his meeting. The government took these fears seriously. Police were dispatched to Royston and the Home Office sent Maberly a stern warning against unlawful proceedings. In the event the meeting was exceedingly quiet despite the presence of nearly two thousand people many of whom expected a riot. The themes of his speech were familiar: the cruelty of the workhouse, the unconstitutionality of the Poor Law Commission, the danger of central government interference in local affairs and so on. He defended the allowance system as the only way of making sure that there was 'a point below which the wages of a poor man cannot sink'.[3] He appealed to the small retailer who, he said, would lose trade, and to the small farmer whose rates, he claimed, would be raised to pay for the new law. Altogether it was an appeal well calculated to rouse popular feeling and perhaps to create an alliance between the laborers and small ratepayers. But nothing came of it. There were no riots, the Board of Guardians did not find themselves suddenly pressed to relax

[1] Royston Union, Hertfordshire: MH 12.4639 Aug. 1835 correspondence; Bishop's Stortford Union, Hertfordshire: MH 12.4536 Dec. 1835 correspondence; Saffron Walden Union, Essex: MH 12.3706 Dec. 1835 correspondence. The two workhouse fires are unusual in that they came long after the formation of the Unions. Very possibly they were inspired by news of the riots in Suffolk, which had begun about a week before.

[2] F. H. Maberly, *To the Poor and Their Friends* (London 1836); MH 12.4693 June 1836 correspondence.

[3] Maberly, *To the Poor*, 34.

the rigors of the law, and the building of the workhouse and the general administration of the Union went on much as before.

It is arguable that Maberly simply came on to the scene too late and that, had he started his campaign a year earlier, he might have succeeded in building an anti-Poor Law alliance and sustaining popular discontent. Perhaps, though all the experience of 1835–6 pointed to the conclusion that popular resistance could be put down with relative ease and that once crushed it was beyond reviving. As for the possibility of creating an alliance between the agricultural laborers and other classes, this was, in the long run, even more remote. So long as the efficacy of the New Poor Law in ending the abuses of the old law and reducing the rates was not proved, and so long as the possibility of sustained popular opposition had to be reckoned with, an alliance was at least possible. But the curtailment of the allowance system together with an often dramatic reduction in rates in most Unions within a year after their formation, removed most of the ratepayers' doubts, while the ease with which disturbances had been ended removed the fear of social unrest. Support for the New Poor Law grew and with it the confidence of the Boards of Guardians and the Poor Law Commissioners. Thus, for example, the prospect of anti-Poor Law riots in 1835 had caused the Guardians in most Unions to make concessions which were only gradually withdrawn after the restoration of peace. In Devon, in the other hand, less than a year later, disturbances were viewed with relative equanimity, no concessions were made and the changeover to a more rigorous policy was carried on as if nothing at all had happened. Once the local Poor Law authorities had come to believe in the law they were administering and in their power to administer it, they could not be shaken.

Only where such confidence was lacking did the new law run into serious and lasting difficulties. In Cornwall, the riots, far from making the Guardians more determined, had frightened them. Moreover, in Cornwall and much of Devon as well, the workhouse had been comparatively little used and was looked upon as alien by all classes of society. These factors combined to make the imposition of the New Poor Law at its most stringent all but impossible. Three Cornish Unions refused to replace their old, small and inadequate workhouses while one Devon Union bordering on Cornwall, as well as the two Cornish Unions where riots had occurred in 1837, had none to begin with and refused to build any. This meant that out-relief to all classes of paupers including the able-bodied had to be continued. There could be no workhouse test, no prohibitory order; indeed, as the Assistant Commissioner for the area was forced to admit, 'the main principles of the Poor Law Amendment Act . . . have not been and cannot be applied'.[1]

But Cornwall was only a small corner of England. That five Unions there and one in adjacent Devon did not build workhouses hardly worried the Poor Law Commissioners when they compared this failure with the extraordinary success of their policy elsewhere. These half dozen recalcitrant Unions in the two counties of the extreme southwest could not be matched in the approximately two dozen counties which made up the remainder of southern and central rural England. The Poor Law Commissioners had triumphed far beyond anyone's expectations and few would have questioned their confident assertion, made in 1836, 'that . . . we should be able by midsummer next to bring the act into operation in every part of the country'.[2]

[1] Falmouth Union, Cornwall: MH 12.1338 Wade to P.L.C. 6 Feb. 1841.
[2] P.L.C., Second Annual Report, 4.

III The origins of
northern opposition

It was not only on the basis of their extraordinary success in the
South of England that the Poor Law Commissioners expected to
have an easy passage in the rest of the country. The industrial
districts of the North, which, along with London, were the only
remaining areas of importance still under the Old Poor Law at the
end of 1836, appeared unlikely to present any major obstacles. Few
of the abuses which prevailed in southern England and which it
had been the main object of the government to eradicate were
present to any great degree in the North. The allowance system
was a rarity and there was nothing in the North to compare with
the classes of paupers and small tradesmen who lived directly or
indirectly off the rates. As a result the cost of poor relief was
strikingly low in the area; of the ten counties where relief costs were
less than five shillings per head in 1836, no less than eight were
north of the Trent.[1]

In such conditions it seemed quite possible that the transition
to the new machinery and new policies of the Poor Law Amendment Act would take place almost without anyone noticing.
Certainly what little experience the Commissioners had already
had with industrial areas pointed to that conclusion. A number of
Midland towns had been re-organized under the new law during
1836 and all of them had begun relatively well. The Commissioners
were above all pleased with their almost unqualified success in
Leicester and Nottingham where conditions most closely resembled those in the textile districts of the North.[2] In both towns
the strictest economy was practiced from the very beginning and
the Boards of Guardians readily accepted the principle of a rigorous test for able-bodied applicants. Nottingham in particular
became a prize exhibit of the Poor Law Commissioners. What anti-
Poor Law feeling there had originally been quickly vanished and,
as the Assistant Commissioner for the district proudly reported
back to London, the Board of Guardians were soon carrying 'out

---

[1] P.L.C., Third Annual Report, *B.P.P.*, 1837, XXXI, 262.
[2] Nottingham Union: MH 12.9944 May–Sept. 1836 correspondence;
Leicester Union: MH 12.6468 May–Aug. 1836 correspondence.

your wishes both in spirit and letter more rapidly and cordially than any other Board of Guardians I ever saw'.[1] One man was elected to combine the offices of clerk, relieving officer and workhouse master. Through his efforts primarily, but with the full backing of the Board, the workhouses were classified and less eligibility was put into practice through a new regime of workhouse discipline. Indeed, the Nottingham Union had become so advanced by the end of 1836 that the Poor Law Commissioners felt able to issue the outdoor relief prohibitory order.

Such successes were encouraging, but, perversely, they should also have been viewed by the Commissioners as a source of some concern. The very ease with which the transition from the old to the new law had been made in places like Nottingham was proof to opponents that the new law was not needed. Northern rates were low, northern overseers and churchwardens were both honest and efficient. Why then replace what was known to work well with a system that had not been proved? This was by no means a new line of argument. It had been used in Parliament by a number of northern members who otherwise favored the Poor Law Amendment Act but felt that the North should be excluded from its provisions. There was of course no way of knowing how many northerners held such views but among them were such prominent Liberals as Edward Baines, who was not only an M.P. but the proprietor of the influential *Leeds Mercury*, and, significantly, while the Commissioners remained unconcerned, a number of supporters of the new law with greater personal experience of the North were less sanguine. Assuming the worst, they began a propaganda campaign aimed especially at a northern audience. This differed markedly from similar efforts undertaken in earlier years in southern England. There the emphasis had been on the savings in rates and the improvement in the moral condition of the poor which the New Poor Law would bring. In the North, however, neither of these arguments could effectively be used and the advocates of the new law had to fall back on subtler arguments concerning the law's potential as a preventer of abuses which might arise or were actually becoming prevalent.

The most interesting of the many pro-Poor Law pamphlets aimed at northern opinion was the anonymously written *Voice from the North of England*.[2] It admitted that rates were low but claimed

[1] MH 12.9944 Gulson to P.L.C. 24 July 1836.
[2] *Voice From the North of England on the New Poor Law* (London

that, considering the unexampled prosperity which the region had enjoyed in recent years, they could have been lower still. It admitted that relief was ordinarily well administered but noted that the creation of Unions and the use of full-time officials would make it even better. It admitted that abuses of the kind and on the scale of those in the South had no parallel in the North but noted that the payment of rents and above all the granting of allowances to the notoriously underpaid handloom weavers were dangerous precedents which, if allowed to continue, might well pauperize the North as similar practices had the South. Indeed it could be argued that the situation in the North was potentially more dangerous in that any use of the rates to subsidize the wages of ordinary factory workers would give an unfair advantage to any manufacturer who could thereby lower his wages bill. Such a thing had never yet happened but there was no guarantee, the Poor Law Commissioners argued, that it would not, unless of course the New Poor Law was introduced into the manufacturing districts.[1]

The opponents were very quick to point out that all of these pro-Poor Law arguments were simply matters of opinion and conjecture. To talk of possible future abuses was a very different thing from the reform of existing abuses which had been the justification of the New Poor Law in rural southern England. The allowances granted to handloom weavers were not, opponents asserted, an abuse in the ordinary sense. The handloom weavers were a special class, quite distinct from any other in industry. They performed a function which was being replaced by machinery; they were therefore a dying class living off declining wages, and the granting of allowances to them was simply a way of softening the blow. No one in Lancashire or Yorkshire thought of extending similar benefits to other types of workers in different sorts of jobs. This much had been admitted even by the pro-Poor Law assistant to the Poor Law Inquiry Commission and the opponents felt that in raising such issues the Poor Law Commissioners were at best misrepresenting and at worst were totally ignorant of the conditions and needs of industrial areas.[2]

1837). It appears that this pamphlet was written by R. M. Muggeridge, the head of the migration office in Manchester. It was not, however, an official P.L.C. publication and at least one Assistant Commissioner had reservations about its views on relief policy. MH 12.14720 Note by Alfred Power on the back of a letter from Wagstaff to P.L.C. 18 Oct. 1838.

[1] P.L.C., 1834 Report, 43.
[2] On the Old Poor Law in the North, see: Report of Assistant

The question of whether the new law was needed in the North was however only half the issue. Even if the need for some reform was granted, there remained doubts concerning the applicability of the Poor Law Amendment Act outside of agricultural districts. Opponents claimed, not unreasonably, that the Poor Law Inquiry Commission had been established in response to a crisis in rural affairs, that it had dealt only cursorily with the problems of industrial areas and that its recommendations had been made with rural not urban problems in mind. Rural problems such as surplus labor, seasonal unemployment and substandard wages were not by and large the problems of the North where there was a chronic labor shortage and high wages in periods of prosperity and mass unemployment or part time employment in periods of depression. It followed, so the opponents argued, that less eligibility and particularly less eligibility enforced through the workhouse system could not be sensibly applied to the North, however beneficial it might prove to be in the South. When trade was good the workhouse would be empty apart from the aged, the sick and children; when times were bad no reasonable workhouse would be large enough to hold the mass of able-bodied factory workers which the application of a workhouse test would bring in.

The Poor Law Commissioners appeared at the time to have seen the force of such arguments. In their official pronouncements they denied any intention of enforcing a prohibitory order in the North. The workhouse was represented in the mildest possible terms, primarily as a refuge for the old and sick and as a deterrent for the lazy and improvident. In so representing their aims the proponents of the New Poor Law, including the Commissioners themselves, were either inconsistent or dishonest, perhaps a little of both. There was in fact no clear-cut Poor Law Commission policy on the subject. Assistant Commissioners in the various industrial districts differed, as indeed did the Commissioners in London. Some suggested that a rigorous workhouse test should be the aim in the North quite as much as in the South. Others felt that the workhouse test should be applied except in times of severe depression. No nationally appointed poor law official advocated anything more lenient than the latter policy and a majority or near

Commissioners Henderson and Tweedy to the Poor Law Inquiry Commission, *B.P.P.*, 1834, XXVIII. On northern attitudes towards the new law, see, for example: HO 73.53 passim, but especially, Power to Chadwick 10 May 1837.

majority led by Chadwick and the more enthusiastic of the Assistant Commissioners unquestionably supported the former position.[1]

Proof of this came at a critical time during 1837 when the industrial Unions of the North were being organized. The recession of late 1836 turned into a severe depression in a number of districts during the early months of 1837. Among the areas most deeply affected were the east Midlands hosiery towns such as Nottingham and Leicester, where the machinery of the New Poor Law was functioning and could be used by the Commissioners to try out its policies in urban conditions. Nottingham was the key.[2] The Assistant Commissioner for the district, Gulson, was a firm backer of the workhouse test as was the all-powerful Barnett, the clerk cum workhouse master cum relieving officer of the Nottingham Union. Nottingham had, moreover, a relatively large workhouse and a highly co-operative Board of Guardians. It was, from the Commissioners' point of view, the perfect place in which to test and demonstrate their policies.

In the early stages of the depression there was no question of relaxing the workhouse test which was unquestionably seen as a deterrent. 'The workhouse system', Gulson wrote happily to London, 'has . . . developed in a wonderful degree the ability of the artisans still to find means of maintaining themselves.'[3] Even so, it still remained an open question whether or not, as pressure increased, the rules would have to be changed. But whatever might happen eventually, this much was agreed, that change would be delayed as long as possible even if a strict adherence to the workhouse test meant a degree of overcrowding in the workhouse, the renting of additional space and even perhaps the encouragement of emigration away from Nottingham. Of these expedients the

[1] The endless debate among the administrators of the law on this most important question of policy was discussed at some length by the Webbs in their *English Poor Law History*, Part II, Vol. I, 142–52. Much more information is now available. The strict view was taken by Chadwick and probably a majority of the Assistant Commissioners, while a more lenient or at least more gradual policy usually had the support of two out of the three Commissioners. Finer, *Chadwick*, Book III, Ch. I; the opinions of the Assistant Commissioners on a proposed general order of the P.L.C., which can be found in HO 73.53 Aug.–Oct. 1837 correspondence.

[2] For events in Nottingham, see: MH 12.9944 Jan. 1837–Mar. 1838 correspondence; P.L.C., Third Annual Report, 7–9; P.L.C., Fourth Annual Report, *B.P.P.*, 1838, XXVIII, 23–6.

[3] MH 12.9944. Gulson to P.L.C. 27 Jan. 1837.

first two at least were extensively tried. The central workhouse ordinarily had about 260 inmates but by crowding it and renting additional space the Board of Guardians was able, at the worst period, to house 900 people. But even this was not enough and by April 1837 the Board was facing a crisis and had to ask the Poor Law Commissioners to suspend the prohibitory order.

The Commissioners were saved from having to grant a suspension at this time by the creation of a privately supported relief fund which was used to employ no less than 200 heads of families on road works. The pressure on Union funds and Union facilities was relieved and a rigorous application of the principles of the New Poor Law was maintained. That this had been achieved only with the greatest difficulty and, at the moment of severest pressure, solely through the intervention of private charity, could not, however, be denied. Even Barnett had to admit 'that but for the subscription we could not by any means have avoided outdoor relief to a considerable extent to the able bodied poor'.[1] Nor was this the end of the matter. During the summer pressure continued to mount, the private relief fund ran out, and Barnett and Gulson reluctantly concluded that a temporary suspension of the prohibitory order and the extension of other forms of outdoor relief such as soup kitchens could no longer be avoided. None the less the long struggle to avert this had not been in vain. There was no question of the suspension of the workhouse test being anything but temporary and, little more than a year later when unemployment eventually receded, the suspending order was revoked. The Commissioners had, therefore, good reason to be pleased. Throughout the crisis, the workhouse had remained the basis of relief policy, the labor test had been used solely as a supplement to it, and even at the worst of times all able-bodied paupers had been subjected to some sort of test.

Even so, Gulson and Barnett were anxious about the future. In 1837 a strong Board of Guardians, the private relief fund and the determination of Gulson and Barnett had averted any mitigation of the rigors of the law for many months and had ensured that any mitigations would be regarded as a crisis measure only. But Boards of Guardians might not always be so firm—already, as a result of the depression, a few anti-Poor Law Guardians had appeared on the Board—and men of Gulson's and Barnett's doggedness might not always be available. Moreover, now that it had

[1] MH 12.9944. Barnett to P.L.C. 2 May 1837.

become clear that the Commissioners would suspend the work-house test during an economic crisis, there was good reason to believe that local pressure for such a suspension would come much earlier in future crises. There was, Barnett and Gulson believed, only one way of ensuring against these eventualities, by building a huge new workhouse capable of holding at least 800 inmates. That such a house would be a white elephant in times of prosperity did not trouble them; they were concerned with maintaining the integrity of the New Poor Law even at the worst of times, and the worst of times in Nottingham, as 1837 proved, could be very bad indeed.

To those in the North who watched the steady progress of the New Poor Law with anxiety the reaction of the Poor Law Com-missioners to the depression in Nottingham was a particularly ominous sign. It seemed to give the lie to all the assurances of the Commissioners that the law would be flexibly administered in the North. It was, moreover, a clear demonstration of just how great were the powers of the Commissioners over local authorities. But the northern opponents hardly needed the example of Nottingham to confirm their worst fears. There was, in the migration scheme, quite as good an object lesson far closer to home. The migration clauses of the Poor Law Amendment Act were never as important as either their supporters or opponents had at first expected. The depression of the late 1830s put an end to the early efforts at trans-ferring surplus rural workers to urban areas, and once dead they were never revived. But in 1835–6 migration and, to a lesser extent, emigration were thought of as fundamental to a solution of the problem of rural poverty.

Detailed planning for extensive migration began in response to a request from a Lancashire manufacturer, Henry Ashworth of Bolton, for additional hands.[1] In a series of letters to Chadwick starting in June 1834 he sketched out his views not only of the Poor Law and migration in particular but of the effects which they could have, if properly administered, on the economy as a whole. Industrial progress in the North, he argued, was hampered by a labor shortage and consequently high wages. In such circum-stances the working classes had no inhibitions about openly

---

[1] This correspondence in its entirety is in the files of the Bolton Union, Lancashire: MH 12.5593 June 1834–May 1836 correspondence. It was reprinted in part, with much additional commentary, in P.L.C., First Annual Report, 21–3, 183–204, 212–20.

organizing trade unions and belligerently demanding higher wages, better working conditions and the like. In this situation, Ashworth suggested, the Poor Law Commissioners could be of considerable help. Extensive migration would increase the supply of labor and perhaps 'have a tendency to equalize wages as well as prevent in a degree some of the turnouts which have been of late so prevalent'.[1]

The Commissioners responded enthusiastically to Ashworth's initiative. Migration offices were established in Manchester and Leeds to act as clearing houses for requests for hands in the North and offers of laborers from the South. Poor Law Commission sponsored delegations of agricultural laborers visited the industrial districts and laudatory accounts of these tours were printed and distributed in the areas of labor surplus. But though the administrative machinery was in large part based on suggestions originated by Ashworth and other manufacturers, the intentions of the Poor Law Commissioners in setting it up were by no means identical with those of the prospective employers of migrant laborers. Ashworth's appeal to the Poor Law Commissioners had been prompted largely by his desire to undermine the great trade union movement of the early 1830s, just then reaching its peak. The Commissioners wisely did not wish to associate themselves with one party to this struggle or to endanger the long-run success of the migration scheme by precipitant action. They therefore insisted on elaborate contracts between migrants and possible employers which included provision for housing, a guaranteed period of employment, and a rate of wages which, though often below prevailing scales, was still relatively high. Perhaps partly as a result of this and certainly in consequence of the long negotiations which usually preceded any successful migration, the number of laborers and their families who actually made the move was small.[2]

[1] MH 12.5593 Ashworth to Chadwick 21 March 1835.

[2] On the migration scheme as a whole, see: A. Redford, *Labour Migration in England 1800–1850* (Manchester 1964), Ch. VI; P.L.C., Second Annual Report, 409–42; P.L.C., Third Annual Report, 90–9. The reports of fact finding tours in the North by southern laborers are particularly interesting: R. A. Kersey, *Letter to the Venerable Archdeacon Lyall . . . in Consequence of a Visit to Manchester* (Hadleigh 1835); W. Noakes, *Report of a Journal to Manchester* (Sandwich 1836). For examples of Unions which were particularly active in the migration scheme, see: Docking Union, Norfolk: MH 12.8249 1835–36 correspondence; Cosford Union, Suffolk: MH 12.11793 1836 correspondence; Leeds, Yorkshire: MH 12.15224 Dec. 1835–Aug. 1837 correspondence; Stockport Union, Cheshire: MH 12.1138 1835 correspondence.

Even so, relatively unimportant as the migration scheme was in the overall history of the New Poor Law, it was of considerable importance in another respect. It provided the opponents of the law in the North with their first effective issue, their first concrete example of the local workings of the dreaded Commissioners in London. The assurance that the relief of rural overpopulation and not the lowering of industrial wages was the object of the migration scheme was easily brushed aside; the overzealous supporters of the law, as so often before, provided the opposition with more than ample evidence of evil intent. The Ashworth letters had been published not only in the press but in the official annual reports of the Poor Law Commissioners. Nothing more was needed. A series of bitter pamphlets attacking migration was published in 1836 and the following year, and in the speaking tours of northern political agitators the migration scheme, indeed the New Poor Law as a whole, began to emerge for the first time as a major issue.[1]

None of these signs of public disquiet caused the Poor Law Commissioners much concern, for the new law had aroused similar controversy in the South. Working-class discontent was to be expected and the belief, as common among the middle as the working classes, that the New Poor Law was irrelevant to the North had to be taken into account and where possible overcome. If serious resistance was ever to arise, however, middle-class disquiet about the implications of the law would have to be transformed into outright opposition, and this in turn would have to be linked with working-class discontent, which itself would have to be organized and channeled almost exclusively into anti-Poor Law activity. As we have seen, the Poor Law Commissioners were confident that the fulfillment of all these conditions was even less likely in the North than it had been in the South.

In practice, however, just the reverse proved to be the case, for there were special factors present in the North late in 1836 that had been absent in southern England one or two years before. One of the most obvious and perhaps the most important of these was the existence in the North of organized protest. No area in England, not Birmingham, not even London, was as productive of popular movements. The contrast with the rural South could not have been much greater. The attempts of the early 1830s to

---

[1] M. Fletcher, *Migration of Agricultural Labourers* (Bury 1836); MH 12.15224 Baker to P.L.C. 12 April and 14 June 1837.

organize rural discontent collapsed with the prosecution of the Tol-
puddle martyrs in 1834, and thereafter, as we have seen, the few
overt demonstrations of that discontent which did take place were
uncoordinated and ineffective. But an almost equally disastrous setback for the trade union movement in the North in 1834 did not
lead to a collapse of organized movements of protest and reform;
after a brief period of inactivity, the energy was simply redirected
into other channels and particularly into a revival during 1836
of the factory reform movement. This continued vitality of
northern reformism should perhaps in itself have given the
Commissioners some cause for concern. On the other hand, there
was no reason to assume that popular agitation would be turned
away from the factory reform campaign or that, if it was, it
would be turned against the Poor Law rather than to one of the
traditional subjects of agitation such as trade unionism or political
radicalism.

This at any rate was the Commissioners' assessment of the situation and in normal economic conditions it would probably have
been the correct assessment. But economic conditions were far
from normal in the North late in 1836 and the Commissioners,
whose early successes had been made possible in large measure,
and more than they perhaps realized, by the unusual prosperity of
the mid 1830s, suddenly found that their luck in this respect had
run out. Shortly before the arrival of an Assistant Poor Law Commissioner in the North there was a sharp downturn in trade. The
extent of this recession is difficult to gauge owing to the lack of full
and accurate statistics, but enough is known to make it possible to
draw some conclusions.[1] The economy reached a peak about the
middle of 1836 and began to decline thereafter, until, by early
1837, it was markedly depressed. This was not, it should be emphasized, a general depression. A number of important sectors of
the economy continued to flourish, in some cases even increasing
their activity. This was the case in railway building, for example,
largely because lines projected or started in the boom conditions
of the early or middle 1830s were followed through during the last
years of the decade. Equally important was the continued rise in
cotton production which, like the sustained railway boom, was

[1] For a detailed discussion of the recession of the late 1830s, see:
A. Gayer, W. W. Rostow and A. J. Schwartz, *The Growth and Fluc-
tuation of the British Economy 1790–1850* (Oxford 1953), Vol. I, Ch. I;
R.C.O. Matthews, *A Study in Trade Cycle History* (Cambridge 1954),
Chs. IV, VIII, IX (Parts 4 and 7), X, XII (Parts 3 and 4).

largely the result of commitments made in earlier more prosperous years. So long as there was a profit, however small, it was
more advantageous to the mill owners to keep their expensive
plant in operation than to leave it idle.

But in spheres where the return on large investment was not a
major factor, the recession was immediately and sharply felt.
Building activity in the North, having reached a peak in 1836, fell
away drastically in 1837 and kept on falling for the remainder of
the decade. More severely affected, perhaps indeed the greatest
sufferers of all, were the handloom weavers of the textile districts.
Even at the best of times they had been hard pressed for a generation. Too numerous in any case and fast being replaced by power
loom weaving, they were in a most exposed position. A recession,
let alone a depression, was bound to worsen an already intolerable
situation. Under the pressure of falling profits, employers cut
costs where it was easiest to do so, in the piece work rates of
weavers. This, coupled with the gradually rising price of food as a
result of a succession of poor harvests, pushed a great many
weavers well below the subsistence level.

Thus, while it may be inaccurate to speak of a depression in the
late 1830s, it can be said that the general prosperity of the middle
years of the decade was over and that certain sections of the
economy and of the working population were suffering acutely.
The effects this was likely to have on the prospects of the Poor Law
in the North are fairly obvious. Mass unemployment would not be
a problem since most mills continued to work, even if occasionally
on short time. But severe unemployment in some trades, such as
building, and insufficient wages in others, particularly handloom
weaving, were just as clearly going to be a problem. In such circumstances the New Poor Law was bound to become a focus for
discontent and an object of agitation.

But it was not only the depression that turned the New Poor
Law into a major popular issue late in 1836, for, at the same time,
the recently resuscitated factory reform movement was entering a
period of crisis which made the adoption of some alternative issue
almost a necessity. Indeed, to a large extent, the factory reform
movement had been on the defensive ever since its revival, which
had been as much a desperate move to save the few gains already
made as a sign of renewed vitality.[1] The Factory Act of 1833 had

[1] The best account of the revival of the factory reform movement is in
C. Driver, *Tory Radical* (New York 1946), Ch. XXIV.

been scheduled to come gradually into effect during the three following years. First, ten-year-olds and finally, in 1836, twelve-year-olds were to be limited to an eight-hour day. But as the final year approached the pressure from employers to water down the law increased, largely because it had proved difficult to operate the mills efficiently when the regulated hours of children were so much shorter than the unregulated hours of adults. To the factory reformers this was further proof of the need to regulate the hours of all workers, but to the employers and, as it turned out, the government as well this problem was seen as a justification for backtracking and removing the restrictions on twelve-year-olds. The reformers, who had always thought the bill inadequate, now found themselves its main defenders and in 1835 they resuscitated the old factory reform committees to fight for its preservation. Preservation alone, however, was not enough to rally the old forces, and to counter a government bill aimed at partial repeal they put forward their own proposals for further reform. In the end nothing came of either the government's or the reformers' proposals but this did not end the activities of the revived Lancashire and West Riding Short Time Committees.

The 1833 act, though once more theoretically secure, was constantly evaded and only indifferently enforced. Inevitably then, with further reform out of the question for the moment, the factory movement turned to the issue of enforcement. Throughout the late months of 1836 this was the major point of agitation in the North and, as it became clearer day by day that local magistrates were often actively hostile to the law, the leaders of the movement, Richard Oastler in particular, became increasingly violent and aggressive. Oastler reached his peak in a speech at Blackburn in September in which he declared that further evasions of the law could only be met by drastic measures. 'If', he advised his audience, 'your magistrates should refuse to listen to your complaints under the factory act . . . bring [me] your children and tell them to ask their grandmothers for a few of their old knitting needles which I will instruct them how to apply to the spindles in a way which will teach these law-defying mill owner magistrates to have respect even to . . . the factory law.'[1] This was strong stuff, too strong as it turned out for many of the more timid reformers; but it was also, surely, as much a sign of desperation as of determination and conviction. The factory reform movement had in practice

[1] C. Driver, *Tory Radical* (New York 1946), Ch. XXIV, 127.

reached a dead end. It could not realistically hope for any new measure of reform; it was in fact reduced to pressing for the implementation of a law which it had originally opposed as inadequate. Without some new incentive to activity the popular reform movement in the North was probably in some danger of disintegrating, as, for example, it had done for some time after the trade union debacle of 1834.

Of this, however, we can never be sure, for the needed stimulus was provided late in 1836 by the arrival in the North of Alfred Power, the Assistant Commissioner charged with the responsibility of introducing the new law into the textile districts. Nothing could have better served the needs of the leaders of the factory reform movement. The Poor Law offered them not only a much-needed alternative issue around which to build a campaign, but it could be fitted almost perfectly into the campaign they were then waging. It promised to be, at one and the same time, both a new issue and a new aspect of an old issue, new evidence in fact that what they had been asserting all along was true. The migration scheme could be interpreted as an attempt to introduce child labor into the North *en masse* in order that a relay system in the factories could be established, and, more generally, it was easy to show how the workhouse system and restrictions on out-relief could be used to drive down wages and force workers to accept almost any factory conditions. It was essentially in such terms that the New Poor Law was first introduced to mass audiences in the North and for some time opposition to it was represented as an extension of the factory reform campaign.[1]

This did not last long, of course. With an Assistant Poor Law Commissioner already touring the area, resistance had to be organized immediately or not at all, and, in any case, expediency dictated a fairly rapid shift to what promised to be a more fertile field of agitation. Once this process was complete and resistance to the New Poor Law was established as an independent and, for the moment at least, as the most important popular movement in the North, the early links with factory reform tended to be forgotten. All the same, the smooth transition from one issue to the other was of inestimable importance to the anti-Poor Law movement in its early stages. It meant that the transition period could be short, a matter of weeks rather than months, and that the

---

[1] Fletcher, *Migration*, 4–5; R. Oastler, *Eight Letters to the Duke of Wellington* (London 1835).

leadership of the factory reform campaign could be transferred with little or no difficulty to the service of the new agitation.

This almost complete continuity of leadership is perhaps the most striking characteristic of the transition period. Very few of the factory reformers did not become active in the anti-Poor Law movement and, with really only one exception, all of the major anti-Poor Law leaders had been prominent in the factory reform campaign.

The exception, Feargus O'Connor, was a very special case.[1] Up to a point it may be said that his career in northern politics did begin as a result of the anti-Poor Law agitation, though even this is questionable since political reform was always at least equally important in his program. Still, even if it is accepted that it was the anti-Poor Law movement that drew him to Leeds and allowed him to win a place in northern political life, it is nonetheless true that this move was not the beginning but only a new phase of his career. He began as a radical M.P. from Ireland but was deprived of his seat in 1834 because of an inadequate property qualification. Thereafter, until his move to Leeds in 1837, inconstancy seems to have been the one constant feature of his political career. Frustrated personal ambition and frustrated hopes for radical action led him to quarrel with those men such as O'Connell and Lovett upon whom a career as a radical in Irish or London politics most depended. He attempted to get around this by founding a rival to Lovett's Working Men's Association, but, when this venture failed, O'Connor found himself in effect shut out of London radicalism. A move to the North, which, characteristically, he had been toying with even while centering his attention on London, now seemed the only answer. Thus, late in 1837, he moved permanently to Leeds. Clearly it was the potential for radical politics and for his own advancement that the North offered, rather than the anti-Poor Law agitation as such, that drew O'Connor to the West Riding.

O'Connor was however the only anti-Poor Law leader to arrive late; all the others had founded their public careers in earlier years on other issues. John Fielden, a radical factory owner from Tod-

---

[1] On O'Connor, as on each of the major anti-Poor Law leaders (except Bull), see the essays in G. D. H. Cole, *Chartist Portraits* (London 1965). But the main source for his early career is D. Read and E. Glasgow, *Feargus O'Connor* (London 1961), Chs. III–VI.

morden on the Lancashire–Yorkshire border, had had the longest
and most varied career.[1] His father had been a woollen manufacturer who made the shift to cotton late in the eighteenth century. The Fielden sons all worked for their father in various
capacities and John, the most talented of the children, inherited
the overall management of what soon became a very large and successful firm. He was, however, a most unusual manufacturer. He
entered politics as a critic of orthodox financial policy, a supporter
of universal suffrage and a disciple of William Cobbett, with
whom he was elected to Parliament from Oldham in 1832. Though
a factory owner, he fought for such reforms as the regulation of
hours, minimum wage scales and factory inspection. When the
Factory Act of 1833 failed to achieve most of these ends, he allied
with the great Lancashire trade union leader John Doherty to form
a group ambitiously entitled the National Regeneration Society,
aimed at enforcing an eight-hour day in all factories, if necessary
by general strike action. This movement, like so many others,
collapsed in the great trade union debacle of 1834 and, to a large
extent, Fielden's bitter opposition to the New Poor Law grew
directly out of these earlier setbacks. In attacking the Poor Law in
the House of Commons early in 1837, he reminded his fellow
M.P.s 'that the labouring man has no control whatever over the
price of his labour, and that this House has constantly refused,
under an affectation of principle, to regulate that price for him in
such a manner that he may receive a due reward for the labour that
he performs. As I have found that this House is unwilling to do
that which is to keep the people from poverty', he therefore concluded, 'I will resist this act which punishes them for being poor.'[2]

An entirely different tradition of popular leadership was represented by Richard Oastler, perhaps the most revered of the anti-
Poor Law leaders.[3] He began his public career at about the same

[1] Alone among the major anti-Poor Law leaders, Fielden has not been
honored with a full-length biography. Cole's portrait is helpful, as, to
some extent are: J. Holden, *A Short History of Todmorden* (Manchester
1912) and H. McLachlan, *The Methodist Unitarian Movement* (Manchester 1919). In addition, two of Fielden's rare pamphlets, *The Curse of
the Factory System* (Halifax 1836) and *National Regeneration* (London
1834), as well as a speech he delivered at a banquet given in his honor
(*M.S.A.* 9 June 1838), give a good deal of information about his career
prior to 1837. Fielden's pamphlet on the factory system has recently (1969)
been reprinted and prefaced with a biographical essay by J. T. Ward.

[2] Hansard, *op. cit.*, XXXVI, 1014.

[3] Oastler's early career is definitively treated in Driver, *Tory Radical*,
Chs. IV–XXXIV. Copies of most of his almost innumerable pamphlets

time as Fielden, in 1830. Before that he had led an undistinguished
life, quietly tucked away in the hills above Huddersfield as the
steward of Fixby Hall estate. In 1830 he met John Wood, a
worsted manufacturer, who introduced him to the conditions of
work in factories. From that time on the reform of these conditions
became the consuming passion of Oastler's life. Though conservative in politics and as ignorant of working people as he had been
of their conditions, he was driven by his horror at what he had
discovered to ally himself with working-class radicals and lead a
popular movement for factory reform. Little that did not bear
directly on this question interested him; he was indifferent to trade
unionism and hostile to political reform. But the New Poor Law
was another matter. Oastler believed that, by lowering wages and
introducing cheap labor from rural areas, it would have the effect
of nullifying whatever benefits the worker might derive from factory reform. Indeed, coming as it did in the wake of Parliamentary
refusal to adopt adequate factory legislation, the Poor Law appeared to Oastler, as it did to Cobbett and to many conservatives,
as part of an attempt by financial and industrial interests, abetted
by a governing class which had forgotten its social obligations, to
deprive the working classes of what economic rights and security
they still retained. Because of this Oastler opposed the New Poor
Law from the moment of its introduction in Parliament and it was
not merely expedient but very nearly inevitable that he would shift
his attention almost entirely to fighting the New Poor Law when
finally it threatened to be imposed on the North itself late in 1836.

The Rev. George Stringer Bull was not a leader of Oastler's
calibre but, as the foremost advocate of the social humanitarian
responsibilities of the church in the North of England, he was
scarcely less important.[1] His ideas and public career ran closely
parallel to Oastler's. As with Oastler, his exposure to factory conditions came as a revelation which changed the whole pattern of
his life. Like Oastler he was a Tory who regarded the failure to
ameliorate these conditions as a betrayal of trust on the part of the
governing and propertied classes. Like Oastler he saw the New
Poor Law as born of the same spirit and had begun opposing it
publicly while it was still being debated in Parliament in 1834.

are in the Oastler Collection, Goldsmith's Library, Senate House,
London.
    [1] J. C. Gill, *The Ten Hours Parson* (London 1959), Chs. II–XIV.
Most of Bull's pamphlets are also in the Oastler Collection.

Working out from his parish near Bradford he had long since established himself as one of the most popular orators in the West Riding and well before the end of 1836 he, like Oastler, had all but ceased to talk of anything but the need for a new agitation against the new and now imminent threat of the New Poor Law.

The last of the really important anti-Poor Law leaders to emerge as a public figure was Joseph Rayner Stephens.[1] He was the Methodist counterpart of the Anglican Bull, a strong believer in the social role of the church. For his views on this and other matters, in particular his opposition to a state church, he was dismissed from the Methodist communion. But he promptly established a chapel of his own at Ashton-under-Lyne on the Lancashire–Cheshire border and, free from outside discipline, he devoted his time increasingly to the agitation for factory reform. His rise was meteoric. In a matter of months during the latter half of 1836 he achieved a following and a reputation equal to that of the old-established northern popular leaders. Like them he regarded opposition to the New Poor Law as a logical extension of the factory reform campaign and with them he began to shift his own attention and that of his audiences to the new issue even before Alfred Power first arrived in the North.

All of these men—O'Connor, Fielden, Oastler, Bull and Stephens—were popular leaders of regional and, for a time at least in each of their careers, of national importance; as such, and in certain other respects as well, they were unrepresentative. More typical of the leadership of the popular anti-Poor Law movement as a whole were those men who were able to achieve regional importance and perhaps aspired to a national career, but who remained nonetheless essentially local leaders. Of these secondary figures, Matthew Fletcher, the radical surgeon of Bury in Lancashire, was perhaps the most interesting.[2] Though the son and grandson of manufacturers, and originally a Tory, he broke with his background and modified his views sufficiently that by the

---

[1] Cole's portrait is especially valuable for Stephens, since G. J. Holyoake, *Life of Joseph Rayner Stephens* (London 1881) is far from adequate. See also J. T. Ward, 'Revolutionary Tory: The Life of Joseph Rayner Stephens', *Transactions of the Lancashire and Chesire Antiquarian Society*, LXVIII (1958). In addition, there are some reprints of his speeches and sermons in the Oastler Collection, and a more complete collection of his writings in the Ashton Public Library.

[2] There is a short biographical sketch of Fletcher in *The Charter*, 31 March 1839. Additional information has been supplied by the Bury Public Library.

middle 1830s he was firmly established as a leader not only of the Bury factory reformers but of the local trade unionists and radical political reformers as well. Fletcher's intimate connection with every aspect of local working-class political life led him almost inevitably into assuming a leading role in resistance to the New Poor Law, and, in addition, it contributed to an interpretation of the significance and implications of the new law even more alarmist than the views of Fielden or Oastler. Fletcher believed that the New Poor Law was merely one element of a conspiracy between the government and the manufacturers, aimed not only at undermining the factory acts but, beyond that, at destroying the economic, social and political independence and power of the working classes. If the government should succeed in imposing the New Poor Law in the North, he feared that measures of tyranny such as a national police force and the re-imposition of the Combination Acts would almost certainly follow. Resistance to the Poor Law, then, was necessary not only or even primarily for its own sake but as a means of preserving all those other movements to which he was so deeply committed.

Fletcher was the most explicit and extreme advocate of this view of the New Poor Law, but, in some measure at least, almost all of the local anti-Poor Law leaders shared his fears. This was certainly the case with R. J. Richardson, a printer and stationer in Salford near Manchester, who, like Fletcher, was deeply involved in trade unionism and political radicalism as well as factory reform, and was to play a role in founding a resistance movement to the Poor Law in Salford almost identical with Fletcher's in Bury.[1] Across the Pennines in Bradford, Peter Bussey, at one time or another a joiner and a metal worker but, for the moment, a tavern keeper, was, if anything an even more outspoken adherent of the conspiracy theory of the New Poor Law.[2] His main base of operations was the local radical reform association of which he had been secretary for years, but he too was closely associated with trade unionists and factory reformers before joining the ranks of Poor Law opponents late in 1836. Further south, in Huddersfield, Laurence Pitkeithly played a similar role as the anchor man of popular reformism in all its variety.[3] He is best remembered as one

---

[1] A great deal of information of Richardson's career has been amassed by the Chief Librarian of the Salford Public Library and is now available there.   [2] *The Charter*, 5 May 1839.

[3] The best source of information is Driver's biography of Oastler.

of the group of six workingmen, the founders of the local Ten Hours Committee, who walked to Fixby Hall on a June Sunday in 1831 and convinced Oastler of the need to join forces, thereby launching the factory reform movement as a major force in northern politics. Even at the height of the factory reform campaign, however, Pitkeithly never abandoned his organizing efforts in other causes such as Owenite socialism and political radicalism, and, when the question of resistance to the Poor Law arose, he, like the other popular leaders, adopted it as essentially one more aspect of a wider struggle which, in one way or another, he had been waging for nearly a decade.

An entirely different sort of leadership was provided by the extraordinary number of clergymen who flocked into the new movement. Both Church of England and Nonconformist clergy were involved, but the nature of their involvement differed. Most ministers of the established church who opposed the New Poor Law were a great deal more retiring than George Stringer Bull, whose political and social views they often shared, but whose tactics they rarely followed, preferring to avoid notoriety and confining their activities to their own parishes. Nonconformists were less reserved. Perhaps because they were used to preaching on a circuit, they tended to agitate on one as well. There were many such men but, next to Stephens, the most effective public speakers and certainly the most ubiquitous were William Thornton, a Methodist preacher and factory reformer of long standing, from Halifax, and James Taylor of Rochdale, a Methodist Unitarian and, like most ministers of that small East Lancashire sect, an ardent radical.[1]

There was, finally, another group of regional anti-Poor Law leaders who worked primarily as organizers rather than public agitators, and tend therefore to be overlooked. William Clegg in Lancashire and Samuel Bower and William Stocks in the West Riding were perhaps the most important of these behind-the-scenes coordinators. Clegg, a friend of Robert Owen, had been associated with Fielden in the National Regeneration Society; Bower had long been active in all sorts of reform movements in Bradford; and Stocks, the Chief Constable of Huddersfield, had a long association with Oastler and the Factory Reform Movement.[2]

---

[1] McLachlan, *Methodist Unitarian Movement.*

[2] Information on these men is exceedingly difficult to come by and must be culled from many different sources of which the studies of

Of those men who never achieved even regional prominence but remained throughout of entirely local importance, little need, or for that matter can, be said. Most of them are now what they were outside of their small spheres then, just names. What little we know of them indicates that they were very similar to the secondary level of leaders. Like them, and unlike some of the more famous leaders, these local men were almost always drawn from lower-middle-class or working-class backgrounds, were political radicals and were associated with a wide variety of reform movements. What is most important about these local leaders at this time, however, is what they had in common with all of their better-known associates, that they too were drawn rapidly and almost imperceptibly from whatever movements they happened to be engaged in at the time into the service of the new agitation. The chairman and the movers and seconders of resolutions at a local anti-Poor Law meeting in December 1836 or January 1837 had, more likely than not, performed the same functions at factory reform rallies, radical association meetings, or gatherings of trade union representatives a year or a month before. At no level of leadership, in short, did the anti-Poor Law movement either exclude established public figures or find it necessary to seek out new leaders. Because of this the mounting of a major campaign, which ordinarily might have taken four or five months to prepare, was accomplished in as many weeks.

Much less dramatic but no less important than the sudden emergence of popular anti-Poor Law agitation was growing disaffection among the substantial ratepaying classes upon whom the successful administration of the new law depended. It was the failure of the opposition in the South to win adherents from this section of the community which was perhaps most decisive in ensuring the Commissioners' early successes, and, while there were widespread doubts in the North about the necessity and applicability of the new law, the Commissioners assumed that the magistrates and overseers, the ratepayers and their representatives on the Boards of Guardians would go along. What the Commissioners failed to realize was that, behind all the debate on whether the principles of the New Poor Law could or should be implemented in the North, lay a deep distrust of the centralizing tendencies of Poor

---

Chartism by Gammage, Hovell and Briggs, and Driver's biography of Oastler are the most helpful.

Law Amendment Act, which no amount of reasonableness or flexibility on specific points of policy could really allay. Such fears were, of course, nothing new, nor were they confined to the North. Parliamentary discussion of the Poor Law had returned again and again to this question. But as every Assistant Commissioner who was to have charge of the North quickly discovered, no other area in England clung so tenaciously to its local autonomy or viewed with such alarm the possibly revolutionary implications of the creation of a central authority in the field of poor relief.[1]

Even so, it was a long way from local discontent, however strongly felt, to open resistance and it is highly unlikely that the first would have been translated into the second on a significant scale but for the recession of late 1836. Under any Poor Law, old or new, rates were bound to go up substantially during a recession but the New Poor Law promised to add to this by requiring a complete reorganization of the administration of relief, the hiring of permanent paid officials and perhaps even some major capital expenditures for the building or alteration of workhouses. In the South such reforms had promised to effect immediate and often substantial reductions in the rate burden, while in the East Midlands they had been made before the recession set in. But in the North in 1837 possibly expensive administrative changes which did not hold out the promise of immediate economies, and severe pressure on the rates due to a recession coincided for the first time. With profits and incomes falling and credit growing tighter, many substantial ratepayers who would otherwise have acquiesced, however grudgingly, in the new law decided to resist its introduction, for the time being at least.

This opened the way for a number of hotheaded opponents among the ratepayers to assume a role of influence and leadership they would otherwise not have been able to achieve. The Commissioners, understandably, and typically, tended to identify the whole of the opposition with these self-appointed spokesmen and dismiss it as the work of a few irresponsible agitators. This was wishful thinking; one of the most significant features of ratepayer opposition was the undoubted respectability of many of its leaders. Admittedly this was not the case with the lesser ratepayers and many of the township overseers, but the magistrates, appointed by the Crown, and the Guardians as officials elected under a property qualification were, and were intended to be, drawn from among

[1] On the fear of centralization in the North see: MH 32.63 21 Oct. 1837.

the more substantial members of the community. In the largely urban poor law Unions of southeast Lancashire manufacturers and other employers were the largest single element, often a majority, on the Boards, with shopkeepers and professional men making up most of the remainder. Elsewhere in the textile districts the rural hinterland was larger and farmers and country gentlemen often surpassed manufacturers and merchants as the major group on the Board. Though not enough is known about individuals to allow any correlation to be made between social position within each of these groups and opposition to the law, if indeed there was such a correlation, the fact remains that opponents of the law were drawn from all of these classes in all parts of the textile districts.

Another measure of the extent of disaffection among what the Commissioners liked to call the 'better sort of person' in the North was the press. The overwhelming majority of northern newspapers including all of the Tory and Radical journals declared themselves unalterably opposed to the New Poor Law and advocated resistance to it. They differed of course in their reasons and in their recommendations for opposing the law. All opposition papers of both political persuasions stressed the centralization issue. Most of them attacked the new law on social grounds as well, the Tory papers from a humanitarian paternalist point of view, the Radical papers in terms similar to Fielden's. Finally, the Tory press, happily ignoring its own party's vote in Parliament, could not resist attacking the Poor Law on purely partisan grounds. The pro-government Liberal press, led by the *Manchester Guardian* and the *Leeds Mercury*, was, by contrast, restrained. They supported the new law but only with reservations, or on the grounds that it was not as bad as the opposition claimed, or on the grounds that as the law of the land it must be obeyed.

This lop-sided press line-up probably misrepresented the true state of northern opinion. Actual experience of working the New Poor Law was to prove that many Tories were more concerned with making political capital than with the rights or wrongs of the law itself, and that there existed a large body of Liberal opinion prepared to accept if not applaud the law. Still, the fact that such men kept silent during the winter of 1836–7 is in itself indicative of how unpopular the law was in all ranks of northern society. It was this diversity of support that made the anti-Poor Law movement unique and, potentially at least, quite formidable.

IV   1837: the opposition victorious

The Poor Law Commissioners were undoubtedly overconfident when they first turned their attention to the North, though in fairness to them it should be remembered that they could not possibly have known that the recession of 1836 would get worse or that the factory reform movement would turn its attention and organization almost exclusively to fighting the New Poor Law. Still, they should have acted with at least the same degree of circumspection which they had displayed in first trying out the new law in the South; and this they did not do. Partly through carelessness and partly through circumstances beyond their control, they began very badly. The most serious initial blunder was none of their doing but was made for them by the government. In 1836 Parliament passed an act requiring the registration of births, deaths and marriages and placing the local administrative responsibility for this in the hands of the clerks to the Boards of Guardians. As originally passed, the law was to have come into effect early in 1837. In the South of England this posed no problems since the machinery of the Poor Law had been working for as much as two years in many areas. In the North, on the other hand, not only was the New Poor Law not in operation, it had not even been prepared for. The Poor Law Commissioners, it is true, had the option of making temporary provision for registration until the local machinery of the New Poor Law could be set in motion, but, since the Commissioners hoped to introduce the New Poor Law itself into the North during 1837, they decided, on the advice of Alfred Power, to avoid the duplication of effort involved in a two-stage process and push ahead directly with the establishment of Poor Law Unions, the election of Boards of Guardians and the appointment of Union clerks.[1]

This was an understandable decision, but it had a number of unfortunate consequences. As a result the Commissioners did not have the long period of preparation which they had used so well in the South. In the agricultural districts most Assistant Commissioners had begun sounding out their areas some months before

[1] MH 32.63 25 Nov. 1836.

the date on which the Unions were declared. They had always been able to visit each of the Unions and, within most Unions, a large number of the individual parishes. In the North this was not true. The Assistant Commissioner did not arrive in Lancashire and the West Riding of Yorkshire until October 1836, and the first Unions were declared within two months.

This was difficult enough, but the Commissioners compounded their problems by appointing Alfred Power as Assistant Commissioner for the district. Power was a rigid, unbending man who lacked both a sense of humor and a sense of proportion. He was, moreover, already well-known and heartily disliked in the North. He had been one of the three investigators sent by the Royal Commission on Factories to report on the North in 1833 and during their time in Yorkshire these men had been hounded constantly by representatives of the local factory reform committees. It is hardly likely that when he returned to the North in 1836 Power had forgotten, let alone forgiven, his earlier treatment there; and it soon became clear that the North in its turn had neither forgotten nor forgiven him. In almost every one of the many towns he visited late in 1836 he was greeted by a hostile crowd. His private meetings with the overseers, churchwardens and other local worthies were constantly interrupted by noisy demonstrations outside and, if Power was unwise enough to hold a public meeting, or unlucky enough to have one forced upon him, the speeches were usually drowned out by hecklers.

Perhaps the most notorious of these confrontations took place in early January 1837 in Bury where, news of Power's impending arrival having leaked out, Matthew Fletcher invaded and totally disrupted Power's conference with local officials.[1] Egged on by the crowd which accompanied him, Fletcher harangued and cross-questioned Power on point after controversial point in the New Poor Law, lacing his accusations with predictions of popular violence should the new law ever be introduced in Bury. His performance was very much in the tradition of Oastler's needle speech and, as such, went well beyond what most opponents of the Poor Law were prepared to say at this early date. Only Oastler's own Huddersfield provided an incident which deserved and got the same publicity. Even so, other lesser confrontations, quite as much as those in Huddersfield or Bury, had their effects, perhaps in

---

[1] On Power's experiences in Bury see: *Bolton Chronicle* 14 Jan. 1837; Huddersfield: *L.I.* 14 Jan. 1837.

rousing public opinion, certainly on Alfred Power. The Assistant Commissioner circumscribed still further his travels in the North and understandably preferred to keep his local conferences both small and secret. This unquestionably added to the difficulties already imposed by a limited timetable in getting sufficient information about the district he was to supervise.

Public harassment was not the only reaction which Power's arrival in the North provoked. During the early weeks of 1837 virtually every major town in the textile districts held at least one public anti-Poor Law meeting.[1] These were a good deal less dramatic than actual confrontations with the Assistant Commissioner, but they were in a way even more disturbing omens for the future, since they were not, as public harassment always was, the exclusive province of the popular movement. Many such meetings were called by the local overseers or groups of eminently respectable ratepayers. Moreover, even at such meetings the advocates of moderate measures such as delay or amendment of the law, negotiating with the Poor Law Commissioners, or simply waiting and seeing were out-voted or out-shouted by those argued for diehard local resistance and the petitioning of Parliament for repeal of the law. In large part of course this can be explained by the fact that these were open meetings which the more rabid opponents of the law could easily swamp with their own supporters. This was a favorite technique of the popular anti-Poor Law party and was even used at this time to disrupt public meetings that had no connection with the Poor Law at all. But that is not the whole explanation. Even meetings called under the auspices of the popular leaders were usually attended by what the press called 'more respectable' elements which, whatever their private feelings about the terms employed or the tactics suggested, were willing to cooperate with the advocates of radical courses.

Power was not the sort of man to let himself be rattled by these or any other difficulties or portents, however.[2] If anything, such demonstrations tended to confirm him in his views about the opposition and his determination to push the new law through at any cost. Then, as he was always to do, he dismissed popular antipathy to the Poor Law as unimportant; what had happened in

[1] Accounts of public meetings appeared in all the West Riding and Lancashire papers during Jan. and Feb. 1837.

[2] For Power's strategy see: MH 32.63 29 Dec. 1836; Report from the Select Committee on the Poor Law Amendment Act, B.P.P. 1838, XVIII, Questions 3841–3879.

Bury he regarded as the work of 'a mad doctor and a rabble',[1] nothing more. As for disaffection among more substantial northerners, he recognized its existence but was confident it could be neutralized by diplomatic handling. Thus, for example, far from regarding the haste which the Registration Act had imposed on him as necessarily a disadvantage, Power attempted to turn it to his own uses by assuring the opponents of the Poor Law that they could support the creation of the new administrative machinery, since its only immediate function would be the implementation of the Registration Act. In addition, recognizing that northern opinion was almost unanimously opposed to a workhouse test, he suggested that the introduction of the Prohibitory Order be delayed until the administrative machinery of the New Poor Law was securely established. Finally, Power proposed to the Commissioners in London that the five standard rules relating to outrelief to the able-bodied, which were always issued to newly formed Poor Law Unions when they took over the responsibility for relief, be re-written for northern consumption. Such rephrasing was, however, as Power himself emphasized, to be no more than that; it would certainly not involve any changes in the substance of these regulations. Through these apparent concessions he hoped to lull, blunt, divert or divide potential opposition, anything indeed rather than meet it half way. Superficially so flexible, so open to suggestions, Power was in fact as closed to any views other than his own as was his mentor Chadwick.

It would be unfair to ascribe all of Power's early mistakes to his rigidity. That a number of Poor Law Unions later proved to be inconveniently large and heterogeneous, for example, was almost certainly due to his having to work under pressure. Nonetheless, it is questionable whether such errors would have assumed the importance they later did had Power been genuinely sensitive to local feeling and more willing to accommodate himself to it. Nor is there any reason to believe that, given more time and broader contacts, Power would have become more understanding or amenable. Credit must be given where credit is due, however, and it would be unfair to record his failings without noting his achievements. Despite the enormous difficulties under which he labored in a large, populous and rapidly changing district, he was able to create a large number of Poor Law Unions, the great majority of which proved to be viable administrative units, and to do this in a

[1] MH 32.63 8 Jan. 1837.

remarkably brief period of time. The last of the Unions in the textile districts was declared in January 1837, less than four months after his arrival in the North, and the first elections of Boards of Guardians in all of them was scheduled for February at the latest.

The speed at which the Poor Law Commissioners had been forced to work in the North had clearly been a considerable disadvantage. Nothing substantial had been done to forestall potential opposition and a number of structural weaknesses had been built into the system. There was, however, one possible compensation in this, that the opponents of the law would be compelled to organize at least as rapidly. In the long run this was to prove one of the greatest weaknesses of the anti-Poor Law movement, but in the opening rounds with the Poor Law Commissioners it seemed no handicap at all, since, to a large extent, the opposition had an organization ready-made. Since all of the leaders of the new agitation were drawn from other movements they quite naturally utilized existing Radical Associations, Ten Hour Committees and the like in mounting the campaign of harassment and mass meetings which accompanied Power's first tour of his new district. All that seemed necessary to create an anti-Poor Law movement as such was the transformation of these various committees and associations into an official anti-Poor Law organization. This essentially is how the structure of the new movement was built up during the early months of 1837 and, as might be expected, the transformation was both rapid and smooth.

Such continuity was simplest and most complete in Yorkshire.[1] The most interesting example of this and, moreover, the event which marked the beginnings of an effective anti-Poor Law movement in the West Riding as a whole was a meeting held in Bradford at the end of the first week in March 1837. It was called initially as a meeting of delegates from the major West Riding Short Time Committees, but the official announcement of the meeting did not limit it to factory reform. 'As soon as the business of the Ten Hour Bill is disposed of', it declared, 'the same delegates shall deliberate on the propriety of holding a West Riding meeting . . . to enter into a violent remonstrance against the Poor Law act.'[2] The meeting however went even further than this. It decided in effect to

---

[1] On the organization of Yorkshire see in particular: *L.I.* and *L.T.* Jan.–March 1837. [2] *L.I.* 4 March 1837.

abandon for the time being all agitation for factory reform and to concentrate its efforts on building an anti-Poor Law organization.

In practice this often meant little more than converting already existing factory reform committees into anti-Poor Law Committees. Most West Riding towns had fairly effective short time committees and a number of the most active of these had already become anti-Poor Law committees in fact, sometimes in name as well, as early as January 1837. The task locally was not a formidable one, therefore. Regionally it was even easier. The West Riding meeting of delegates from Short Time Committees simply assumed the title and functions of a West Riding meeting of delegates from anti-Poor Law associations and appointed a few permanent officials, including Samuel Bower as secretary and William Stocks as Treasurer, to plan and coordinate the future growth of the movement. The fact that the meeting felt able to take such steps is good evidence of just how far the transformation must already have gone on the local level. Indeed, apparently the only important new organizational tasks they had to undertake were the creation of local committees in those few areas where none existed and, more important because it was entirely new, the creation of intermediary delegate committees at the Poor Law Union level.

What little evidence we have indicates that this was done fairly rapidly and that within a month or so the outline of this hierarchy of committees was complete. Little is known in detail of how they went about this business. Apparently the main organizational burden fell on the reconstituted short time committees in those major towns—Bradford, Huddersfield, Halifax, Dewsbury and Keighley—which were to be the centers of Poor Law Unions. From them organizers, in some cases it seems full-time paid professionals, went out to build up local committees, and under the aegis of these older, larger committees the Union committees were created. But beyond this little is known. The relationship between the various organizational levels and the role of the Union and regional delegates committees in practice as opposed to theory remain something of a mystery. Up to a point this lack of information is a tribute to the organization; they were, after all, organizing to prevent the implementation of a law and secrecy was not merely a good weapon, it might well be a necessity.

The newly constructed West Riding anti-Poor Law organization had a public function as well; northern opinion had to be aroused against the New Poor Law as it had before been aroused in support of factory reform. A good start had already been made by the more proficient of the local committees to which such things as harassing Assistant Commissioners, holding public meetings and raising petitions were almost second nature by now. But there were limits to what even the best organized local groups could achieve and the need for some major event at the regional level which could give focus and direction to local efforts was obvious. Hence the proposal for a mass West Riding demonstration which was the main reason given publicly for calling the Delegate Conference in the first place and which was approved at their March meeting. Arrangements for the demonstration, scheduled for mid-May on Hartshead Moor in the center of the Yorkshire textile district, were left in the hands of Samuel Bower, who evidently had considerable experience in organizing such events and certainly did an impressive job of coordination in this case.

All other propaganda activity over the intervening two months was directed towards this culminating point of the first phase of the Yorkshire anti-Poor Law movement, and, on the day itself, columns of demonstrators from towns and cities all over the central West Riding converged on the Moor and passed before the speakers' stand in a monster procession that lasted for hours. Estimates of the number who came varied of course; the anti-Poor Law press put it as high as a quarter of a million, but even the Liberal papers had to admit to something near 100,000. The business of the meeting was as prosaic as the meeting itself was impressive. During the six hours it lasted the familiar grounds for opposition were traversed once again and, as usual, a series of resolutions calling for constant vigilance and further petitioning was passed. But while the speeches may have been more of the same, the roster of speakers was much more than that. Almost all of the factory reform leaders who were now to act as anti-Poor Law leaders attended. So did O'Connor who was already beginning to shift his center of activity to the North. So did a number of important London radicals including Bronterre O'Brien and Henry Hetherington. And so, as a reminder of the great agitations of earlier years, did Robert Owen. Thus the Hartshead Moor meeting was not just another, larger anti-Poor Law demonstration; it was a recognition that the anti-Poor Law movement had won itself a position of equality with the greatest of the northern protest movements.[1]

[1] On the Hartshead Moor meeting see: *Ibid.* 20 May 1837.

F

At the same time that resistance was being organized in the West Riding, a roughly parallel development was taking place in Lancashire, with the difference, however, that the Lancashire movement was not as coherent and that it did not, at least at this early stage, go so far.[1] The factory reform movement in Lancashire had never been as distinct from other movements as it had been in Yorkshire. Middle-class radicals, including factory owners, had had an importance in the movement which was rare in the West Riding and, similarly, the links with trade unionism culminating in the National Regeneration Society had always been closer. This overlapping of various movements continued into the anti-Poor Law agitation.

The all-important role which the Short Time Committees played in the early stages in Yorkshire was shared out in Lancashire between Short Time Committees, Radical Associations and, to a lesser extent, trade union committees. Any one of these groups might take the initiative in planning local resistance to the Poor Law and the creation of anti-Poor Law associations tended to be the result of an amalgamation of elements from all three rather than the extention of one under a new name as had happened so often in Yorkshire. In practice it is true this frequently made little difference. Hostile reception committees were as much a feature of Power's travels in Lancashire as in Yorkshire, local meetings were held and local petitions were circulated as commonly in one county as the other, and the itinerant agitators of the North did not confine their activities within the boundaries of any particular county. But in at least one respect, the greater diversity of the Lancashire organization probably hampered its effectiveness. There was no single body comparable to the West Riding Delegate Committee which was in position to appropriate to itself the regional leadership of the new movement. And, whether or not this was the cause, there was no successful attempt at this time to create a county wide organization. What coordination there was between resistance movements in different Unions depended almost entirely on the efforts of individuals, and county wide activities comparable to the Hartshead Moor meeting were not even attempted.

These differences between the two counties were however of relatively small practical importance at least in the early stages of the anti-Poor Law movement. Yorkshire's superiority in regional

[1] On the organization of Lancashire see: *M.S.A.* Jan.–March 1837.

organization and agitation may perhaps have given that county an advantage in the mobilization of public opinion, but, even while the Yorkshire leaders were perfecting their regional structure, the importance of organizing a mass popular movement was receding into the background in the face of a new, more urgent and entirely novel problem, the Boards of Guardians elections. These elections presented a challenge to the opposition which it could not very well ignore. If popular antipathy to the Poor Law was ever to be taken seriously, it would have to be directed against the machinery of the law, immobilizing it or capturing it. But for this task the popular anti-Poor Law movement in Lancashire and Yorkshire alike was woefully ill-equipped. The anti-Poor Law movement had begun on the model of the Factory Reform campaign, as a mass movement primarily concerned with public demonstrations, petitioning and the like. For such purposes its organizational needs were relatively simple and a few strong committees could, in practice, carry the burden for a whole district.

To contest a Board of Guardians election, however, required a tight local organization capable of day-to-day politicking, for which no amount of regional organization, help from stronger neighboring committees, or intervention by outside agitators was an adequate substitute. Few local anti-Poor Law Associations were capable of making the transition from one kind of activity to the other, let alone of sustaining both. Only those Associations which grew directly out of strong, deeply rooted Short Time Committees or Radical Associations were able to do so; the rest followed as best they could, which was often not at all. As a result, any idea of meeting the challenge of the Boards of Guardians elections with a uniform response in all the Poor Law Unions of the textile districts had to be abandoned from the very beginning. Worse still, these differences in the strength of local committees applied as much within Poor Law Unions as between them, and was an even more serious problem on this most local of levels. After all, though opposition on a regional scale was desirable, it was not a prerequisite for effective local resistance. But concerted action within the newly created Poor Law Unions was indispensable, and there seemed no more immediate likelihood of achieving this than of achieving regional coordination.

Organizational deficiencies were perhaps the most serious difficulty faced by the anti-Poor Law movement in dealing with the Boards of Guardians elections, but they were not by any means the only ones. There was, first of all, the problem of class. The contesting of Guardians elections brought the two elements of opposition to the law, the popular movement and ratepayer opposition, into closer proximity than any other aspect of anti-Poor Law activity. Unquestionably they needed one another but the relationship was never a comfortable one except in those few areas where someone—John Fielden was the most notable example—had managed to become a member and leader of both groups. Elsewhere there was a tendency for middle-class opponents of the law to shy away from too close contact with the popular movement. Both Alfred Power and the pro-Poor Law press seized on this potential for division among their enemies and made much of the contrast between respectable elements, whatever their views on the law, and the rabble.[1] Presumably this had some effect. The large number of abstentions in these elections probably derived in part from a decision by some of the ratepayers to have no part either of the law or of its more rabid opponents. And there were a number of Unions in which candidates appealed for votes on the basis of respectability and responsibility rather than their views on the Poor Law itself.

It was not, of course, only the respectable ratepayers who felt uncomfortable in this unwonted relationship. Many of the popular anti-Poor Law leaders were never able fully to reconcile themselves to co-operating with men whom they had attacked as bitter enemies on other issues as little as a few months before. Every popular leader regarded the New Poor Law as a piece of class legislation and most of them accepted Fletcher's analysis of it as a conspiracy at least in part. But, whereas most of the major anti-Poor Law leaders believed that a large number of individuals in the middle and upper classes genuinely opposed the new law and its possible implications, there were others, led by Fletcher, who remained deeply suspicious of their sincerity.

This problem might not have been so important had the Boards of Guardians elections been fought out entirely on the issue of the Poor Law, but this was rarely the case. Many Radicals and Dissenters, otherwise opposed to the New Poor Law, regarded the Registration Act as a piece of radical legislation in their interest, and they were understandably reluctant to risk jeopardizing it by

[1] Class divisions and the need for respectability were emphasized most frequently in the *Manchester Guardian, Leeds Mercury, Bolton Free Press* and *Bradford Observer* during February and March.

allowing its administration to fall into the hands of members of the established church, still less by wrecking it. There can be no doubt that Power's carefully drawn distinction between support for the administrative machinery of the Poor Law as a means of implementing the Registration Act and support for the Poor Law itself was a very beguiling argument in the North. How seriously it undercut the position of the out and out opponents of the law can be gauged by the vehemence of their reaction. Fletcher, for example, felt compelled to warn Dissenters that, should they let the Poor Law in through the back door of the Registration Act, 'their places of worship would become as detestable in the eyes of the people as the cotton mills or union workhouses'.[1]

Local party politics confused the situation still further. With the Tory and Radical press in full cry against the New Poor Law, while the official organs of Liberalism supported it, albeit often reluctantly, logic seemed to demand some sort of coalition between Radicals and Conservatives. There were any number of precedents for this, of course, of which by far the most important was the factory reform movement. Moreover, the beginnings of the anti-Poor Law campaign coincided with the fullest stage in the development of the radical wing of northern Toryism.[2] This Tory-Radicalism, as it was pejoratively and somewhat confusingly dubbed in the Liberal press, is often thought of as a Yorkshire speciality, since Oastler, Sadler and Bull, who were the most famous exponents of Tory-sponsored social reform and of a tactical alliance with working-class Radicals to achieve it, were all Yorkshiremen. But Lancashire was little behindhand in these efforts. At just this time, for example, the ultra-Radicals and Tories of Manchester joined forces to oppose the Liberal-sponsored incorporation of the city, and the proliferation of Tory-supported workingmen's clubs, the so-called Operative Conservative Societies, though it began in the West Riding, at Leeds, in 1835, was as rapid west as east of the Pennines.

The New Poor Law was perhaps the most perfect issue ever

[1] *Blackburn Gazette* 1 Feb. 1837; the best coverage of the religious issue was in the *Manchester Guardian* for February and March 1837.

[2] Of the northern papers the *Manchester Guardian* was the most attentive to the activities of the Tory-Radicals while the *Bolton Chronicle*, *Leeds Intelligencer* and *Manchester Courier* (all Tory papers) made the most of the role of the Operative Conservatives. For a more general treatment of the whole subject see: R. L. Hill, *Toryism and the People* (London 1929).

presented to the Tory-Radicals, for not only did it promise to prolong the anti-Liberal, anti-industrial middle-class alliance of Conservatives and working-class Radicals begun in the factory reform campaign, but, by threatening established institutions and local autonomy, it evoked a wider response among Conservatives generally than the factory reform issue ever had. The winter of 1836–7 can be said to have marked the apogee of Tory-Radicalism and of the alliance between Conservatives and ultra-Radicals. Leading local Tories appeared at almost all the early anti-Poor Law meetings, regardless of their political complexion, and co-operated fully in the harassment of Alfred Power, giving the popular leaders information as to the whereabouts of the elusive Assistant Commissioner and doing little or nothing to deter or punish the crowds once they had caught up with him.

How far down the social scale this bi-partisanship went or made an important contribution to the movement is an intriguing but difficult question to answer. The Tory press made much of the role of the Operative Conservatives in every phase of anti-Poor Law activity from the organizing of mass meetings to canvassing in petitioning drives and the Boards of Guardians elections. On the other hand, the non-Tory press, whether Liberal or Radical, never mentioned the Operative Conservatives except in terms of the greatest contempt. Since the main public function of these societies appears to have been the holding of meetings and dinners in which the paternalism of the distinguished guests was only exceeded by the deference of their working-class hosts, and, since none of the latter appeared in a major capacity in the anti-Poor Law movement, it is legitimate to suspect that the non-Tory newspapers were nearer the truth. However, this does not detract from the rather remarkable fact that in the early stages of the anti-Poor Law campaign a very large proportion of the northern Conservative leadership, including virtually the whole of the party press, publicly associated itself with an agitation run primarily by political radicals and aimed at preventing the implementation of a law. But co-operation in such activities and co-operating in fighting the Boards of Guardians elections differed in one obvious and very important respect. The latter involved, as the former did not, the sharing out of local political power, and, once that issue arose, partisan mistrust, partisan ambition or a combination of the two came to the fore and wrecked the not very well laid plans for united action.

*　　　*　　　*

In combination all these factors produced an extraordinarily confused series of Boards of Guardians elections in 1837. Only the most clear-headed and politically secure opponents of the law were not deflected from what was ostensibly everyone's main concern. Fielden, in particular, argued that the North must not be seduced by the desirability of the Registration Act into creating an administrative structure which could later be used to implement the Poor Law, and that all class, partisan and religious differences had to be put aside in the struggle against the introduction of the Poor Law and of anything remotely associated with it.[1] In short, he advocated total obstruction, which meant in practice a total boycott. Almost no one else went so far or spoke so clearly, and not without reason. Fielden's local bailiwicks, his home town of Todmorden and his constituency in Oldham, were both centers of Poor Law Unions, and both were very nearly uniquely endowed with the requirements of out-and-out resistance. Yet even in Oldham and Todmorden Fielden was not completely successful, at least not at first.

Oldham itself and three of the seven other townships presented no problems.[2] The township overseers, upon whom the proper functioning of the electoral machinery depended, were either sympathetic to the opponents or could be pressured into co-operating with them. They did what was legally required of them, they received and advertised nominations for the office of Guardian, but they refused to act as deliverers and collectors of the voting papers. Since no one could be found to take on these tasks and since there had been very few nominations in the first place, no Guardians were elected in any of these townships. Even so the opposition failed. The handful of Guardians elected in the remaining townships were sufficient to constitute a Board which the Poor Law Commissioners would not have hesitated to use in imposing the new law throughout the Oldham Union.

Luckily for the opponents, however, the January elections were only a preliminary round and, during the few weeks between them and the new elections, required for the new parochial year beginning in March, the opposition managed to extend its control to all the townships of the Union. Protest meetings were held in every town and village in the Union and each of the townships

<hr />

[1] For Fielden's views see: *M.S.A.* 4 Feb. 1837.
[2] For the Oldham campaign see: *ibid.* Feb.–April 1837. For an interesting analysis of the nature of Oldham radicalism see, John Foster,

raised its own petition against the Poor Law Amendment Act. The culmination of this aspect of the campaign was a simultaneous march into Oldham from all the townships of the Union followed by a huge rally in the center of the town at which Fielden gave his blessing to all the efforts of the local opposition leaders. While the solidarity of the people of the Oldham Union against the New Poor Law was being demonstrated in public, the much more difficult task of ensuring that those who differed would be rendered powerless proceeded in private. Great pressure was exerted on the overseers and on any who sought to put names in nomination. In most townships there were ratepayers' meetings which managed to extract pledges from all the ratepayers not to nominate or if nominated not to run. The pressures worked. In most towns there were no nominations at all. In one twelve men were nominated but all withdrew before the election. And in another a Guardian was actually elected but, since he was an anti-Poor Law man, he immediately resigned. Thus, in the March election, no Guardian was appointed from any of the eight townships and the Poor Law Commissioners, faced for the first time in their career with a total boycott, were helpless.

Oldham thereby established itself as the ideal opposition Union, but it was an ideal which few Unions even attempted to achieve and which none achieved in full. Oldham's success, it turned out, had been due to a peculiar combination of favorable circumstances. Size was one. The Oldham Union had only eight townships while the average Union in the district contained about twice this number. The extension of effective control to every township, which had been difficult even in Oldham, was probably an impossibility in at least half the Unions in the Yorkshire–Lancashire textile district. Oldham possessed in addition a great organizational advantage over most other Unions. The leadership of the local anti-Poor Law movement was not disputed between Conservative and Radical opponents but lay entirely in the hands of the powerful and active Oldham Radical Association. Such unity was rare in the northern Unions and where it did not exist the discipline needed in order to carry out a boycott policy proved unattainable. Oldham therefore remained unique, though a number of Unions did attempt to follow its example.

'Nineteenth Century Towns—A Class Dimension', in H. J. Dyos (ed.), *The Study of Urban History*, (London 1968).

One of these was Todmorden, a Union which very closely resembled Oldham.[1] With only six townships, it too was small and, as in Oldham, the local Radical Association dominated political life, including the anti-Poor Law movement. Moreover, as the hometown of John Fielden, it was even more directly under his personal influence than Oldham. But whereas in Oldham the Radical Association had been able to bring all the townships of the Union to accept its policies, in Todmorden this proved impossible. Geography almost certainly played a part in this. The Todmorden Union was strung out along the narrow Calder valley and the hills above it, and, while Todmorden at the upper end was a cotton town on the Lancashire–Yorkshire border, much of the rest of the Union was in the woollen district and far closer to Halifax than to any town in Lancashire. Fielden's influence and the economic and political influence of Todmorden were small in these towns, and the boycott policy, which won immediate acceptance from the overseers and ratepayers of Todmorden and the neighboring town of Langfield, was rejected by the four towns further down the valley. This was not, it is true, a demonstration of support for the New Poor Law. The Guardians elected for these townships claimed to be anti-Poor Law men and they justified their actions by quoting Power's assurance that the only immediate function of the Board of Guardians would be the implementation of the Registration Act. But, whatever their motives, the effect of their actions was to prevent a total boycott in the Todmorden Union.

Having failed to repeat their Oldham performance even in Todmorden, it is hardly surprising that the opponents of the Poor Law were unable to match it elsewhere. They came close however in two Unions, Bury and Burnley, though in both of them opposition organization appears to have been less efficient and less broadly based than in Fielden's territory, so that outright intimidation played a larger role in enforcing a boycott. This was certainly the case in the Burnley Union,[2] where Parson Bull, who crossed the Pennines from Bradford in March to lead the opposition campaign, was able to win immediate support in the chronically depressed and strike-ridden area around Colne, so exciting the populace that

[1] On Todmorden see: MH 12.6272 Ormerod to P.L.C. 31 March 1838; *M.S.A.* and *L.T.* Jan.–March 1837.
[2] On Burnley see: MH 12.5673 Jan.–March 1837 correspondence and Power to P.L.C. 5 Dec. 1837; *M.S.A.* Jan.–March 1837.

neither the Guardians chosen for that area in January nor anyone else could be induced to run for election two months later. The Colne area marked the limits of Bull's influence, however. Further down the Calder valley, in Burnley itself and surrounding townships, the election proceeded in a normal fashion and the diehard resistance of a handful of towns and villages tended to be forgotten in a Union nearly three times the size of the Oldham Union and containing no less than twenty-six townships.

Of the Bury boycott campaign we know far less, which is unfortunate, since the Bury Union, due both to its central location and what happened there, was one of the key areas of resistance to the Poor Law.[1] In the early months of 1837 the Bury anti-Poor Law movement quickly established itself as the most radical and potentially the most violent in the textile districts. In sharp contrast to Todmorden and Oldham, where Fielden had deliberately fostered an alliance between all of those opposed to the Poor Law, the most active anti-Poor Law organization in Bury appears to have been an amalgam of trade unionists, ultra-Radicals and Operative Conservatives, which, it seems, could not or perhaps would not work closely with possible allies from other groups and classes. Instead, its leader, Matthew Fletcher, in keeping with his view of the Poor Law as part of a wider conspiracy, played on fears of class warfare, first in his celebrated cross-examination of Alfred Power, and later in a series of pre-election public meetings where he not only attacked middle-class Dissenters but forecast that the introduction of the law in Bury would be followed by the burning of local cotton mills.

The meager information we have on the actual Board of Guardians election in Bury indicates that it was conducted in the same atmosphere of acute tension and threatened violence. In the first round of elections, as in Oldham, the opposition was unable to prevent many nominations from being made, but the strength of local feeling was amply demonstrated by the large number of nominees who refused to serve and the fact that nearly ninety per cent of the ballot papers were burned or returned unmarked. In the interval between elections pressure was stepped up through a campaign of mass public meetings. This, plus whatever pressure Fletcher and his colleagues were able to apply in secret, had very

---

[1] Events in Bury must be pieced together from the uniformly inadequate accounts in the *Blackburn Gazette*, *Bolton Chronicle* and *M.S.A.* for Feb. and March 1837.

nearly the maximum desired effect. Far fewer nominations were made, more of those nominated backed out before or after the election, and, while a few Guardians were elected and did, it appears (though this is not certain), agree to serve, the overwhelming majority of the Union's twelve townships sent no representatives to the new Board.[1] In order to achieve this result the opposition must have been able to get some measure of co-operation from township officers and at least a few of the more substantial ratepayers, but, whereas in Oldham voluntary co-operation was more common than coercion, in Bury the reverse was almost certainly the case. This, at any rate, was the conclusion of Assistant Commissioner Power, and, largely because of this, the probably incompletely successful boycott campaign in Bury was to prove almost as effective a bar to the introduction of the Poor Law as Oldham's greater achievement. So certain were the Poor Law Commissioners and the Home Office that an attempt to introduce the Poor Law into Bury would lead to mob violence, that it was decided to do nothing beyond implementing the Registration Act.

Oldham, Todmorden, Bury and Burnley were the only Poor Law Unions where a large scale total boycott was attempted with any degree of success. Two others, Rochdale and Ashton, tried but failed, though both seemed likely candidates for a boycott.[2] Ashton bordered on one of the boycotting Unions and Rochdale on no less than three. Both were as compact as their successful neighbors. Both had strong local radical organizations and Ashton, like Bury, Oldham and Todmorden, was the center of activity of one the major anti-Poor Law leaders, J. R. Stephens. In Rochdale, however, though the Radicals adopted the boycott policy, they were unable to convince or pressure the local Conservatives into going along. Once the Tories decided to put up a slate of candidates, the Radicals, led by local Dissenters who feared allowing control of the Registration Act to fall into Conservative hands, countered with a list of their own. In Ashton, for which like Bury our information is scanty, a total boycott was suggested by some of the overseers, probably with the backing of Stephens, who we

[1] It is not clear whether all or only almost all of the Guardians elected resigned, whether, in other words, there was or was not a complete boycott in the end. Compare *Blackburn Gazette* 10 May 1837 and HO 73.55, Power to P.L.C. 21 Sept. 1839.

[2] Ashton: *M.S.A.* 4 Feb. and 27 April 1837; Rochdale: *L.T.*, *M.S.A.*, *M.G.* Jan.-March 1837.

know favored this course of action a year later. But a majority of the overseers were afraid of challenging the government so directly and there is some evidence that Stephens and his supporters were unable to win the co-operation of many middle-class opponents of the law.

This does not exhaust the list of places that attempted a boycott, successful or unsuccessful. There was hardly a Poor Law Union in the textile districts which did not have one or two townships that refused to elect Guardians.[1] A few of these local boycotts were the work of the major anti-Poor Law leaders. Oastler, for example, ensured that his township of Fixby remained unrepresented on the Huddersfield Board. The great majority of these localized boycotts had little in common with the Union-wide efforts, however. Most of them involved small country townships and were the work of a powerful local landowner or of a handful of men able to dominate parochial affairs. Their intention, almost always, was to protect their local bailiwicks from the clutches of London or, for that matter, of the local big city. They do not appear to have aimed, as the organizers of Union-wide boycotts most certainly did, at striking a fatal blow at the New Poor Law in the North. Boycotts in that sense were a sub-regional speciality. Apart from Burnley all of the Unions where a boycott was attempted lay immediately to the north or east of Manchester in the Pennines or at the point where the mountains meet the south-Lancashire industrial basin. Moreover, all of these Unions shared certain characteristics in size and compactness, in their social make-up and high population density, in their high degree of radical political organization, in their being the main stamping grounds of outstanding popular leaders, and in their proximity to one another. Few other Poor Law Unions came near to possessing comparable advantages, no other Unions attempted a boycott so systematically or on such a scale, and it is probably safe to say that had they done so they would have failed.

Luckily for the opposition, the boycott was not the only or the most commonly pursued policy; it was much more usual simply to attempt to pack a Board of Guardians with an anti-Poor Law majority. Though admittedly not the equal of a total boycott, this particular method of resistance had distinct advantages over a partial boycott which seemed to be the only other alternative. The danger in a partial boycott was that it resulted in a Board of

[1] MH 32.63 27 March 1837.

Guardians from which the most determinedly anti-Poor Law townships were excluded and, in those Unions, which were the great majority, where the attempt to impose a boycott was bound to end in only partial success, the opposition was wise to set its sights a bit lower and concentrate its attention on electing anti-Poor Law guardians. For this task it was not necessary to have a politically unified opposition or an organization of more or less equal strength in all the townships of a Union. Nor did the size or compactness of the Union matter very much. The opposition as a whole or the various elements in it could concentrate on the areas of their greatest strength, working out from these in the hope of capturing sufficient townships to give them the needed majority. The packing of a Board of Guardians had one additional, inestimable advantage over a boycott. Most opponents of the Poor Law were not John Fieldens. Even had they been able to command his means, they would have hesitated to follow him in taking the awesome step from mildly obstructionist but still legal opposition into outright defiance and sabotage. They preferred to accept the assurances of Alfred Power that the new administrative machinery would be used in the first instance only to implement the Registration Act, and to hope, Micawber-like, that something would turn up before they would be faced with the Poor Law itself. Packing a Board of Guardians seemed to offer the best of two worlds. It certainly demonstrated opposition, which many hoped might be all that was needed, while avoiding the precipitation of an immediate crisis.

The packing of a Board of Guardians may have been a less ambitious project than preventing one from coming into existence, but it proved little less difficult to achieve. There was, first of all, a large body of opposition opinion which disagreed with the premises of those who advocated capturing control of the Boards. They argued that no Board of Guardians, whatever its views, could remain independent of the all-powerful Poor Law Commissioners. This had been one of the main points in Fielden's case for a total boycott, and many of those, primarily Radicals, who accepted this view believed that, where a total boycott was an impossibility, the administration of the law and the unpopularity associated with it ought to be left in the hands of the Whigs or Tories.[1] A number of the more extreme Tory opponents of the law

---

[1] The best coverage of the advocates of a unilateral boycott was given by the *L.T.* and *M.S.A.* Jan.–Feb. 1837.

took the same line, arguing that the Whigs should be made to carry out their own measure. On the other hand, many Radicals and Tories, primarily for political reasons, and many Dissenters, for religious reasons, disagreed, believing, on the whole, that the risks involved in abdicating power and responsibility were greater than the risks involved in doing battle as Guardians with the Poor Law Commissioners.

This basic tactical division appeared in almost every Poor Law Union in the textile districts and was bitterly fought out in January and February as the elections approached. It accounted in large part for the popularity of the total boycott, which, quite apart from its obvious superiority as a weapon of resistance, seemed to be the only way of bridging over these divisions and preventing a fatal weakening of the unity of the movement. Since, however, a total boycott was an impossibility in most Poor Law Unions, this fundamental tactical difference was only rarely resolved and many advocates of a unilateral boycott maintained their position to the end. This was especially the case among working-class opponents of the Law, both Radical and Conservative, who argued that, given the property qualification for Guardians and the system of multiple voting in the elections, no Board of Guardians, even should it be able to maintain some independence from London, would serve the interests of the poor. How significant an effect these arguments had when it came to the actual balloting, it is impossible to say. That there were abstentions, often on a mass scale, is certain. But we cannot equate this with a deliberate unilateral boycott or use it as an accurate index of working-class disaffection.

The difficulty in assessing the extent and meaning of the unilateral boycott is that it cannot be separated from other factors, in particular partisan rivalry between Conservative and Radical opponents of the New Poor Law.[1] This sometimes bitter partisanship, reinforced and often dominated by religious differences, was the most serious and persistent problem faced by the advocates of a united opposition and, in the end, made a mockery of almost all attempts at and talk of unity. Of only one Poor Law Union, Huddersfield, can it be said with any degree of certainty that there was extensive co-operation between Radicals and Tories in the conduct of the 1837 Board of Guardians election. This of course

[1] On the fragmentation of the radical vote see especially: *M.G.*, *M.S.A.* and *L.T.* Feb.–April 1837.

was the work of the old Huddersfield Short Time Committee, itself an embodiment of the concept of a Tory–Radical alliance and, as such, very nearly unique. Elsewhere, despite constant pleas for unity from the anti-Poor Law press, there was little evidence of it. Conservatives were largely responsible for preventing a boycott in the first round of elections in Oldham and they wrecked the Radical-sponsored boycott in Rochdale. In Rochdale, where non-Tory politics was dominated by anti-Poor Law Radicals, this partisanship did little damage to the cause, since, whichever side won in an election contest, the resulting Board would be committed to resistance.

Such political conditions were rare outside of south-eastern Lancashire, however. Elsewhere in the textile districts, only Preston, the city which had sent Henry Hunt to Parliament only seven years before, had an equally strong ultra-Radical tradition.[1] There, in the central urban townships of the Union, the opposition was led by Joseph Livesey, a Dissenter and political and social radical who was later to achieve national importance as a leader of the teetotal movement. Had he chosen to extend his anti-Poor Law activities beyond Preston, Livesey could easily have become as important a figure as any of the major popular leaders. As it was, though he confined himself to his home town in opposing the New Poor Law, his achievements there were extraordinary. His own private war with the New Poor Law lasted for twenty years and he launched it in 1837 with a fiery campaign of propaganda, petitions and public meetings which very nearly brought an anti-Poor Law Radical victory in the first round of elections and was successful in the second round. Livesey's relationship with local Tories was ambiguous. Though they were officially committed to opposition, and their local paper, the *Pilot*, welcomed an anti-Poor Law victory in the Board of Guardians elections, the Conservatives disliked Livesey's methods, his friends and his supporters, and offered him no help during the election itself. Indeed, the class and partisan enmity engendered by the campaign was so great that the local Tories, in their efforts to undercut Livesey and his supporters, soon became, in effect, the allies of the Poor Law Commissioners in the Preston Union. Luckily for the anti-Poor Law movement, the Radicals were strong enough to be able to manage very nicely on their own.

[1] Preston: *Preston Chronicle* Jan.–April 1837; J. Pearce, *Life and Teachings of Joseph Livesey* (London 1866).

Preston, however, was peculiar both in its strong radical tradition and in having a leader of the caliber of Joseph Livesey. In most Poor Law Unions the situation was reversed; it was the Tories who were able to come forward as the anti-Poor Law party, since Whigs and Liberals rather than anti-Poor Law Radicals dominated the reforming interest in local political life. The great majority of contested Boards of Guardians elections were straight fights between Tories and Whigs or Liberals, and, while the latter were rarely enthusiastic supporters of the New Poor Law, most of them declared themselves willing to give it a trial. This, the most common electoral situation placed Radical opponents of the law in an almost impossible situation and led to considerable vote splitting. Some of the ultra-Radicals voted for Tory opponents of the New Poor Law, others, especially Dissenters, backed Liberal candidates and a large proportion almost certainly abstained. How the Radical vote was actually shared out depended on local circumstances such as the size of the Dissenting interest and the prominence given to religion in the election campaign, the degree to which Liberal candidates, though willing to work with the New Poor Law, were committed to resisting its harsher aspects, and, finally, the extent to which Liberal–Radical political divisions corresponded with and were exacerbated by middle-class–working-class social divisions and the degree to which the Tories were willing and able to take advantage of this.

Class, political and religious cleavages, boycotts, attempted boycotts and hotly contested elections naturally received the most attention during the Boards of Guardians election campaign. But it should not be forgotten that in every Union some townships and in a few Unions nearly all townships appointed Guardians without a contest and in an atmosphere of peace and quiet. Most of the individual townships that had no contests were in rural or semi-rural areas where an individual land-owner, more occasionally an individual manufacturer, or a handful of influential ratepayers were able to dictate the choice of a Guardian. The situation was somewhat different in those Unions where a majority of townships managed to avert a contest. In such cases peace was maintained by some sort of deal between local factions to share out power among them. This did not mean that the divisions which led to contested elections elsewhere were not present in these Unions. But where the outcome could be predicted fairly accurately and the almost certain winners were willing to accord the almost certain losers a generous allocation of Guardianships and a fair percentage of jobs under the New Poor Law, there was little reason to force the issue in an election and at least one very good reason for not doing so, the expense of conducting an election.

Despite all these local peculiarities, there were clear regional or sub-regional patterns in the results. In general, the larger towns and cities returned Liberal Guardians while rural areas were usually solidly Tory. Thus, the larger the rural hinterland around the central urban townships, the greater was the chance that the Board of Guardians would have a Tory anti-Poor Law majority, while in the more urban Unions a Liberal Board more or less favorable to the New Law was likely, except of course in Preston and those Unions north and east of Manchester where anti-Poor Law Radicals rather than Liberals were able to assume control. The Liberals did particularly well in Yorkshire.[1] The elections in the Bradford and Halifax Unions, which many hoped or feared would result in Tory victories due to mass defections by anti-Poor Law Radicals, produced instead sweeping Liberal victories extending well beyond the urban core into the out-townships of these Unions. Religion was a big factor in both Unions and the strong Dissenting vote may have been decisive in bringing about this result. In addition, there is a good deal of evidence that most anti-Poor Law Radicals as well as many working-class Conservatives abstained rather than vote for the Tory candidates. Dewsbury and Wakefield also appear to have elected comfortable pro-Poor Law majorities, probably for much the same reasons. Only two Unions, Huddersfield, which had an electoral campaign quite unlike that of any of its neighbors, and Keighley, the most rural Union in the Yorkshire textile district, returned anti-Poor Law majorities.

In Lancashire the Liberals did less well, being bested by the Radicals as well as the Tories.[2] Anti Poor Law Radicals not only dominated those Unions in south-eastern Lancashire where complete or partial boycotts had been enforced, but they made an almost clean sweep in Rochdale and managed to extend their

[1] For the results in Yorkshire see *L.I.* and *L.T.* for early Feb., late March and early April 1837; HO 73.53 Power to Chadwick 10 May 1837. Additional information on Halifax and Bradford are in the *Halifax Express* 11 Feb. and 1 April 1837, and in the *Bradford Observer* 9 and 16 Feb. 1837 respectively.

[2] For the results in Lancashire see, in addition to Power's letter to Chadwick cited above, *M.G.* and *M.S.A.* for early Feb., late March and early April. Additional information on Bolton is in the *Bolton Chronicle* 11 Feb. and 8 April 1837.

victories far enough beyond the city of Preston to win control of that Union as well. The Liberals, on the other hand, won decisively only in the predominantly urban Poor Law Unions along the Lancashire–Cheshire border. Ashton, despite Stephens' machinations, Stockport and Chorlton-on-Medlock all elected probably overwhelming Liberal pro-Poor Law majorities. Elsewhere the Tories were far more successful than they had been in the West Riding in confining the Liberals within their urban strongholds and overwhelming the Boards with country Tory Guardians. The Bolton Union, though it had an unusually bitterly contested election, was fairly representative of this more usual Lancashire pattern. In the central townships the Liberals were never in any serious trouble, despite a vigorous Tory campaign to win over disaffected Radicals, but the out-townships were swept by the Tories and provided them with more than enough Guardians to completely dominate the affairs of the Union. Warrington and probably Haslingden went the same way, and the Blackburn Union, though it appointed its Guardians without a contest, belongs in a similar category. It is likely that much the same thing happened in the Wigan, Chorley and Clitheroe Unions, all of which were predominantly rural in character, but the significance of probable Tory victories in these Unions is not certain, since the degree of Tory militancy in opposition to the Poor Law in a particular locality tended to be more or less directly proportionate to the extent of urbanization, industrialization and political competition in that locality. In short, a Tory victory in Chorley or Clitheroe was unlikely to mean quite the same thing as a Tory victory in Bolton.

The problem of finding out what happened, let alone the significance of what happened in the 1837 Boards of Guardians election is greatest in these peripheral Unions, but is by no means absent even in the center of the textile districts. Many of the results cited above are strong probabilities, not certainties. In a few cases, as in Leigh, the results were too close to draw definite conclusions; more often the problem is simply lack of adequate information. Of the two main sources for the elections, Power's letters to the Poor Law Commissioners are unsatisfactory because of his tendency to be optimistic and discount the strength of opposition except in those Unions where it was really militant. The northern press is more rewarding in so far as it went, but most Poor Law Union centers did not have papers at this time, the great majority of papers outside the metropolitan centers of Leeds and Manchester were nearly exclusively local in their coverage, and even the Leeds and Manchester papers had their shortcomings. They depended on local correspondents, sometimes good, more often bad, and the extent of their coverage dropped off sharply beyond a fairly narrow radius.

Another, and ultimately the most important reason for this un-certainty about the significance of the election results is that the Boards elected in 1837 were given little opportunity to display their sentiments. The only immediate aim of the Commissioners was the implementation of the Registration Act and the role of the Guardians in this was limited to the election of a clerk who was also to act as registration officer. Once this was done the Guardians ceased to have any specific function until such time as the Poor Law Commissioners chose to introduce the New Poor Law itself and in most Unions the election of a clerk was followed by many months during which the Guardians did not meet at all. There-fore, almost the only way in which a Board of Guardians could demonstrate its dislike of the Poor Law during the early months of 1837 was by refusing to elect a clerk. Motions to this effect were proposed in many Boards but with only one exception they were defeated and usually by substantial majorities. This almost universal reluctance to sabotage the Registration Act was not, however, an accurate reflection of attitudes towards the Poor Law itself. In Keighley, for example, the Board easily defeated a motion to delay the election of a clerk; yet, little more than a month later, the Guardians (as well as a turbulent crowd outside) used one of Power's periodic visits as an occasion for heaping abuse on him, his employers and the law. Only the hot-heads were willing to go further and force an immediate confrontation by opposing every directive from London, but the hot-heads were almost everywhere a minority, even among the anti-Poor Law Guardians.[1]

The one exception to this rule, the Huddersfield Union, was a special case in other respects as well.[2] It was one of the largest

[1] On Keighley, see: *L.I.* 25 March 1837; MH 12.15158 Feb.–March 1837 correspondence.

[2] The main sources on Huddersfield in 1837 are the files of the P.L.C. (MH 12.15063) and the Home Office (HO 40.35 and HO 41.13). The only important published accounts are in Driver, *Tory Radical*, Chs. XXV–VII, and, from the government point of view, P.L.C., *Third Annual Report*, Appendix A No. 7. Newspaper accounts, of which that in the *L.I.* was the fullest, add comparatively little to this.

Unions in the area, ranking fourth in population and second in area. It included no less than thirty-four townships which to-gether took in the Colne valley, its major tributaries and the hill country in between. Apart from Huddersfield itself and a few of the adjacent towns, none of the townships was very large and a few were nothing more than isolated villages remote in every respect from Huddersfield. The Union was as diverse socially and economically as it was geographically. Some of the townships were almost entirely agricultural communities, a few were prosperous mill towns little affected by the recession, while others were semi-industrialized and burdened with a large number who lived in-creasingly precariously in whole or in part from handloom weaving.

The Huddersfield Union's size and diversity, either of which alone would have made it a difficult Union to deal with, were closely linked with another, equally vexing problem. One of the main sources of opposition to the New Poor Law all over the country but especially in the North, was the system of Poor Law Unions. Urban and rural townships felt that they had little in common, the larger centers resented the possibility of being out-voted in the management of their own affairs by the host of smaller towns and villages around them, the smaller townships feared losing their identity, and so on. A relatively small, compact or homogeneous Union might hope to avoid such divisions, but the larger and more diverse a Union, the greater were its chances of descending into bitter factionalism. The system of representation only exacerbated the problem. By law each township had to be represented by at least one Guardian while the larger townships were allotted additional Guardians, in proportion to population so far as was possible. Once again this presented few problems in the smaller Unions where it was often feasible to allot Guardians strictly in accordance with the population of the various townships and still end up with a Board of manageable size. But, the larger the Union, the more the Commissioners were forced to depart from strict proportionality, and in Unions the size of Huddersfield the system broke down completely. Townships with as few as 500 people and as many as 4,000 people both had one Guardian while Huddersfield with 25,000 people had only five Guardians. Small wonder that the Huddersfield townships were more persistent in their petitions to the Commissioners than any others in the North, and, while it is true that they could not agree on a solution—the larger towns wanted more Guardians for themselves and the smaller ones sought escape from such a huge Union—there was at least one source of unity among them, their shared animosity towards the authority which had placed them in this position.[1]

As if this were not enough, Huddersfield was perhaps better prepared for giving practical expression to this local discontent than any other Poor Law Union in England. The Huddersfield Short Time Committee, which had assumed the direction of the early stages of the anti-Poor Law campaign was of course the home committee of Oastler and Pitkeithly and as such by far the most professional of all the factory reform organizations in the North. Its conduct in early 1837 was to provide a model for other anti-Poor Law committees in much the same way that, years before, it had inspired the Yorkshire ten hours' agitation. Largely through its efforts, the Board of Guardians election in March, and perhaps in January as well, resulted in a majority, though a small one, which was not only anti-Poor Law but, for the most part at least, prepared to prove it.[2]

The first sign of trouble came at the first and only meeting of the preliminary Board of Guardians elected in January. The Guardians decided by a very close vote to adjourn without electing a clerk. No one, including the chairman of the Board or Power, was sure of the meaning of this decision. It could be interpreted as hostile to the New Poor Law or simply as a wish to delay decision on an issue which was not resolved (the Registration Act was then being reconsidered in Parliament).[3] After the March election, however, any doubts were quickly dispelled, for the non-election of a clerk, which may in February have been an accident, became in April the primary goal of the opposition. But the opposition majority was exceedingly small and, with Power present to put the Commissioners' case, the Board if left to itself might well have elected a clerk. The opposition therefore decided to back up its allies on the Board with popular action. A threatening and noisy but otherwise quite peaceful crowd invaded the meeting, completely disrupted it and forced the Board to adjourn temporarily until order could be restored. How great an effect this had on the Board's decisions later that day it is of course impossible to say, but, considering that the motion not to elect a clerk was passed by a margin of only three votes out of a total of thirty-nine,

---

[1] MH 12.15063 Jan. 1837 correspondence.
[2] *L.I.* Jan.–March 1837.
[3] MH 12.15063 Swan to P.L.C. 18 Feb. 1837.

the chances are that the intervention of the crowd was decisive. In any case, a clerk was not elected and the Board added insult to injury by voting, this time by a much greater margin, to adjourn for two months.[1]

Power was furious and his first inclination was to strike back hard by getting the Poor Law Commissioners to issue an order commanding the Board to act, thereby forcing the Guardians into a position where either they would elect a clerk or expose themselves to prosecution for not obeying the law. But the state of popular feeling in Huddersfield was such that Power himself had second thoughts and, in any case, the Poor Law Commissioners were not yet ready to force the issue. The most they were willing to do at this early stage of the proceedings was warn the Board of the possible consequences of its action. 'Any further postponement of the necessary proceedings', the Commissioners pointed out, 'will be in direct contravention not only of the Order of Union but of . . . the Registration Act.' And, what is more, 'if the provisions of the Registration Act should fail of being carried into effect through their [the Guardians'] default, they alone will become responsible for defeating the intentions of the legislature'.[2]

Though rather more than friendly advice, this warning from the Commissioners was still something less than a direct threat. Nonetheless, it was enough to frighten many of the Guardians, and the Board, in its meeting of June 5, would probably have reversed its earlier decision and elected a clerk but for the fact that the opposition was prepared to bring even greater pressures to bear. The mobilization of popular discontent, as used for example at the April meeting of the Huddersfield board, was nothing new in anti-Poor Law activity. Popular demonstrations and marches had been used against Power when he first came to the North, in the Oldham boycott campaign, and in attempts to influence the election of Guardians in townships all over the area. Actual violence had so far been rare, but threats of violence and the incitement to violence were commonplace and had been so in the North ever since Oastler's 'needle' speech of the previous autumn. But the preparations for the June 5th Board of Guardians meeting, though they grew out of these earlier efforts, were on an entirely different scale. The opponents had come to see the Huddersfield confrontation as the first serious test of their strength and as a key to

[1] MH 12.15063 Power to P.L.C. 5 April 1837.
[2] *Ibid.* P.L.C. to B.G. 3 June 1837.

their success elsewhere. They poured everything they had into the preparations for it. The great meeting at Hartshead Moor in May was not only the first effort of the newly organized West Riding Anti-Poor Law Association, it also marked the opening of a campaign of unrelenting pressure on Huddersfield. It was followed throughout the central West Riding, but particularly in the Huddersfield area, by constant small meetings, demonstrations and, evidently a favorite pastime, burnings in effigy of Power and local supporters of the new law. Then, a few days before the meeting of the Board, Oastler placarded the Union with posters calling on the people to assemble *en masse* in the center of town about an hour before the Guardians were scheduled to meet.[1]

All these preparations had the desired effect on both parties. The pro-Poor Law Guardians were terrified while the opposition, whipped up by almost a month of unceasing agitation, were belligerent and confident. Something in the order of 10,000 people showed up for Oastler's rally on the morning of the 5th. He addressed the crowd at length, in his usual fashion combining highly emotional calls for resistance with solemn warnings not to break the peace, and he then led a mass march on the workhouse where the Board of Guardians was meeting. Oastler demanded admittance to the meeting while the crowd milled about, gradually closing in on the workhouse. The Guardians refused Oastler's demand, the crowd responded by throwing stones and the Guardians, fearing worse, took the opportunity to escape by the back door. The crowd now split, part of it remaining to wreck the workhouse, while the rest followed the Board to its new meeting place at the Albion Tavern, pressing in on the frightened Guardians, shoving them and throwing stones. Once in the tavern, however, the Guardians soon found that they were little better off. The crowd outside grew larger and their mood uglier. A local magistrate, Battye, realizing he had nothing with which to back up his authority, and in any case no great friend of the New Poor Law, refused to read the Riot Act. The Board was, in effect, imprisoned and, as time passed, became more amenable to any suggestion which might extricate it in safety from the tavern. Oastler was admitted to the meeting, stated his case and further emphasized his control of the situation by calling successfully on the crowd to disperse. It hardly need be said that the motion to elect a clerk was defeated that day. The vote was not even close, as it had

[1] *Ibid.* Tinker to P.L.C. 8 June 1837; *L.I.* 27 May, 14 June 1837.

been two months before; only eleven Guardians dared defy the opposition.[1]

This was a major defeat for the Poor Law Commissioners, in fact the most serious they had yet suffered; but it was not, or so they thought, irretrievable. The Board was to meet again in a week's time and the Commissioners, far from being dismayed by what had happened, already had a plan for undercutting the position of the growing anti-Poor Law majority on the Board. It depended on a legal subterfuge. According to the Commissioners, the adjournment of the meeting without having elected a clerk was 'a direct contravention of the law'. This being the case, they argued, no such illegal act could be binding 'on such portion of the board as may be willing to act in execution of the law'.[2] In other words, a quorum (three members or more) would be legally entitled to push through the election of a clerk no matter what a majority of the Guardians said or did. Had this been proposed some time before, it might have worked; but after June 5th it was too late. The Anti-Poor Law Association and the opponents on the Board were in complete control. As on June 5th, a crowd collected outside the Guardians' meeting place, but now, a week later, there was no violence. There was no need for violence. The Board made only the feeblest attempt to exclude non-members from the meeting, and it made no attempt to elect a clerk. The Commissioners' problem was no longer that they could not win a large minority, let alone a majority, to their side; on June 12th not even the requisite three members could be found who would dare publicly to support the law.[3]

The Poor Law Commissioners were now forced to admit what the opposition had realized the week before, that the battle in Huddersfield had entered a new phase. Heretofore, the victories of the opponents had been won by keeping one jump ahead of the Commissioners. The Commissioners' policy of entreaties, followed by threats, followed by legal subterfuges had failed not because it was inherently unworkable but because it had not changed as fast as the opposition's tactics. And the Board of Guardians, subjected to increasing pressure from both sides, naturally yielded to those

[1] MH 12.15063 Tinker to P.L.C. 8 June 1837; Lockwood to P.L.C. 8 June 1837; P.L.C. to Russell 21 June 1837.
[2] *Ibid.* P.L.C. to B.G. 10 June 1837.
[3] *Ibid.* Tinker to P.L.C. 14 June 1837; Morehouse to P.L.C. 14 June 1837.

pressures which were strongest and most immediate. But, throughout this early period, the Board did at least continue to function and could arguably have been won over by the Poor Law Commissioners if the Commissioners had seized the initiative. After June 5th, however, this was no longer true. As a result of the violence on that day, the Board of Guardians had begun to disintegrate. It is no exaggeration to say that many Guardians now feared for their lives and, bitterly angry at the government for not protecting them, they were thereafter unwilling to expose themselves to the crowd in the service of a law to which few of them in any case felt deeply committed. Some of the Guardians resigned; most simply did not turn up at the Board meetings after June 5th. The anti-Poor Law majority, once so slim, took complete control by default.[1]

Once started, such a process was very nearly impossible to reverse, and to do so would require government efforts far beyond anything yet attempted. The Board as a whole would have to be put under extreme pressure and, above all, the Guardians would have to be protected and indeed isolated from popular pressure and the threat of mob action. The first requirement was easily met. Late in June the Commissioners issued an order to the Board of Guardians, commanding them to meet at the Albion Hotel in Huddersfield on July 17th and not to adjourn until they had elected a clerk. But the other requirement was rather more difficult to fulfill and to do so required the co-operation of the Home Office, since nothing less than a show of force would suffice. London police were sent to Huddersfield and a detachment of cavalry were stationed nearby in case any serious trouble should arise. But the Home Office demanded a high price for its assistance. The Home Secretary, Lord John Russell, believed that the opponents should be rendered ineffective in more ways than simply by sending in outside forces. The carrot as well as the stick would have to be applied. 'It is obvious', he declared, 'that if you shall endeavor to compel unwilling Guardians to assume the administration of relief among an excited community you run the risk of strengthening prejudice against the law.'[2] From this it followed that the election of a clerk in Huddersfield ought to be separated as far as possible from the Poor Law issue and Russell

[1] *Ibid.* P.L.C. to Russell 21 June 1837; Shaw to P.L.C. 28 June 1837; Kent to P.L.C. 3 July 1837.
[2] *Ibid.* Russell to P.L.C. 27 June 1837.

therefore recommended that the Poor Law Commissioners put off the implementation of the Poor Law itself in Huddersfield at least until early 1838 and that the decision to do this should be communicated to the Board of Guardians as a means of inducing them to proceed to the election of a clerk. The Poor Law Commissioners agreed; they could do little else. They even instructed Power not to attend the meeting in order to underline the fact that its sole function was to elect a clerk under the Registration Act.[1]

It didn't work. The Commissioners failed to get even the conditional victory to which they had resigned themselves. Two candidates were nominated for the clerkship but during the course of a meeting which lasted off and on for seven hours no seconders could be found. And the clerkship, though ostensibly the only subject of the meeting, was of secondary importance as far as the opposition Guardians were concerned. Their aim was to circumvent the order from London and eventually they hit upon a petty but nonetheless legal technicality which allowed them to do so. The Poor Law Commissioners' order, they claimed, was invalid because the place in which the Guardians had been told to meet did not exist. There was no Albion Hotel, only an Albion Tavern.[2]

This, certainly the most humiliating defeat suffered by the Poor Law Commissioners in Huddersfield, was achieved entirely without violence. In part, of course, the absence of any disturbance was due to the presence of the London police. But even more perhaps it was due to the fact that, as on June 12th, violence was now superfluous. The crowd had done its work and needed to do no more; the mere threat of violence was enough to keep the pro-Poor Law Guardians away or inactive. And the threat of further violence, despite the presence of the police, was always there. Every Board of Guardians meeting was attended by a sullen and insulting crowd. The burning of effigies went on throughout the summer in the towns and villages around Huddersfield. And finally, as a reminder of what could happen, there were two serious riots in the West Riding that summer. Neither of them were specifically anti-Poor Law riots; they occurred in connection with the general election occasioned by the death of King William IV. But they were anti-Poor Law riots in all but name. The first occurred

---

[1] On government preparations, see: *ibid*. Frankland Lewis to Russell. 7 July 1837; Russell to Harewood 5 July 1837; HO 41.13 June-July 1837.
[2] MH 12.15063 Power to P.L.C. 18 July 1837; Swan to P.L.C. 19 July 1837.

at Huddersfield where Oastler himself was a candidate and the Poor Law was made the major issue. It was a close contest, so close indeed that in the early counting Oastler went ahead. But gradually his lead was cut and when at last he fell behind his Whig opponent, the crowd went wild. The polling officials and anyone known to be a Whig sympathizer were pelted with stones. The police intervened but by this time the presence of the police could not stop it. At length a detachment of cavalry was brought in and the Riot Act was read, but even then it was some time before the crowd could be dispersed and the town pacified.[1]

This incident took place late in July, but before the month was over another and far more serious riot took place in nearby Wakefield. In the contest there for the West Riding seats Oastler was not a candidate but he was determined to make the Poor Law the major issue there just as he had done in Huddersfield. The whole central West Riding was placarded with notices calling on the people to march to Wakefield on nomination day. Oastler himself led a march from Huddersfield in the early morning and by noon some 30,000 or more were packed into the courthouse square and the streets nearby. The riot was probably started by a group of drunken Whig supporters trying to push their way through the crowd, but the origins do not really matter, for, within minutes, it turned into a general street fight between Whig and Tory supporters with Oastler conspicuously at the head of his own anti-Whig contingent. After some time and a good deal of damage, the fighting petered out of its own accord and troops arrived only to find the nomination day speeches resumed as if nothing had happened.[2] But, of course, enough had happened that no one in the West Riding was likely for some months to fly in the face of popular feelings. The government recognized this and recommended that no further action be taken in the Huddersfield Poor Law dispute. The Poor Law Commissioners reluctantly accepted the status quo and there was no attempt from London to interfere with the one remaining 1837 meeting of the Huddersfield Board of Guardians, held in September. The result therefore was a foregone conclusion. The meeting was dominated by the opposition, the motion to elect a clerk was defeated by eight votes to two and the Board ended its deliberations by voting to adjourn for an unheard of four months.[3]

[1] *L.I.* 29 July, 5 Aug. 1837.
[2] *Ibid.* 5 Aug; R. Oastler, *A Letter to Viscount Morpeth* (London 1837).
[3] MH 12.15063 Swain to P.L.C. 12 Sept. 1837.

V Concession and counterattack

The last meeting of the Huddersfield Board of Guardians in 1837 was something of a victory celebration by the opposition. It was the culmination of a year-long series of virtually uninterrupted successes of which this was by far the sweetest. In the boycotting Unions opposition defiance of the Poor Law Commissioners had not yet been challenged by the government, but in the Huddersfield Union the opposition had been challenged, and the opposition, not the government, had won. Despite the early scepticism of many anti-Poor Law leaders, the belief or hope that a small majority, perhaps even a minority of Guardians, if well led and backed by good organization and the co-operation of the overseers and ratepayers, could resist pressure from London had been fully vindicated. The normal functioning of a Board of Guardians had been so delayed and disrupted that those Guardians favorable to the New Law had become completely demoralized and the Poor Law Commissioners, finding no sure allies on the local level, had turned away in frustration and disgust.

There were, to be sure, limits to the effectiveness of this kind of resistance. The Commissioners would ignore a Board of Guardians for a while, but not for very long. Sooner or later the Assistant Commissioners and the Commissioners in London would hit back, and, when determined, they were not above resorting to the same tactics as the opposition, countering evasion of the law with threats of legal action or resorting to subterfuge in order to win their point and cow a recalcitrant Board. On more than one occasion such moves by the Poor Law Commissioners had very nearly pushed the Huddersfield Guardians into submission. If fought out in isolation, such battles between a Board of Guardians and the authorities in London would almost certainly have led to defeat for the Board, because the Commissioners had, in the end, both the right and the power to impose their will. But the battle had not been fought in isolation; at critical moments, and especially on June 5, the continued resistance of the Huddersfield Board had not been due to the determination of the Guardians at all, but to the timely intervention of a well-led mob. This particular use of the mass demonstration, though not of course the mass demonstration itself, was a really new contribution of the Huddersfield resistance movement. It was the opposition's ultimate weapon and, in combination with a divided Board of Guardians, apparently an unbeatable one.

In fact, however, the use or threat of mob action was as fragile a weapon as Board of Guardians' resistance, for, just as the Commissioners were capable of bringing tremendous pressure to bear on opposition Guardians, so the government could, if it chose, easily outbid the opposition in the use or threat of force. Yet this is precisely what the government did not do in Huddersfield in 1837. While the Poor Law Commissioners gradually raised the stakes in their battle with the Guardians, the use of the mob, which was the opposition's answer to pressure from London, was not in its turn countered by the introduction of superior forces on the government side. Or, rather, when this was finally done, it was both too little and too late. The reasons for the government's restraint are complex. In part it was due to conditions within the Huddersfield Union. Unquestionably the magistrates, who did not disguise their distaste for the New Poor Law, failed to do their duty.[1] On a number of occasions prior to the disastrous Board meeting of June 5, pro-Poor Law Guardians, fearing violence, had asked the magistrates to call on the central government for military or police aid in preserving order. The magistrates had refused. On the day of that all-important meeting only one magistrate was in attendance and he, having made no provisions for a force to back him up in case of trouble, refused to read the Riot Act. Unable and perhaps unwilling to make his authority felt, he had no alternative, as one Guardian put it, but to 'place the board under the merciful protection of Richard Oastler'.[2] After that the government became alarmed. It no longer waited for requests for assistance, and offered to supply police from London at a moment's notice. But the magistrates replied that such help was not needed and the government contented itself with stationing troops nearby in case there should be any trouble. This in itself was not enough, however, to revive the shattered morale of the pro-Poor Law Guardians, who no longer trusted the magistrates

[1] On the role of the magistrates see: MH 12.15063 Tinker to P.L.C. 14 June 1837; P.L.C. to Russell 24 June 1837; Russell to Harewood 5 July 1837; Battye to P.L.C. 11 July 1837.
[2] *Ibid.* Tinker to P.L.C. 8 June 1837.

to call in help, even though now readily available, should it be needed.

But collusion between the magistrates and the opposition, and the magistrates' dereliction of duty, though important factors in preventing proper law enforcement, were not the whole story. The slowness of the Home Office in taking action was as much self-imposed as imposed upon it by the delaying tactics of the magistrates. The stationing of troops and even their intervention in a particular place was entirely a government responsibility, and either action could have been taken without reference to the local magistracy. Yet the government delayed and did not act on its own initiative until after the riot of June 5. The use of the London police was in a different and more difficult category since, theoretically, they could not be employed outside of London unless sworn in as special constables by local magistrates. But the government could, if it chose, have forced the hand of reluctant magistrates by dispatching the police unasked, only letting the magistrates know of this when the police were about to arrive. This indeed is what the Home Office finally did in Huddersfield, though not until early July when police intervention could prevent further incidents but not erase the effects of earlier ones.

In view of what had happened at Huddersfield, Home Office policy seems inexplicable, but the government had good reasons for pursuing a cautious policy in general as well as in this particular case.[1] The fundamental problem of law enforcement was that local resources were inadequate in any extraordinary situation. The only way in which a magistrate could supplement the usually tiny force of local constables was by swearing in special constables or calling up the yeomanry. But, as civilians drafted into public service, they lacked discipline and were subject to local political pressures and the fear of later reprisals from the populace. If brought face to face with a mob, they were, in practice, unreliable. Understandably, then, most magistrates were inclined to call on the central government for aid at the slightest hint of trouble. And in its turn, the government was suspicious of all requests for aid and usually tried to avoid taking the burden from the local magistrates on the reasonable grounds that to do so would

[1] On the government's attitude towards intervention and the problems of local law enforcement see: F. C. Mather, *Public Order in the Age of the Chartists* (Manchester 1959), 62–5, 75–87, 105–11, 146–8, 158–60, 164–9, 173–7.

weaken both their authority and their determination, thereby inviting the lawlessness it was intended to avoid.

Intervention, should it nonetheless prove justified and unavoidable, also had its problems. The government had only two forces at its disposal, the London police and the army. The former were exceedingly unpopular outside of London while the use of the latter was an extreme measure which the government wished to avoid if possible. Moreover, both the London police and the troops available for domestic duties were severely limited in numbers and the London police could rarely be spared for long periods of time. It was therefore in the interests of the government to limit strictly both the scope and duration of direct interference in local peace-keeping operations. But this proved exceedingly difficult in practice, for, while intervention by the police or army was usually enough to quell a disturbance immediately, no one could foretell the consequences of withdrawing these forces, and the magistrates almost always tried to hold onto them for as long as possible. The maintenance of scattered small forces which this implied and which the magistrates always called for in times of trouble, was the last thing the government wanted, and with good reason. The effectiveness of the home army lay very largely in concentration and mobility; to disperse it and, still more, to tie it down vitiated its strength. As a general rule, then, the government resisted the temptation to intervene forcibly in local affairs unless every other means had been tried and found wanting.

Most of these general considerations applied with equal force to the Huddersfield situation, though the particular circumstances were rather unusual. For example, the Huddersfield magistrates, far from seeking aid from the government, rejected it when it was offered. This, however, was only another and more devious method of abdicating responsibility, and the government was even less inclined to take on the burden in such circumstances than in the more usual case of inaction through fear. Thus, while the government eventually offered its assistance, every such offer was accompanied by lengthy admonitions to the magistrates to do their duty both as law enforcement officials and as ex-officio members of the Board of Guardians, and it was only when these failed to have any effect that the government began to act on its own. Even then the government moved cautiously, for it did not intend to get too deeply involved in the local affairs of Huddersfield or to relieve the magistrates (or the Guardians) of their unpopular responsibility for implementing the orders of the Poor Law Commissioners. Sooner or later, after all, they would have to undertake these duties and, to give them the excuse that they had acted only because of government compulsion, would have only made the law even more unpopular and the long run task of its local administrators even more difficult.

Nonetheless, Huddersfield had proved so intractable, that, had it been possible to deal with it in isolation, the government might well have decided to risk the consequences and intervene more swiftly and forcefully. But Huddersfield could not be considered in isolation, for there was the real possibility of similar situations arising throughout the industrial North. Should this happen, the government, having once allowed local magistrates to evade their duties and itself taken them over, would have been hard put to it to avoid the same development elsewhere. Most of the magistrates, even in the industrial districts, were drawn from the local landed gentry and one of the recurring complaints against them was that they often tended to take the side of the opponents against the Liberal supporters of the law. Such men could not be trusted to deal severely with anti-Poor Law disturbances and even their neutral or pro-Poor Law colleagues might be frightened into inactivity or, worse still, led into it by the belief that the government would bail them out. Thus the government might easily find itself placed in the unwelcome and dangerous position of having to take on the responsibility for local law enforcement over a wide area with all that that implied in terms of political embarrassment, growing opposition to the New Poor Law, expense and the wide dispersal of troops.

In the hope of avoiding this the government sought to preclude the possibility of any further direct confrontations with the anti-Poor Law movement and, to this end, the Commissioners in cooperation with the Home Office altered their tactics in approaching the problem of implementing the Poor Law itself in the North. What had happened in Huddersfield was not the only thing that entered into their calculations; indeed the change in policy was a gradual one dating back some months in its origins. As early as April, in view of the Boards of Guardians election results, Power and the Commissioners had begun to consider the possibility of delaying the introduction of the Poor Law into the most agitated Unions until the remainder were secure. The resulting disruption of the Commissioners' timetable did not seem likely to be great, however. Power estimated that only four Unions, Preston, Huddersfield, Bolton and Oldham, would prove really difficult and that in the remainder the Guardians would be able to take over the administration of relief well before the end of the year.[1]

Later in the spring the situation was complicated by the emergence of a new form of resistance. While Huddersfield was still fighting the election of a clerk and dominating the anti-Poor Law news, Power was busily engaged elsewhere making preparations for the introduction of the Poor Law itself. With complete Boards of Guardians in existence almost everywhere and clerks appointed in all Unions apart from Huddersfield, only one important task remained, the collection from the individual townships of their estimates of average annual expenditure on the poor, on the basis of which a fair allocation of Union costs could be made. Power encountered no problems in obtaining these figures from most Unions. In a number of individual townships, however, and in a significant proportion of the total in some Unions, the overseers, usually backed by the local vestry or by ratepayers' meetings, refused to comply. The great majority of these recalcitrant townships were small and peripheral, but there were a few exceptions, of which by far the most important was Salford.[2]

Salford was in a peculiar position at this time in that, largely for administrative reasons, it had not been placed in a Poor Law Union early in 1837. Therefore, when Power decided to organize a Salford Union in May, he was not faced with a deadline as he had been elsewhere in the North four or five months before, and, given time, he decided to revert to normal Poor Law Commission procedure by taking the averages before rather than after the formation of the Union and the election of a Board of Guardians. This gave the opposition in Salford not only more time to organize but a unique opportunity as well. Opponents of the law elsewhere might aspire to delay or wreck the New Poor Law through the non-election of a clerk, or the packing of a Board of Guardians, or the boycotting of the Guardians' elections; in Salford the opposition could hope to prevent even the creation of a Union by withholding the information on which that Union would be based.

[1] MH 32.63 15 April 1837.
[2] On overseers resistance in Salford and similar similar efforts in Ashton and Bolton see: *M.S.A.* 4 Feb., 27 May, 10 June 1837; MH 12.5593 Woodhouse to P.L.C. 3 June and 1 Nov. 1837.

H

Luckily for the opponents of the law in Salford, they were sufficiently united and broadly based to take advantage of the situation. As in Bury, the popular movement was an amalgam of trade unionists, political radicals and factory reformers. In addition, the major local opposition leader, R. J. Richardson, had established excellent relations with Conservative opponents of the Poor Law and was able to maintain them throughout 1837, possibly because there was no Board of Guardians election to bring potential rivalry out into the open. In any case, during the spring of 1837, Radical and Tory opponents of the law co-operated in winning control over the local vestry and overseers, and in organizing mass demonstrations, public petitions and all the other more usual expressions of anti-Poor Law feeling. Thus, when Power called on the overseers and vestry to supply him with the averages and other information, he was met with a policy of total non-co-operation and wisely decided to retreat and leave Salford to its own devices, at least for the moment.

Clearly a new category of opposition had been established and Power was compelled once again to revise his original plans.[1] A three-stage approach seemed called for, involving an initial move in those Unions, still, he believed, the great majority, where the Guardians and overseers were reasonably amenable, followed by individual attacks on Unions with reluctant Boards or non-co-operative overseers, after which the final attack could be made on the centers of die-hard resistance. That this would entail further delays was certain, but Power remained convinced that these would not be great. Salford, after all, was unique. In most Unions overseers' non-co-operation was limited to two or three townships, which, moreover, tended to be rural or semi-rural in character and of relatively little importance in their Unions as a whole. In most cases, then overseers' resistance was an irritant rather than, as in Salford, a possible danger and Power was convinced that increased pressure from London or, if necessary, legal action to compel compliance could crush it easily and relatively quickly. He saw no reason to abandon his hope of bringing the great majority of Unions under the Poor Law before the end of 1837.

It was at this point that violence in Huddersfield and with it the Home Office entered the balance, tipping it subtly but decisively in favor of a still more cautious approach and further delay. On

[1] MH 32.63 29 July 1837.

the face of it the Home Office view of the Huddersfield situation and its implications for the North as a whole did not differ substantially from the position to which events had brought Power by late June or early July. Lord John Russell's letter to the Poor Law Commissioners of June 27, in which a pledge of Home Office support for the Commissioners in Huddersfield was combined with a polite but firm admonition not to alienate local opinion further by pushing ahead with the Poor Law, ended with a general comment on the situation in the North as a whole. It came almost as an afterthought. 'This observation [on the strategy to be followed in Huddersfield]', he remarked, 'may be considered as containing the result of my opinions upon other similar cases.'[1] Power could quite legitimately regard this as an endorsement of his own views on how to treat the centers of die-hard opposition and there was nothing in Russell's remarks which implied that Power's plans for rapidly introducing the Poor Law elsewhere were mistaken.

Russell may have intended and the Poor Law Commissioners certainly appear to have understood a different interpretation. After Huddersfield their main concern seems to have been to avoid a repetition of what happened there, regardless of the consequences this might have on their timetable elsewhere in the North. While Power still argued for quick action in a majority of the northern Unions, the Commissioners began to set their sights a good deal lower. Even the apparently safe Unions were now to be treated as Power had intended to approach those that were doubtful, through a series of carefully planned, slow and individual attempts to introduce the New Poor Law. Any idea of handing over the administration of relief to the Boards of Guardians in a majority of the Unions in the textile districts before the end of 1837 was finally abandoned. The most that the Commissioners sought to do in the fall of 1837 was establish a number of model Unions here and there throughout the textile districts, in the hope that these would provide examples for the remaining Unions and a means of peacefully undermining the strength of the opposition.

If such Unions were indeed to be models, however, then their successful transition to the New Poor Law was indispensable, and, to ensure this, the Commissioners made one final major concession, and a concession moreover in a hitherto sacrosanct area, relief

[1] MH 12.15063 Russell to P.L.C. 27 June 1837.

policy. The usual orders directing a Board of Guardians to assume control over poor relief contained five clauses prohibiting or restricting certain practices. Relief in aid of wages in money, though not in kind, was prohibited, as was the payment of rent as part of relief, and also relief to paupers with a settlement in the Union but resident elsewhere. The order also required that half of all relief to widows and to able-bodied paupers working for the parish be given in kind. Throughout southern England and even in the industrial Midlands these five regulations had been included as a matter of course in the orders issued to the Board of Guardians. In the North, on the other hand, these restrictions had been a subject of controversy from the very beginning and, as has already been mentioned, Power was willing to alter their wording though not their substance in an effort to allay suspicion and opposition. Despite continued pressure from the Boards of Guardians throughout the spring and summer, he maintained this position on the grounds that the authority of the Poor Law Commissioners and the effectiveness of the Poor Law would be seriously undermined by any substantial change in such basic relief rules. Nonetheless, at some point during the summer, the Commissioners decided to overrule their Assistant Commissioner and not merely revise these standard relief regulations, but omit them entirely. Instead, the Commissioners simply 'left it to the discretion of the several Boards of Guardians to realize the objects of these rules in such a manner and to such an extent as they might find compatible with the circumstances of the . . . Union'.[1]

This was an extraordinary concession, far more important than the delay which the Home Office forced on the Commissioners in the wake of the Huddersfield riots. That had been merely a stay of execution; this altered the terms of the sentence. In explaining this grant of almost complete local discretion, the Poor Law Commissioners did not, as might be expected, admit that northern resistance had influenced their decision in any way. They justified it on the grounds that,

some of the peculiarities which . . . [distinguish] the northern manufacturing districts from other parts of the country appeared to us to weigh strongly against the issue of the usual regulations, particularly when taken in connection with the depressed state of trade . . . It appeared to us that considering the very casual nature of the circumstances under which relief is generally afforded to the able-bodied in

[1] P.L.C., Fourth Annual Report, 30 and Appendix A, No. 7.

the manufacturing districts, and considering also the extensive inter-
mixture of the settled population . . ., the advantages derivable from
the issue of the five regulations would not be commensurate with the
inconvenience which would have attended their strict enforcement.[1]

This in itself was quite an admission from a body which only a
year before had insisted that the measures envisioned in the Poor
Law Amendment Act were equally applicable in all parts of the
country. But, while the Commissioners' recognition of special
conditions in the North unquestionably did play a part in their
decision to drop the five restrictions, it was the Huddersfield
opposition which drove them to this and to the adoption of a
policy of piecemeal progress in the North.

By and large, the Unions in which the Commissioners first chose
to issue their watered down regulations were well selected. In the
last four months of 1837 five Unions were brought successfully
and uneventfully into operation for Poor Law purposes. Three of
these, Chorlton-on-Medlock, Wakefield and Leigh, had never
caused any difficulties and involved little or no risk. The other two,
Blackburn and Warrington, both had Tory dominated anti-Poor Law
Boards of Guardians, but offered no resistance, perhaps because
of the Commissioners' extraordinary concessions, which had in fact
met many of their specific objections. But in one Union, Bradford,
the Poor Law Commissioners miscalculated badly. On the face of
it Bradford seemed as safe a Union as any, despite the fact that it
had started out as one of the likeliest centers of resistance.[2] It was
the headquarters of Parson Bull, of a vociferously anti-Poor Law
magistrate Matthew Thompson, of a militant local Radical
Association led by Peter Bussey, and of the West Riding Anti-Poor
Law Delegates' Committee. Bull had played a leading role in
organizing the Colne boycott, both he and Thompson had been
involved in the creation of the West Riding Committee, and both
men, along with Bussey and various local associations, had held
numerous meetings and worked hard to influence the Board of
Guardians' elections in January and March.

But since the spring the situation in Bradford had changed
almost beyond recognition. The Board of Guardians, despite the
efforts of the opponents, was predominantly in favor of the law or

[1] *Ibid.*, 29–30.
[2] On Bradford, see: MH 12,14720; HO 40.35; HO 41.13; P.L.C.,
Fourth Annual Report, Appendix A, No. 8.

at least willing to suspend judgment. Bull himself had almost ceased to speak and agitate, while Thompson had changed his mind, or his tactics, sufficiently that he now declared his willingness to give the law a trial. The entire Union had become extraordinarily quiet, and not only superficially so. Power was cautious; he studied local conditions and he 'had received very satisfactory assurances that [Bull would abstain] from taking any part in encouraging violence . . . before [Bradford] was brought into operation'.[1] Power's information was correct; Bull took no part. Yet there was violence.

The first sign of trouble came on October 30, in connection with the first meeting of the Board of Guardians for Poor Law purposes. During the meeting, which, because it was the organizational meeting, lasted a considerable length of time, a crowd gathered outside and, in spite of attempts by the magistrates and local constables to break it up, grew larger and noisier as the day wore on. There was no violence, however, until after the end of the meeting, when Power emerged from the courthouse and was immediately assailed with mud, stones and umbrellas. Power was by this time quite used to such incidents and managed to make his way out unhurt, though not, as he noted, through any help from the local constables who stood by and watched.[2]

Had this been the end of it, Power would probably have risked going ahead as if nothing had happened. But throughout the following week crowds gathered at every opportunity and the Guardians began to panic much as they had earlier in the year at Huddersfield. Another Huddersfield was the last thing the Poor Law Commissioners could afford and therefore, though reluctantly, Power felt it advisable to call in outside help. The difficulty was, what sort of help. It would have to be powerful, since, in Power's view, no reliance could be placed on the local magistrates and constables, who were few in number, afraid to act and, more often than not, anti-Poor Law. But to call in the London police had serious disadvantages, for they were hated locally and their presence might even worsen the situation. Nor was the army much to be preferred from this point of view. Indeed, Power now found himself in the sort of dilemma which the government and the Poor Law Commissioners most dreaded. 'Some Guardians', he wrote, '[have intimated] that they will resign if any extra-

---

[1] MH 12.5673 Power to P.L.C. 5 Dec. 1837.
[2] MH 12.14720 Power to P.L.C. 30 Oct. 1837; *L.I.* 4 Nov. 1837.

ordinary aid is called in to enforce the peaceable execution of the law; whilst others have said they will not attend if such [disturbances] as occurred on Monday are allowed to take place.' With many misgivings, Power concluded that, on balance, 'there is far more risk of a falling off in the Guardians on the employment of a police force from London than from the dread of future disturbances'[1] and he consequently recommended that police be sent, but kept in Leeds until needed in Bradford. Troops, too, he believed should be sent, but without publicity or the intention of making an unnecessary show of force.

The police, in fact, were never used as such; they were enrolled as special constables and used as spies. But continuing unrest in the city compelled the authorities to fall back on the troops. Their presence did not have the desired effect however. Bradford did not quieten down immediately and there was another riot, far more serious than the first, before the worst was over. On November 20 the Board of Guardians met again, but this time behind a double guard of special constables and troops. Even this formidable obstacle was not enough to deter the crowd which gradually pushed its way forward until it was almost at the courthouse doors. Words were exchanged, the crowd pressed in on the soldiers and stones were thrown. The Riot Act was read but the crowd could not be dispersed. The Board hurriedly finished its business and left, escorted by the military, in the hope of drawing off enough of the crowd to end the trouble. But the crowd remained at the courthouse, as, unwisely, did the clerk. With the troops gone, the crowd besieged the courthouse, breaking all its windows and imprisoning the clerk. Finally, after about two hours of this, the troops returned to rescue him. But by this time the crowd rather than the soldiers had control of the streets, and at one point, in order to force their way through, the troops had to open fire.[2]

Luckily no one was hurt and, far from marking the opening of an even uglier phase in the struggle, this event proved to be the end of trouble in Bradford. All later meetings of the Board of Guardians passed off quietly, the Guardians regained the self-assurance which had begun to crack after the events of October 30, and Bradford soon became the model Union which the Poor Law Commissioners had expected it to be. Nonetheless, the riot of

[1] MH 12.14720 Power to P.L.C. 5 Nov. 1837.
[2] *Ibid.* Wagstaff to P.L.C. 20 Nov. 1837; Power to P.L.C. 21 Nov. 1837.

November 20 had been by far the most serious incident in the year-old Poor Law struggle and, though its effects on Bradford itself were slight, its implications for the Poor Law Commissioners and the anti-Poor Law movement were considerable. Much the most important immediate result was yet another alteration in government policy in the area.

The strategy developed by the government late in 1837 as an answer to its defeat in Huddersfield had been based at least in part on wishful thinking. It had been hoped that Huddersfield could be kept an isolated case to be dealt with judiciously in isolation, that its effect on the North had been, and could be kept, small, and that, so long as the Commissioners moved cautiously and at first only in the quietest areas, the Poor Law could be introduced without further trouble and without the direct intervention of the central government. But the events in Bradford undermined every one of these hopes. The apparently spontaneous character of the riots was particularly worrying. Either they were evidence of the existence of an efficient undercover opposition organization of which next to nothing was known, or they were genuinely spontaneous. Neither alternative was encouraging, for the government was now compelled to recognize the existence of either a degree of organization or a strength of popular feeling far beyond what it had been willing to admit previously. Hardly less disturbing was the immediately demoralizing effect of the riots on what had been a model Board of Guardians. At the first sign of serious trouble, it, like the Huddersfield Board, had begun to crack up. And finally, in order to stop violence and shore up the crumbling position of the local authorities the government had found it necessary to intervene rapidly and in force.

In the light of these developments, the government was forced to revise its policy. The overall aims and to an extent the means were not changed; it was still hoped, as in September, to bring the North slowly, Union by Union, under the New Poor Law, and in the process to avoid direct confrontations with the opposition and the use of government forces wherever possible. But, as a direct result of the unqualified success of its intervention in Bradford, the government altered its tactics in one very important respect. Resistance would no longer be answered with calculated withdrawals or concessions designed to disarm the opposition, as it had been throughout much of 1837. Instead, should a situation arise which threatened to deteriorate as Huddersfield had done, the government would not hesitate to intervene swiftly and in sufficient strength to prevent it happening.

The first signs that the government was adopting a much tougher policy appeared almost immediately after the Bradford affair was over. Ordinarily, military intervention was followed by a gradual withdrawal of troops from the disturbed area, but late in 1837 the government actually added to its strength in the North by dispatching troops to key centers throughout south Lancashire and the West Riding.[1] This was followed in early January by the first practical application of the new militancy. The scene, appropriately, was Huddersfield where the Board of Guardians, adjourned for four months, was about to meet again. It is likely that, but for Bradford, the government would have let this meeting pass unnoticed, as they had a similar meeting in September. The Poor Law Commissioners were counting on the Boards of Guardians elections of March 1838 to improve their position throughout the industrial districts and a few more months of patience had seemed, even in Huddersfield, to be the most advisable course. In the light of what had happened at Bradford, however, the further deferment of the inevitable showdown in Huddersfield appeared less desirable, and by mid-December at the latest the decision to force the issue in January had been taken.

The Poor Law Commissioners and the Home Office could not afford to be defeated again and took the most elaborate precautions to ensure their victory.[2] The Home Office, in consultation with Power and Lord Harewood, the Lord Lieutenant of the county, appointed two new magistrates, Sutcliffe and Starkey, both of them local manufacturers and avowed enemies of Oastler. But packing the magistracy and the Board with allies was not enough; it was also necessary to ensure that they would be able to make their presence felt. The Commissioners had, in short, to dictate the course which the meeting would take in so far as that was possible. Two methods were used. In the first place the Commissioners stepped up pressure on those members of the Board known to be friendly or at least neutral. And, secondly, they refined and extended the legal trickery of the previous June. Then, a minority of three had been authorized to act against the will of the

---

[1] For evidence that the government and the P.L.C. were adopting a tougher policy at this time, see: HO 73.54 Power to P.L.C. 5 Dec. 1837 and P.L.C. to Russell 4 Jan. 1838; HO 40.35 and HO 41.13 Dec. 1837.

[2] MH 12.15064 P.L.C. to Swain 23 Jan. 1838; Fox Maule to Huddersfield Magistrates 13 Jan. 1838.

majority. Now, according to the Commissioners, such a minority could, if it chose, ignore even the existence of that majority. The Commissioners advised the chairman of the Board that,

it is competent to you and . . . it is your duty . . . to refuse to put to the meeting any motion or amendment the obvious effect of which would be to defeat or postpone the election of a clerk; and secondly that, whatever course may be adopted by the majority of the guardians in contravention of the law, . . . the candidate having the majority of votes will be duly elected although less than three may have voted for him, provided that three guardians at least have taken part in the election.[1]

The rest of the Commissioners' instructions were in much the same vein. They had, so they hoped, anticipated every possible direction which the meeting might take. But even this was not enough. The Board clearly would not act unless protected, to the point of being sealed off from, the mob. A promise of aid in case of trouble would not be enough. The Board demanded the presence of force and was given more than it requested. Two troops of cavalry were sent into Huddersfield well before the meeting and on the day itself they were ranged in front of the court-house. The government had indeed come a long way from the time, only six months before, when it hesitated even to show its forces.

All this activity did not of course go unnoticed or unanswered in the opposition camp. Oastler, as he had done nearly eight months before, arranged a mass demonstration to coincide with the meeting of the Board. His placards were, if anything, even more inflammatory than they had been in 1837. He outlined (quite accurately, in fact) the tactics which the pro-Poor Law group would use and in answer to these was full of dark hints of 'plans of opposition . . . which at present it would be neither wise nor prudent that I should mention'.[2] But there was apparently nothing behind these threats. Even he admitted that a clerk might be elected and, reading between the lines of his placards, it is clear that he could think of no way to prevent it and nowhere to go should it happen. And it did happen, almost like clockwork. The Board met and the usual motion to adjourn without electing a clerk was made. The chairman refused to put the motion, two men

[1] MH 12.15064 P.L.C. to Swain 23 Jan. 1838.
[2] *Ibid*. Oastler's placard is included in the January correspondence.

were then nominated for the clerkship and, by a small margin in a small total vote, one of them was elected. The crowd outside was informed of all these proceedings, but it did nothing. The Poor Law Commissioners, after a year of delays and humiliations, had finally outbid the opposition and won.[1]

[1] *Ibid.* Power to P.L.C. 29 Jan. 1838.

VI Towards a national movement

The Commissioners' victory in Huddersfield marked the end of the first phase of the Poor Law struggle and a devastating defeat for opposition as conducted throughout 1837. Suddenly it appeared that all the opposition's victories were illusory, that they had been won as it were on sufferance and that the government, if it chose, could displace the opposition even from its positions of greatest strength. All the weapons of the opponents could, it seemed, be blunted. It was not enough to have the magistrates on their side; the government could simply create new ones. It was not enough to win a majority on the Board of Guardians; the government could impose the law with the co-operation of only three. It was not enough to have overwhelming popular support and a disciplined mass following capable of intimidating the Guardians, overseers and ratepayers; the government could introduce police and troops and intimidate even more effectively. It was not enough even to have all of these things, for the government, by concentrating all its forces, could separate and crush each strand of resistance. Indeed the opponents seemed to be left with only one sure method, the total boycott, and the very perfection of that weapon ensured that it could rarely be forged. The resistance movement in most Unions would have to make do with much less ambitious schemes, much as Huddersfield had done. But few Unions would be able to match Huddersfield's resourcefulness even in the use of these lesser techniques, and, since Huddersfield had failed, what chance had any others to succeed?

This apparently hopeless prospect for the opposition was not, however, solely the result of the policies developed by the government in the winter of 1837-8. Even had the opposition won another round in Huddersfield, this could not have obscured the fact that the terms of the struggle elsewhere were changing in favor of the Poor Law Commissioners. This was, to some extent, inevitable. The opposition had fought on peculiarly favorable ground throughout the greater part of 1837. The New Poor Law itself had not been at stake, what resistance there was was resistance in anticipation of events, and therefore the opposition could choose to resist or not without risk to its prestige or following. It could, in short, elect to do battle solely in the areas of its greatest strength. When, however, the Poor Law Commissioners decided, as they did in the autumn, to implement the Poor Law itself, the advantage in the battle automatically shifted. The Commissioners, not the opponents, chose the field, and the opponents had to resist as best they could or not at all. The defeat in Bradford, and still more the ease with which the administration of relief had been handed over to the Boards of Guardians in other Unions, indicated just how much the situation had changed even before the election of a clerk in Huddersfield had reversed the one serious defeat suffered by the Commissioners. Indeed, it was primarily as a result of their, for the most part, easy victories elsewhere that the government and the Commissioners had the confidence to embark on a concerted drive against the Huddersfield opposition as early as January. And with victory there, the future course of government policy was set. It now seemed possible that the Commissioners would be able to weed out the Unions where resistance was least likely, thus completely isolating the main centers of opposition and allowing the government to concentrate all its efforts on their subjugation.

Clearly resistance as conducted in 1837 was not adequate to meet the new situation and, had the Commissioners developed and carried out their new plan of attack sooner, achieving their string of victories in a matter of weeks rather than months, they might have so demoralized the opposition as to begin its disintegration. As it was, the slowness with which the Commissioners adapted to the situation in the North dulled the effect of their victories, allowing the opposition time to build on its early successes to the point where it could survive and to some extent even derive fresh impetus from its later defeats. By early January the opposition leaders had already adjusted their thinking to the new situation which had been developing so clearly since September and, great a setback as the election of a clerk in Huddersfield undoubtedly was, it did not lead them to conclude that their cause was hopeless or even that their methods were necessarily the wrong ones.

Huddersfield, where the opposition had possessed every advantage, had fallen, but Huddersfield, it could be argued, had been as much a special case for the government as for the opposition, since only the complete isolation of the opposition there had allowed the government and the Poor Law Commissioners to give their full attention to crushing it. If, on the other hand, the opposition could be strengthened sufficiently even in the weakest Unions so that the Commissioners would have an easy time of it nowhere, and, if resistance could be co-ordinated between those Unions where it was strongest so that the government would never feel free to concentrate its resources in one or two places, then a repetition of what had happened between September 1837 and January 1838 was not inevitable. Indeed, given such a strengthening of the opposition, even victory still seemed possible. Huddersfield, fighting alone and against tremendous odds, had managed to avoid defeat for nearly a year and, in the process, wring major concessions from the government. If some resistance could be mounted in every Union, and if even as few as half a dozen Unions could be transformed into centers of persistent opposition, then the government, seeing no end or physical limits to the struggle and fearing too great a strain on its resources, might back down again and this time force the Poor Law Commissioners to grant even more substantial concessions.

The opposition leaders were convinced that such a development was possible. Even in their defeats they saw some signs for hope. Though ineffective, the largely spontaneous riots at Bradford did at least demonstrate that mass support for the opposition, which had been used to great effect in the early months of 1837 and later on at Huddersfield, was still there, ready to be tapped. And, in Huddersfield, not only the mass of the population but most of the local officials—constables, overseers and magistrates—as well, had stood firm against the new law; their defeat had been achieved not by winning them over but by circumventing them. Admittedly, the public officials in other Unions had displayed nothing like the same determination, but this, like the lack of any but sporadic popular resistance, could be blamed on the fact that the necessary focus for effective opposition, a large anti-Poor Law faction on the Board of Guardians, existed in only a handful of Unions. And this, in its turn, was blamed on the woefully inadequate organization which was all that the opposition in most Unions had been able to patch together in time for the Board of Guardians' elections of 1837. But given time and a much better idea of what they would have to contend with, the opposition leaders saw no reason why they should not be able to mobilize resistance throughout the North as effectively as they had in a few Unions at the beginning of the year. And, if this could be done, then every Board of

Guardians could be turned into a potential threat to the Poor Law Commissioners, and the policy of piecemeal implementation of the Poor Law would be rendered unworkable.

Such ambitious plans would have been inconceivable even as little as three months before. In September 1837, when, in response to the Commissioners' first unopposed attempts to introduce the Poor Law into the North, the opposition leaders began to look into the problem of extending and perfecting their organization, they found that in most respects the anti-Poor Law movement was no better off than it had been in April. It was still strong only in those Unions where it had inherited strength from pre-existing radical or factory reform associations, and efforts to expand the organization into other areas had ceased with the end of the March Board of Guardians election campaign. Late in the spring, for example, the creation of a South Lancashire Anti-Poor Law Association on the model of the West Riding Delegates' Committee was proposed by Fielden, Stephens and other prominent leaders, but their suggestions met with no response and, after a time, the project was dropped. This, rather than a determination to be better prepared for later battles, was typical. The notoriety of the anti-Poor Law movement during the summer was misleading; Huddersfield, and Huddersfield virtually alone, was responsible for it. Elsewhere the movement was inactive or all but non-existent. Thus, before it was possible even to think of spreading effective resistance beyond Huddersfield, the opposition had to regain the position and popular following it had held during the spring.[1]

The first major contribution to this was the arrival in the North of Feargus O'Connor. He had, it is true, been North before, most recently in early 1837, and he had done well during his brief visits. The established popular leaders welcomed him, and, perhaps more important, the crowds took to him. Nonetheless, he had returned to London, still hoping for a career of popular leadership there. But another defeat for his London ambitions impelled him North once more, this time permanently. He ran for Parliament at Preston in the July election, and lost; he then turned to a scheme for founding an ultra-radical newspaper in Leeds, and here he succeeded. When he took it over in August, the scheme was foundering. Its original backers, Joshua Hobson, a radical

[1] On the organizational problems of the Lancashire movement in early 1837 see: *M.S.A.* 29 April, 24 June 1837.

publisher in Leeds and formerly an associate of Pitkeithly in Huddersfield, and William Hill, a Swedenborgian minister, had given up hope of raising the necessary capital. O'Connor, on the other hand, saw a way of turning this liability into an asset. He decided to go to the people to raise the money. Throughout much of September he travelled from town to town in the manufacturing districts, speaking on any and all possible radical issues and raising small sums through the sale of shares in his promised newspaper.[1]

It worked. On November 18, 1837, the first issue of the *Northern Star* appeared. The impact of this paper was immediate and startling; within a few months it had become the leading radical newspaper of the North and the all-but-official spokesman of every sort of protest movement. By the time it was five months old it had a circulation of 10,000, an extraordinary figure before the repeal of the newspaper tax, and it was one of the few papers in which all the activities of the anti-Poor Law movement, the Workingmen's Associations and similar groups were regularly advertised. The *Northern Star*, and through it Feargus O'Connor, did not achieve this pre-eminence by filling any great gap; the field was if anything oversubscribed. Most of the northern Conservative papers were supporters of factory reform and, still more, of the anti-Poor Law movement. Not only *The Times* nationally, but the *Leeds Intelligencer*, *Manchester Courier* and other lesser provincial papers locally, gave full coverage and support to their activities. At the other end of the political spectrum, the Radical weeklies were even more forthcoming in giving space and encouragement to every variety of popular protest, and they played a role in the early stages of the anti-Poor Law movement far beyond that normally given to newspapers. The editors of the two leading northern Radical journals, Robert Nicoll of the *Leeds Times* and George Condy of the *Manchester and Salford Advertiser*, were both leading figures in local Radical politics. Both had been active factory reformers. Nicoll was a member, along with Hobson, of the Leeds Radical Association, and Condy had been one of the founders of the National Regeneration Society and closely associated with Fielden ever since. Early in 1837 both men put their papers almost completely at the service of the newly founded anti-Poor Law movement, Condy to the extent that the *Advertiser* became a semi-

[1] Read and Glasgow, *O'Connor*, Chs. VI–VII; *M.S.A.* and *L.T.* Sept. 1837.

official organ of the movement, a role of enormous importance in the absence of a county-wide organization in Lancashire.[1]

The *Northern Star*, in short, cannot be said to have filled a vacuum. But it did come to occupy a very special place. For one thing, its coverage of the minutiae of local movements throughout the North was much more extensive than that of any other paper, and still seems impressive. Moreover, it gave its readers the feeling of being in contact with the latest and most exciting developments of reform and Radical politics. It provided a platform for all the most important local leaders as well as a northern outlet for major figures from other parts of the country. But, above all, the *Star* owed its success to the fact that it was a truly popular newspaper. The way in which it had been launched and skilful editing by Hill made it a distinctly working-class radical paper. It addressed itself to the working man and was proud of its reliance on him. Small wonder that it, more than any other newspaper, was in a position to mobilize popular support for the anti-Poor Law movement and shape its future course.

The foundation of the *Northern Star* was not, however, the only or, for that matter, the first service that O'Connor's fund-raising and political lecture tour performed for radical causes in the North. In the wake of his agitation there was a noticeable increase in the number of public meetings held throughout the district. At first these tended to be small, local in character and, like O'Connor's meetings, concerned with any number of issues of which the Poor Law was only one. But by early November at the latest, the major regional leaders had begun to intervene in the hope of revitalizing the campaign of mass demonstrations against the Poor Law which had been moribund since March. In this they were greatly helped by the Commissioners' early attempts to introduce the New Law into the North, and especially by the riot at Bradford on October 30, which was the first dramatic event in the Poor Law struggle since the July Board of Guardians' meetings in Huddersfield.[2]

Assured of growing popular support, the opposition leaders were then able to turn to the task of solving their organizational problems with justified confidence. In Lancashire, where the need to

---

[1] On these newspapers and their editors see: D. Read, *Press and People* (London 1961) and the chapters on Manchester and Leeds in A. Briggs, *Chartist Studies* (London 1959).

[2] For the gradual revival of public agitation, see: *M.S.A.* and *L.I.*, Oct.–Nov. 1837.

strengthen resistance was greatest, the proposals for creating a county-wide organization which had come to nothing in the spring were taken up with alacrity in October.[1] Early in November, a group of delegates from the most active Lancashire Unions met to discuss ways and means of better co-ordinating their own activities and of linking them with opposition in the West Riding. They decided to call on all local committees to send delegates to a further meeting, to be held on November 22, at which it was hoped to form a permanent regional body. The South Lancashire Anti-Poor Law Association, which was set up as a result of this second conference, was different in many respects from its older West Riding counterpart, for the needs of the two counties were not identical and, in any case, the needs of the opposition as a whole had changed in the intervening eight months. There were very few Unions in the West Riding textile districts and most of these, or at least the major towns in each one, had fairly well-developed anti-Poor Law associations even before the regional committee was founded. Thus, though it did assume some responsibility for extending the local and Union committee structure, the Yorkshire body's primary functions were to co-ordinate resistance and in general to act as a medium of communication between the handful of Unions it served. As such it did not seek publicity and was often well advised to shun it.

In Lancashire, on the other hand, though there were many Unions as well, if not better, organized than any in Yorkshire, the number of Unions was far greater and in at least half of them few, if any, preparations had been made for resistance. In the spring this had not seemed too serious a problem; the opposition leaders counted on their strongholds, Ashton, Oldham, Todmorden, Rochdale, Preston and Bury in particular, to see them through. But with the initial success of the Commissioners' policy of by-passing the most troublesome Unions, the opposition took fright and realized it would have to extend itself or die. In practice, therefore, the South Lancashire Association tended to lead something of a double life. On the one hand, like the West Riding Committee, it provided a link between existing associations and operated in semi-secrecy, while, on the other, it hoped to rouse public opinion and recruit new adherents, and therefore actively sought publicity. Of its two roles the latter was immediately the more important and always, of course, the more evident. The

[1] *M.S.A.* 11, 25 Nov., 2 Dec. 1837.

Association opened offices in Manchester, had a paid full-time staff and started its work with a public campaign to raise a fighting fund. The President, R. J. Richardson, and the Treasurer, William Clegg, made a point of attending as many meetings as possible and assiduously cultivated the press. But the most important function of the Association at this time was missionary activity. Within weeks of its foundation, the Association started sending trained organizers into the inactive Unions to set up local and Union committees, and get them in turn to send representatives to the central office in Manchester. By late January the process was complete and Lancashire had nearly as comprehensive an organization as did the West Riding.[1]

The founders of the South Lancashire Anti-Poor Law Association were exceedingly lucky in their timing, for, in the interval between the two organizational meetings in November, the second of the Bradford riots took place. It did what probably no amount of organizational planning and exhortation could have done. Within a matter of days, the competition between issues ceased. The *Northern Star*, founded as much to preach political radicalism as anything else, opened its career by devoting almost its entire space to Poor Law news. The South Lancashire Association, rather than having to overcome local intertia in spreading its organization, found that all it need do was channel the rising tide of anti-Poor Law feeling, and its main problem was in keeping pace with local sentiment. A great protest meeting held at Bradford in early December and attended by Oastler, O'Connor and Bull proved to be, not an extraordinary response to an extraordinary situation, but the first of a long line of larger, longer and noisier meetings.[2]

This surge of activity, far from being carefully planned, developed with its own momentum and carried the leaders along with it. Dozens of meetings were held every week and Oastler, O'Connor, Stephens, Fletcher, Richardson and the others were run ragged attempting to attend as many as they could. Rarely did these meetings last less than four hours, and never less than that if one of the great men spoke, for their speeches were usually two, sometimes even three, hours long. Always the crowds demanded more and, in the highly charged atmosphere of the meetings or through the pages of popular papers designed to be read aloud, the leaders

[1] *Ibid.*, Dec. 1837–Jan. 1838.
[2] *M.S.A.* and *N.S.*, Dec. 1837–Feb. 1838.

responded. The long arguments against the New Poor Law, based on Cobbett's reading of history or Eldon's reading of the constitution, were still used, but they were drowned out by a new stridency. The major anti-Poor Law leaders no longer felt it necessary to convince their audiences, their aim now was to move them.

Almost any issue of the *Northern Star* and almost any meeting can be taken as typical. The pages of the *Star* for these months were littered with italicized phrases, sentences all in capital letters, horrific stories of starvation and cruelty in workhouses, alarming rumors about the government's intentions, and long, only semi-coherent diatribes against the 'coarse food law' and its perpetrators, the 'three-headed devil king' of Somerset House. The editorials, some of them written by O'Connor, and even the ordinary news reports were pitched in this key, but it was Oastler above all who set the new tone. In a series of open letters to Lord John Russell, often as long as three closely packed columns of small print, he abandoned argument completely in favor of a cataclysmic view of the future. 'If', he wrote,

you dare to put that threat [to enforce the Poor Law] in execution, you will throw down the glorious fabric of the British Empire, you will untie the knot which binds society together. You will blot out the parchment title to Property—you will throw back the family of man to its first claimants, and all things will again belong to all men.

If the church, the throne, and the aristocracy are determined to rob the poor man of his liberty, of his life, and of his children, then is the church no longer of Christ;—then are the nobles no longer safeguards of the People;—then are they all worse than useless;—then with their bitterest foes would I cry, DOWN WITH THEM, DOWN WITH THEM ALL TO THE GROUND.[1]

The meetings were little different. As it was winter, and a bad one at that, most of them were held indoors. But occasionally a hall holding a few thousand was found and in these circumstances the masters of crowd oratory came into their own. Stephens, with his training as a popular preacher and his gift for biblical rhetoric, was particularly effective. The Poor Law, he declared,

ought to be resisted to the death, even if the first man that might be slaughtered in opposing it should be Lord John Russell himself . . . If

[1] *N.S.* 20 Jan. 1838.

it was to come, let it come; it should be an eye for an eye, a tooth for a tooth, limb for limb, wife for wife, man for man, and blood for blood—so help them God and their country![1]

Few dared go as far as this, though O'Connor, Fletcher and a handful of others showed little more restraint. But the fact that Oastler and Stephens felt both able and, in a sense, compelled to go to these extremes, and were, moreover, able to carry their audiences with them, shows how greatly the movement had been transformed in a very few months. Admittedly, there had been talk of violence and calamity before, but it had always been qualified, limited and oblique. By early 1838, however, such self-imposed restrictions had been discarded, and what had been hinted at the previous year was now stated openly. Much of this undoubtedly was calculated. Stephens, Oastler and O'Connor were accomplished leaders of crowds and, though what they said was certainly backed by their own passionate convictions, the language of their speeches and writings was chosen very deliberately. Stripped of rhetoric, their threats amounted to very little. They talked of violence, but it was a curiously unreal sort of violence. They described in vivid detail the disasters which would follow on the introduction of the Poor Law in the North, but refrained from specifying the tools of that promised vengeance or from assuming for themselves the role of avengers. Even Oastler's famous, often repeated threat that, should he ever request relief and be required, as a condition of receiving it, to be separated from his wife, he 'would kill the [relieving officer] on the spot',[2] even this, his most direct threat, was couched in the conditional. In all their fiery speeches nothing was said about arming the people against oppression or about how to counter force should the government introduce it. They were bluffing. Their real aim was to frighten the government, if possible, and, more realistically, to frighten local officials and ratepayers. And their stated aim was even milder, amounting to nothing more than the petitioning of both houses of Parliament for the repeal of the Poor Law Amendment Act.

In this, then, as in so much else, the new campaign harked back to the activities of the year before, though the organization of this petitioning, like the organization of most things, was far more

[1] *Ibid.* 10 Feb. 1838.
[2] *Ibid.* 3 Feb. 1838.

sophisticated and professional in early 1838. For one thing, the opposition leaders were now concerned with providing a framework for their activities. It was arranged that Fielden in the Commons and Stanhope in the Lords would move the repeal of the Poor Law early in the new year, thus providing the opponents with an objective and a date towards which they could build their petitioning campaign, something they had not had the previous year. The actual conduct of the campaign also was changed, especially in Lancashire, where the county association assumed control and, once its organization work was substantially completed, devoted almost all its efforts to the project. There was, to be sure, no attempt to impose uniformity of procedure over the whole area, probably because the South Lancashire Association was not yet powerful enough to do so. As in 1837, each town raised a separate petition, written in similar though by no means identical terms, and each town tried to stage its own public meeting in support of its own petition. At this stage, the only evidence of an advance over 1837 was in the size and number of these meetings and petitions.

The culmination of the campaign was an innovation, however. On February 5 two important meetings were held in Manchester.[1] The first, a public meeting, was intended as a fitting climax to three months of demonstrations. Almost everyone of any note, locally or regionally, was there and the size of the audience and the length, number and provocativeness of the speeches outdid anything which had preceded it. The other meeting, less publicized but more important, was a gathering of delegates from all of the constituent Lancashire Anti-Poor Law Associations at which, amid much fanfare and many speeches, the local petitions were handed in and tabulated before being sent off *en bloc* to Parliament in time for the repeal debate. It was the closest that any popular movement had yet come to the concept, which was to be so important only a few months later, of a single huge petition. Compared with their experimentally minded Lancashire colleagues, the West Riding Delegates' Committee did little and was self-effacing in what it did; the main burden, as indeed in most things in the Yorkshire anti-Poor Law movement, was carried by the local associations. But they did their job well and the West Riding campaign, as measured in the number of meetings and the size of petitions, was hardly less impressive than Lancashire's,

[1] *M.S.A.* 10 Feb. 1838.

which alone produced petitions from 107 places, signed, so they claimed, by 122,847 people.

It hardly need be said that all these efforts made very little impression on Parliament. In the Commons, for example, Fielden's repeal motion received a mere 17 votes. What is surprising in retrospect is not so much the smallness of this vote but the exaggerated hopes which the Poor Law's northern opponents had pinned to this great petitioning campaign and their consternation at the meagerness of the results. They had not of course seriously hoped for victory but they had genuinely expected defeat of a kind which would give them hope. This total miscalculation of their prospects was due in part simply to a refusal to face facts. As resistance to the Poor Law began to run into trouble, the temptation to escape into something like a mass petitioning campaign must have been overwhelming. Increasingly, unable to resist the Poor Law Commissioners at the local level and unwilling or afraid to advocate direct violent resistance, the opposition leaders sought out means of resistance which fell within the bounds of legality and, of the alternatives available to them, petitioning seemed by far the most attractive. It was relatively easy to organize, it gave the opposition an opportunity to show off its popular following, it provided a pretext for frequent mass demonstrations and its adoption in the winter of 1837-8 had the additional advantage of allowing the opposition a breathing spell during which it could put aside the frustrating business of deciding what to do with its organization now that it had one.

It would be unfair, however, to dismiss the petitioning campaign as nothing more than a vast exercise in political escapism. The opposition had what appeared at the time to be good reasons for believing that Parliamentary opinion must be more equally divided than in fact it was. To some extent in this they were the victims of parochialism and wishful thinking. The size of their popular following and the nearly universal disquiet about, if not outright opposition to, the New Poor Law in the North gave the popular leadership of the movement an exaggerated idea of the extent of national antipathy to the law. But, while their expectations were undoubtedly exaggerated, they were not, as the predictions of rural revolt against the law back in 1834 had been, erroneous. There were signs in 1837 that the halcyon days of the Poor Law Commissioners had passed, and not only in the North.

And for the first time the possibility of a national anti-Poor Law movement began to be discussed, and again not only in the North, nor, for that matter, only among the law's opponents.

Some of the indications of a possible turning point in the fortunes of the New Poor Law were to be sure visible only to the eyes of those most anxious to discern a change in the climate of opinion. Here and there in rural southern England a few Poor Law Unions which had come under the law quietly enough in 1835 or 1836 elected anti-Poor Law Boards of Guardians in 1837 and began to question the authority of the Poor Law Commission and the wisdom of its orders. But there were very few such places and they were widely scattered; they could easily and legitimately be dismissed as chaff rather than straws in the wind. Other developments could not be so easily explained away. The textile district of Lancashire and Yorkshire was not the only region that demonstrated a new determination to resist the New Poor Law in 1837. As has already been mentioned, the long string of virtually uninterrupted victories for the Poor Law Commissioners in southern England was not broken until they reached Cornwall where a combination of widespread local prejudice against the workhouse system and popular unrest not merely delayed but prevented the introduction of the full rigors of the new law. In the context of rural southern England, Cornwall was a curious anomaly of little importance, but in its temporal context resistance in Cornwall had a wholly different significance, for the riots which touched it off took place in February 1837, at the time when Lancashire and the West Riding of Yorkshire were electing their first Boards of Guardians.

More important, if only because it involved a far larger area, was the resistance which developed in a majority or near majority of Welsh Poor Law Unions during the spring and summer of 1837. Violent opposition was rare in Wales. There was a serious outbreak in the Llanfyllin Union, Montgomeryshire, which closely followed the familiar pattern of rural anti-Poor Law violence in England.[1] One of the relieving officers was attacked in an outlying village and, a few days later at the weekly Board of Guardians meeting, a mob collected, tried to prevent the paupers from going before the Board, and assailed the Guardians and a visiting Assistant Commissioner with mud and stones when they left their meeting place. What distinguished this series of incidents from

[1] HO 73.52 April 1837 correspondence.

similar events in earlier years in southern and eastern England was that the local authorities in the Llanfyllin Union did little to suppress violence at the time or to enforce the Poor Law later on and that both during the period of violence and afterwards the great majority of the local population was sympathetic to the aims and methods of the New Poor Law's opponents. It was perhaps because of this that violence was so rare in Wales. Violence was superfluous in an area where, more likely than not, the Guardians, magistrates and overseers were self-declared and active opponents of the law.

Nowhere outside the North was opposition to the Law so broadly based, for Wales, like the North, had its own peculiar Poor Law traditions and practices in which all sections of the community were interested or implicated.[1] Since the greater part of Wales was a net exporter of population, parish relief to paupers with a legal settlement there but resident elsewhere was common and most ratepayers were reluctant to put an end to it for fear that the paupers would be returned. Even more common was the granting of out-relief exclusively in money rather than kind, a practice which was explained or excused on the grounds that the distribution of relief in kind would be enormously difficult and expensive in the thinly populated and mountainous countryside of Wales. Finally and most deeply entrenched of all was the custom of paying rent out of the rates. For a large proportion of the employers, laborers and owners of cottages in northern and central Wales this had become an integral and indispensible feature of the local economy. Indeed, so habitual was the practice in some areas that it was organized by the overseers on an annual contract basis.

In addition to these departures from the letter and spirit of the New Poor Law, Wales harbored an intense local antipathy to outside interference which was matched only in the North of England, if even there. The New Poor Law was constantly referred to in Wales as a piece of English legislation wholly unsuited to the Welsh. As in the North, moreover, localism went deeper than this. Because of the low density of population, the Poor Law Commissioners created large Poor Law Unions in all parts of Wales other

---

[1] The most interesting general reports on conditions in Wales are: MH 12.15673 Day to P.L.C. 17 April 1837; MH 12.16486 Day to P.L.C. 8 Aug. 1837; MH 12.15564 Day to P.L.C. 1 Sept. 1836; MH 12.15734 Head to P.L.C. 25 Sept. 1836; MH 12.16709 9 Oct. 1836.

than the industrial south. This meant that outlying settlements were often separated from their Union centers by many miles of rough terrain, a fact that was almost as bitterly resented as dictation from London. The Assistant Commissioners, far from trying to assuage this resentment, exacerbated it. They treated their Welsh charges with a contempt that had no parallel in England. One Assistant Commissioner, for example, after an especially frustrating day-long encounter with an obdurate Board, acidly observed, 'I should say not that the Bill was unfitted for Wales, but that the Welsh were unfitted to the Bill.'[1] The locals were not, however, quite so oafish as he imagined. They readily fathomed his private sentiments and heartily reciprocated them. Relations between the representatives of Somerset House and even the most amenable of Boards of Guardians were rarely cordial.

Intractable as it was to become, opposition in Wales took time to build momentum and at first the Principality seemed likely to be as docile as most of southern and central England had been. In all of the Unions declared in the late months of 1836 and very early in 1837 the Assistant Commissioners applied immediate and usually successful pressure on the Boards of Guardians to approve the building of new workhouses.[2] After the election of new Boards in late March and in most of the Unions brought into operation thereafter, the situation changed dramatically. Magistrates, clergy and dissenters banded together in what one Assistant Commissioner called an unholy alliance to arouse the lower orders and capture control of the Boards of Guardians.[3] To a remarkable extent they were successful. In a majority or near majority of the 47 Welsh Poor Law Unions the 1837 elections were won by anti-Poor Law slates of candidates.

In southern Wales these victories had little practical effect, since most of the Poor Law Unions there had been in operation for some time and the process of reorganization, including commitments to the building of new workhouses, had been carried too far to be easily reversed.[4] In the eight counties of northern and central Wales, on the other hand, reorganization had rarely pro-

[1] MH 12.15564 Day to P.L.C. 20 Oct. 1837.
[2] Conway Union: MH 12.16023 Lloyd to P.L.C. 3 June 1837; Newtown and Llanidloes Union: MH 12.16597 Day to P.L.C. 11 Feb. 1837; Presteigne Union: MH 12.16709 Phillips to P.L.C. 27 March 1837; Wrexham Union: MH 12.16104 Luxmoore to P.L.C. 20 April 1837.
[3] MH 12.16326 Clive (?) to Frankland Lewis 28 Aug. 1837.
[4] *Ibid.*

ceeded beyond preliminary stages before opposition was aroused, so that it was possible not only to resist the imposition of new regulations but even to undo much of what the Assistant Commissioners had already achieved. In a number of Unions where earlier Boards of Guardians had approved the building of new workhouses, their successors, sometimes on the basis of a legal technicality, but if necessary in defiance of the letter of the law, refused to be bound by these agreements. Since the Commissioners did not have the power to compel a Union to build a workhouse, they wisely let the matter drop for the time being.[1]

In any case, the Commissioners were having enough difficulties in fields where supposedly their powers were unlimited. A number of Boards openly declared their intention to continue relieving non-resident paupers and give out-relief in money rather than kind, regardless of the orders sent from London. In at least one Union, according to Assistant Commissioner Day, any 'attempt to enforce unqualified obedience [to the regulations on relief in kind] would end in the absolute resignation of the whole board'.[2] To go further and attempt to prohibit the paying of rents would, he believed, lead to open revolt. Day was right. Whether because they were personally involved or through fear of popular reaction, most Guardians refused even to consider ending this practice. Not even the northern Boards of Guardians, Huddersfield always excepted, had dared defy the Poor Law Commissioners so directly.

As with workhouses, the Commissioners decided not to press the issue. Even before the Llanfyllin riots and the emergence of the full flood of Boards of Guardians' resistance, the Commissioners were afraid that the prohibition of rent payments might be enforceable only through military intervention. Afterwards they were convinced of it and equally certain that they would have no sure local backing if they did attempt to enforce their regulations. So, rather than issue their rules and see them flaunted, they made concessions. The fourth and fifth standard relief regulations abolishing non-resident relief and rent payments were withdrawn in the most troublesome Unions. This did not mean that the Poor Law Commissioners or their assistants gave up; they merely changed their tactics. Where formerly they had used pressure, now

[1] MH 12.16023 Owen to P.L.C. 12 Jan. 1838; MH 12.16075 Neave to P.L.C. 25 March 1838.
[2] MH 12.16486 Day to P.L.C. 8 Aug. 1837. For other examples of open defiance see: MH 12.15673 July 1837 correspondence; MH 12.15564 Thruston to Chadwick 17 July 1837.

they tried to persuade or bribe.[1] Their favorite technique was to offer or threaten one thing in the hope of getting another. Boards of Guardians were promised an extension of the relaxation of the relief regulations if they would agree to the building of new workhouses. The imposition of a labor test was threatened as a means of driving a recalcitrant Board into abolishing rent payments or building a new workhouse. The difficulty was that two could play at this game. Most Boards quickly learned how to give way in one area in order to avoid pressure in another and then gradually revert to normal in all areas once the pressure was off. Promises were made and then forgotten; practices were altered only to reappear under some ingenious cover or no cover at all.[2] With a dozen or more Boards of Guardians all doing this simultaneously, it was impossible for the Assistant Commissioners to keep up. By early 1838 the administration of the Poor Law in northern and central Wales had become a war of nerves in which the Poor Law Commissioners might not actually lose but which they had little prospect of winning.

Outside of the textile districts of Lancashire and Yorkshire, Wales was the prize exhibit of the New Poor Law's opponents, but it was not the only area which gave them cause for hope. During 1837 resistance appeared in individual Unions or groups of Unions in other parts of the North to such an extent that it began to seem possible that the whole of England north of the Trent might slip from the Commissioners' grasp. Urban areas, as might be expected, led the way. The Tyneside region had been brought into operation in 1836 and perhaps because of this had experienced few initial difficulties. But during 1837 ratepayer resentment at interference from London and the emergence of a popular radical anti-Poor Law movement led the Assistant Commissioner for the

[1] For examples of the Commissioners' policy of concessions (often mixed with bribery) see: Anglesey Union: MH 12.15673 P.L.C. to Day 22 April 1837; Bangor and Beaumaris Union: MH 12.15964 Day to P.L.C. 10 Nov. 1837; Williams to P.L.C. 30 June 1838; Builth Union: MH 12.15734 P.L.C. to Price and others 13 April 1837; Conway Union: MH 12.16023 Day to P.L.C. 3 Dec. 1838; Dolgelly Union: MH 12.16503 November 1837 correspondence; Machynlleth Union: MH 12.16504 Oct. 1837–July 1838 correspondence.

[2] Examples of continued resistance from the Welsh Boards of Guardians are: Anglesey: MH 12.15673 Day to P.L.C. 13 March 1840; Bangor: MH 12.15964 July–Dec. 1838 correspondence; Caernarvon: MH 12.15998 Day to Lefebvre 20 April and 5 June 1839; Conway: MH 12.16023 Day to P.L.C. 17 June 1839; Llanrwst: MH 12.16075 March 1838 correspondence.

district to revise his earlier optimism at least to the extent that he now foresaw a long and difficult transition period before the New Poor Law would be secure in the North-east.[1]

Sheffield and its surroundings were even more troublesome to the Poor Law Commissioners.[2] A local movement combining Tories led by Samuel Roberts, perhaps the most prolific of anti-Poor Law pamphleteers, and radical workingmen was formed early in 1837 with the active support of the local Radical paper, the *Sheffield Iris*. Modelling its activities on those of its neighbors to the north, the Sheffield opposition circulated petitions and staged mass meetings in the hope of creating the same kind of atmosphere that had immobilized Huddersfield. They were very nearly successful. The overseers and churchwardens were cowed into backing away from their early support of the Law and, by the time of the first Board of Guardians election scheduled for late June, the pro-Poor Law vestry clerk was no longer certain that he could prevent violence or, as he had originally hoped, a contested election. His worst fears were not realized. Behind the scenes bargaining did prevent election contests and there was no violence. The Assistant Commissioner for the district rightly counted this a major victory but he was also compelled to recognize that local supporters of the law had had too close a call to feel secure or be willing to go very far in implementing unpopular policies.

Some measure of opposition had been expected on Sheffield, if only because of its proximity to the textile district of the central West Riding. Barnsley, for example, which lay between Sheffield and Huddersfield, became so agitated during the summer of 1837 that Power was forced to recommend to the Poor Law Commissioners that action there be delayed for at least a year.[3] What the Commissioners did not expect and the opposition hardly dared hope for was the resistance which developed in rural areas of the North during the spring and summer of 1837.[4] Much of the area north and east of Leeds and most of the Vale of York immediately to the east of the textile district was already divided into Poor Law

[1] Newcastle Union: MH 12.9096 July 1836, March 1837 and March 1838 correspondence; Easington Union: MH 12.3052 Walsham to P.L.C. 13 July 1837.

[2] Sheffield Union: MH 12.15465 May–July 1837 correspondence; Ecclesall Union: MH 12.14938 June 1837 correspondence.

[3] MH 12.14674 Power to P.L.C. 19 Aug. 1837.

[4] On the Gilbert Unions of Yorkshire see: MH 32.63 24 and 31 Jan. 1837. For opposition in other rural areas see: Bridlington Union: MH 12.14256. Furby to P.L.C. 6 Nov. 1838; Helmsley Union: Ward to

Unions in accordance with Gilbert's Poor Law Act of 1782. However, according to the Poor Law Amendment Act these Gilbert Unions could only be dissolved and reorganized under the auspices of the Poor Law Commissioners with the approval of the existing Boards of Guardians. Elsewhere in rural England this approval had usually been readily given but in Yorkshire Power was met with an almost unanimous refusal to co-operate which left him and his employers powerless. In addition to this bloc of recalcitrant Gilbert Unions there were a number of individual Poor Law Unions formed during the course of 1837 which displayed an equal determination to resist the introduction of the New Law. There were not many of these but their wide distribution, the fact that an alliance between ratepayers and laborers appeared in all of them, and, above all, the danger that they would link up with urban centers of resistance in a general regional revolt against the Poor Law gave them an importance far beyond their numbers.

However different these many centers of resistance to the Poor Law may have been, they had one thing in common; all were at least a hundred miles from London. It was almost as if an invisible barrier protected the capital and therefore the government from feeling the full effects of provincial disaffection. For this reason perhaps the most heartening development of 1837 for the opposition was the emergence of resistance in London itself. The reorganization of the London area with its almost innumerable small parishes was probably the most formidable administrative task of the Poor Law Commissioners. It was certainly the most delicate politically. Hundreds of overseers and churchwardens saw their authority threatened and most of them proved ready, even anxious to lead popular opposition to the New Law. In the early months of 1837, as the Poor Law Commissioners made preparations to introduce the new administrative machinery, parish officials organized protest meetings all over the London area. The City of London was most active. There representatives from all the threatened parishes banded together to circulate petitions, hold mass meetings and, above all, to use their geographical position and powerful contacts to bring direct pressure to bear on the government and Parliament.[1]

P.L.C. 15 July 1837; Pocklington Union: MH 12.14344 Revans to P.L.C. 14 March 1837.
[1] For opposition in London see: *The Times* Jan.–Feb. 1837.

The simultaneous appearance of opposition in Cornwall, Wales, the North of England and London had a tonic effect on the opponents of the law in national politics, most of whom had all but given up hope. By mid-1835, once it had become clear that a rural revolt against the New Poor Law would not materialize, the steady stream of anti-Poor Law pamphlets which had followed the passage of the law began to dry up and the Parliamentary opposition gradually abandoned its attempts to keep the issue alive by proposing anti-Poor Law motions and pestering the government about alleged abuses during question time. For the better part of two years opposition at the national level can hardly be said to have existed at all. Its revival in 1837 was sudden and rapid. Anti-Poor Law pamphlets, largely but by no means entirely from the North, reappeared in numbers rivalling those of 1834 and in Parliament in February the opposition launched the first major debate on the Poor Law Amendment Act since its passage by moving for the appointment of a Select Committee of Inquiry into the operation of the act. The government was sufficiently confident about the outcome of an inquiry that it readily acceded to the demand and further ensured its position by packing the Committee and a succeeding Committee appointed for the new Parliamentary session later in the year with known supporters of the New Poor Law.[1] Even so, the Parliamentary opponents of the law now had a national forum in which to present their case and growing confidence that outside discontent would go far towards making that case for them. By early 1838 they had become sufficiently optimistic about their overall prospects that Lord Stanhope was beginning to work out plans for the foundation of a national network of anti-Poor Law associations.

All of these plans and assumptions were based, however, on a wildly optimistic misreading of the true situation. Impressive though some of the local resistance movements were, the opposition leaders tended to overestimate most of them and, still more, their potential for coming together into a national movement. In the North for example there was never any realistic prospect that the region as a whole would go the way of the textile districts. The opposition which threatened to develop in Newcastle did no more than that. If ever there was an opening for effective opposition in Tyneside and County Durham, the caution with which the

[1] Hansard, *op. cit.*, XXXVI, 986–1052, 1065–1102.

Assistant Commissioner handled the district and the firmness of those Guardians who favored the New Poor Law closed it off. The southern West Riding, apparently so much more volatile, was little different really. For all the talk of organized resistance and support from the *Sheffield Iris*, there was nothing substantial to pit against local supporters of the law backed by Assistant Commissioner Gulson. Samuel Roberts, who was surely not only the most prolific but also the most incoherent of anti-Poor Law pamphleteers, proved to be no leader at all and an anti-Poor Law organization in an effective sense never really emerged. The near panic which immediately preceded the election of Guardians was wholly unjustified by events in Sheffield, Ecclesall or Rotherham; it was the nearness of Huddersfield rather than anything which happened in their own locality which very nearly immobilized the supporters of the new law in the Don valley. Away from the cities the opposition's prospects were even dimmer. The Guardians of the Gilbert Unions openly defied the Poor Law Commissioners but having done so they were content, even anxious, to lie low and hope that they would be left alone in future. Much the same was true of the individual Unions under the New Poor Law where resistance developed. Opposition in such places was usually the work of one or two powerful landowners who resented outside interference but had no desire to link up with a popular movement tinged with political radicalism.

The situation in Wales was somewhat different. There can be no doubt of the strength of local feeling against the New Poor Law or that this was translated into organized effective resistance on a regional scale. But Welsh opposition, though real enough, remained Welsh. Nowhere except perhaps in Cornwall was the opposition so inward looking. Its appeal, like the practices it sought to preserve, was essentially local. It makes an interesting chapter in Welsh history—and occasionally a melodramatic one. There is nothing in the history of English resistance to the New Poor Law, for example, which quite equals the incident in the Machynlleth Union when the clerk to the Board of Guardians, having been fired, entered the house of the Chairman of the Board, armed and on horseback, and, in an attempt to ride into the Chairman's study, shot one of his servants.[1] But though often fascinating and important in itself and as a background to Welsh Chartism and the Rebecca riots, opposition to the Poor Law in

[1] MH 12.16564 Jones to P.L.C. 2 Jan. 1839.

the principality never influenced or threatened to join forces with opposition across the border.

Even more disappointing to those who hoped for the emergence of national opposition was London. If ever there was an opposition which conformed to the Poor Law Commissioners' description of all opposition as being the work of men who had done well out of the Old Poor Law and were afraid of losing their income or their jobs, it was the London opposition. From beginning to end it was led and supported almost exclusively by overseers and church-wardens in the dozens of small parishes threatened by administrative rationalization. Opposition in London never had serious backing and it died away very rapidly once the transition was actually made.

At no time, in short, was there any real prospect that scattered local opposition to the New Poor Law would develop and coalesce into something on which the advocates of opposition in national politics could rely. That this was the case should not be allowed, however, to obscure the fact that the reverse was equally true. Fielden, Lord Stanhope and their colleagues never provided the kind of leadership that could have drawn together and mobilized a national movement even had the ingredients for such a movement existed. Anti-Poor Law propaganda was almost wholly negative and its quality was abysmal.[1] The reasoned, detailed and constructive criticism with which at least a few journals and pamphleteers had answered the New Poor Law in 1834, had given way by 1837 to wholesale undifferentiated denunciation. At best it was a re-hashing of Cobbett's singular historical theories; at worst and most often it was nothing more than scandal mongering. The local anti-Poor Law press was filled with lurid tales of alleged abuses, cruelty and mismanagement which were then picked up uncritically by pamphleteers and some of the more prominent regional and national anti-Poor Law papers.

Worse still, the Parliamentary opposition adopted the same tactics as its chief method of attack on the law. Almost the whole time of the 1837 Select Committee was occupied and wasted in a

---

[1] A typical and by far the best known example of opposition scandal mongering at this time was the Bridgewater case, for which see: J. Bowen, *The New Poor Law: The Bridgewater Case* (London 1839). The entire history of an only slightly less notorious alleged scandal can be found in the files for the Kendal Union: MH 12.13581 1837–38 correspondence. See also the pamphlets of Bull, Oastler and Samuel Roberts, all of whom were reaching their peak of production at this time.

K

long investigation of alleged abuses in a few Unions where the opposition had not even bothered to check its facts beforehand.[1] This far more than the fact that the Committee was packed with supporters of the law accounted for the opposition's inability to make effective use of what could have been a major forum for their views. The opposition performed rather better on the Select Committee appointed in 1838, perhaps because it had just suffered a serious setback in the defeat of Fielden's repeal motion.[2] Apart from the testimony of George Stringer Bull the opponents of the law tended to be less sweeping and more concrete in their criticisms. Assistant Commissioners were subjected to some very searching cross-examination on such things as the impact of the New Poor Law on wages in areas of labor surplus, and Fielden took care to ensure that the areas to be investigated in detail were thoroughly researched in advance. Even so the opposition made no headway, and not surprisingly. Its motives and methods were too suspect. The Unions to which Fielden sent his team of investigators were, for example, not only those in which the costs of poor relief had fallen most drastically, but they also happened to be in Bedfordshire, the home county of the Russell family. Beyond that there could be no doubt that even when the opposition leaders talked of revision or amendment what they really hoped for was to discredit and destroy the New Poor Law. During the debate on Fielden's repeal motion one M.P. rather plaintively pointed out that, while he was profoundly disturbed by the workings of the New Poor Law, he could not join with its out-and-out opponents because they had failed to propose a constructive alternative.[3] This was the greatest problem of the opponents of the law in national politics and their unwillingness or inability to come to grips with it was their greatest failing. Thus, while the disastrous defeat of Fielden's motion certainly vastly underrated the strength and extent of national feeling against the law, it was a fair and accurate reflection both of the effective political power of the opposition in the country and of the sagacity of its national leadership.

The leaders of the opposition in the North, however, far from London, caught up in their own movement and convinced that it

[1] On the proceedings of the 1837 Committee see: Report from the Select Committee on the Poor Law Amendment Act, *B.P.P.*, 1837, XVII.

[2] On the proceedings of the 1838 Committee see: Report from the Select Committee on the Poor Law Amendment Act, *B.P.P.*, 1838, XVIII.

[3] Hansard, *op. cit.*, XL, 1396–8.

was only the tip of the iceberg, were unable to comprehend such subtle distinctions. They expected the vote to reflect popular opinion at least in some measure and when it failed to do so they were profoundly shaken. Hence the confusion and bitterness of the post mortem meetings held in March, for one of which, a meeting of the South Lancashire Association, we have a fairly full record.[1] Fielden and Stanhope both sent letters to the meeting, urging that a new campaign of petitioning be opened. In addition Stanhope stressed the need to go ahead with plans for the creation of a national anti-Poor Law organization. Oastler also addressed the meeting by letter, suggesting that Fielden be requested to demand that a delegation from the North be allowed to appear and plead its cause at the bar of the House of Commons. Stephens, at the meeting, supported Oastler's plan. Richardson argued that the North would now have to embark on a vast campaign of simultaneous or aggregate meetings as a means of demonstrating the extent of opposition support. Clegg proposed tying the two suggestions together by holding mass meetings at which delegates to be heard at the House of Commons would be selected. Fletcher, on a completely new tack, favored a run on the banks. Only one of these many suggestions, further petitioning, was rejected outright. Of that everyone had had more than enough. Everything else, as well as resolutions advocating overseers' resistance and a boycott of the upcoming Boards of Guardians elections, was agreed to. Little came of this program however. A few meetings were held to select delegates to go before Parliament, but this petered out very quickly. Stanhope held a meeting in London to launch his National Association, but that was the last that was heard of the plan.[2] Fletcher's run on the banks never materialized. No one, it is clear, believed any longer in the possibility of a national movement or that the government or Parliament could be reached. The North was now recognized as being what it had really been all along in opposing the New Poor Law, on its own.

[1] *M.S.A.* 17 March 1838.
[2] *N.S.* and *M.S.A.* 17, 24 and 31 March; for Stanhope's attempt to build a National Anti-Poor Law Association see: *Great Meeting at the Crown and Anchor on the Inhuman Poor Law Act* (London 1837).

VII 1838: the North on its own

The collapse of a national resistance movement did not, as might have been expected, weaken the determination of the northern opposition. A few of the important popular leaders did begin to argue that the cause was now hopeless, but the great majority still believed that much could be achieved by the North acting alone and that the winter campaign, while a failure in its ostensible purpose, had been enormously successful in arousing public opinion and broadening the organization of the northern movement. There was, in any case, little time for reflection or debate; new Boards of Guardians for the new parochial year had to be elected in the last week of March.

As a result of all that had happened since September 1837, the opposition election campaign was not only better organized but more purposeful than it had been the year before. The total boycott, which had proved the only sure means of countering the Poor Law Commissioners, was now put forward as semi-official policy. The *Northern Star*, the South Lancashire Association and almost all the popular anti-Poor Law leaders united in endorsing it. But even the much-improved anti-Poor Law organization was unable to spread it very far. The Oldham Union and the two intransigent townships of the Todmorden Union maintained their boycotts with no great difficulty, but it was quite another matter to extend a boycott to Unions where Boards, whatever their composition, had once been elected. Only Ashton managed it and Ashton of course was peculiar in a number of respects.[1] An attempt at a boycott, though frustrated, had been made the year before, the local opposition leaders had never lost sight of this as their ultimate goal, and well before the election Stephens and the local Radical Association joined forces to ensure that the near miss of 1837 would not be repeated. Moreover, Ashton, as Stephens' home territory, had been kept in an unusually high state of excitement all through the winter, and the combination of intimidation with tighter organization had the desired effect. In no other Poor

[1] For the advocacy and use of the boycott in 1838 see: *N.S.* 7 and 14 April; *M.S.A.* 31 March, 7 and 14 April 1838; MH 12.5413 Worthington to P.L.C. 7 April 1838.

Law Union, however, does it appear that a total boycott was newly attempted. Elsewhere there were only scattered individual boycotts and, though these were quite as common as they had been the year before, their significance was again limited. The boycott as a weapon of all out resistance remained a speciality of one important but small area on the eastern border of Lancashire.

Outside of this district, Huddersfield rather than Oldham provided the pattern for resistance, and Huddersfield itself again led the way.[1] The central Union anti-Poor Law Association issued detailed instructions to the township committees, informing them of all the procedural intricacies of the law, and it acted throughout as a clearing house, providing information or, if need be, candidates and canvassers to the less well-organized townships. Other Unions followed Huddersfield's lead as best they could, which was usually a good deal better than in 1837. The general confusion and conflicting aims and tactics, which had been so characteristic of the first Boards of Guardians elections, were much less in evidence. Most of the Radical Workingmen's Associations which had sprung up all over the textile district in the late months of 1837 worked very closely with the official anti-Poor Law committees. Relations between Radical and Conservative opponents of the Poor Law were also reasonably good, certainly far better than they had been the year before. In large part this was due to the fact that the Registration Act was already in operation, thus making religion a less important factor in the elections. More cynical explanations would be that by this time the weaker party in any given locality had realized the futility of direct competition or that some arrangement had been made for sharing out patronage under the Registration Act or New Poor Law. Whatever the reasons, bipartisan opposition did emerge in a number of key Unions, allowing the opposition to strengthen its hold in Rochdale and Huddersfield for example, and playing a major role in the opposition's most important single advance, the capture of the Dewsbury Board of Guardians.[2]

Unhappily for the anti-Poor Law movement, the drawing together of its various components and the tightening of its organization was matched by similar moves on the part of groups which

[1] On opposition tactics in the Boards of Guardians elections see: *N.S.* 10 March, 7 and 14 April; *M.S.A.* 31 March, 7 and 14 April 1838.
[2] For evidence of greater bipartisanship see: *N.S.* 7 April; *M.S.A.* 31 March 1838.

supported the Poor Law or at least opposed its opponents. Moderate Liberals and, as the opposition called them, sham Radicals, who
had often been intimidated into silence or political isolation the
year before, proved much more determined in 1838. In addition,
the militancy of Tory opposition to the new law had waned
noticeably, in part as a result of the Commissioners' concessions,
in part because of a growing concern with the need for law, order
and respectability in the conduct of local affairs. In a number of
Unions where the opposition to the law was particularly powerful
and particularly violent, this reaction was strong enough to create
a coalition of moderate Liberals and Tories in the weeks immediately preceding the election.[1]

In Huddersfield and most of the opposition strongholds this had
little effect. In Bury, however, a slate of candidates, who declared
themselves opposed to the Poor Law but equally opposed to
illegal resistance, was nominated and, despite a vicious campaign,
refused to withdraw before the election, thus breaking the back of
the boycott in that Union. In Preston Livesay's opponents were
unable to win a majority but were able nonetheless to take control
of the machinery of the Board of Guardians. In the election of a
chairman for the new Board, the presiding magistrate, after a
bitter personal attack on Livesay and his friends, disallowed the
votes of all Guardians whose elections were being challenged.
Since all of these happened to be Livesay's supporters, the result
was the appointment of this same magistrate as the new chairman.
The remaining setbacks for the opposition came in the fringe
areas of the textile district where predominantly Tory Boards
more or less committed to opposing the new law had been elected
in 1837. In one of these Unions, Keighley, the opposition suffered
a clear-cut defeat in a hard-fought election contest between pro-
and anti-Poor Law factions. Elsewhere the process was subtler, a
matter of new Guardians coming in who were either less militant
in their opposition to the new law or more amenable to pressure
from London.

The election results could hardly be called dramatic and they
certainly fell far short of the hopes and expectations of both the
Poor Law Commissioners and the northern opposition. With only
four Unions, five if one counts Preston, having changed hands, the
situation remained frustratingly like that of the year before. But it

[1] Bury: *N.S.* 14 April; *M.S.A.* 7 April 1838; Keighley: *N.S.* 14 April
1838; Preston: *Preston Chronicle* 14 April 1838.

was not quite 1837 all over again. The softening up of the peripheral Unions together with the hardening of positions in the
center of the textile district produced a clear regional pattern in the
results which had only been barely discernable a year before. The
Poor Law Commissioners, to be sure, could only count on support
from those few Unions under the control of Liberal Boards, but
they could now also move with some assurance in most of the
peripheral areas. The opposition, on the other hand, had secure
control of a solid block of Unions in the heart of the industrial
North and could be fairly certain of carrying the population of
this area with it in whatever course of action it decided to take.

Anxious to avoid provoking northern public opinion during the
election period, the Commissioners had not directed any Board of
Guardians to assume control over poor relief since January. But
once the election was over, the Commissioners immediately set
about planning for new advances on this front, very much as if the
three to four months' hiatus had not existed. Their strategy as
developed in late 1837 was not altered; if anything the hardening
geographical division revealed by the election results confirmed
the Commissioners' confidence in it. The Union by Union selective approach was adhered to, with the safe Unions being brought
into operation as quickly as possible, the doubtful ones handled
with greater care, and the potentially dangerous ones dealt with
one by one.[1]

With the first two categories the Commissioners were uniformly
successful throughout the late spring and summer.[2] They made
their first move in Stockport, a Union securely under Liberal
control and unlikely to give any trouble. This was followed in July
by the introduction of the new law into Haslingden, which, though
dominated by Tory anti-Poor Law Guardians, was one of those
peripheral Unions where the Commissioners' prospects had improved since the election of a new Board. Wigan, also a peripheral

[1] For the Commissioners' estimate of the election results and of the
Poor Law's prospects in the spring of 1838 see: MH 12.5413 Power to
Frankland Lewis 25 April 1838; HO 73.55 Chadwick to Phillips 2 Feb.
1839; MH 32.64 14 April, 7 May and 10 June 1838.

[2] Stockport: MH 12.1138 May–June 1838 correspondence; Haslingden: MH 12.5840 June 1838 correspondence; Wigan: PUW 1/1 June–
July 1838; Burnley: MH 12.5673. Power to P.L.C. 5 Dec. 1837, 2 July
1838, Shaw to P.L.C. 16 April, 29 July 1838; Keighley: MH 12.15158
May–July 1838 correspondence; Preston: *Preston Chronicle* 23 June and
7 July 1838.

Union and adjacent to Warrington where the new law was already in effect, was brought into operation uneventfully in August. The Commissioners were almost equally successful in three other Unions, Burnley, Keighley and Preston, where the risks were far greater. In all three an attempt to introduce the new law during 1837 would undoubtedly have produced determined, even violent resistance. But the withdrawal of Parson Bull from active intervention in Burnley and the defeat of the opposition by means fair or foul in Keighley and Preston had deprived it not only of much of its strength but, as it turned out, of much of its spirit as well. The worst that the Assistant Commissioner and local supporters of the Poor Law had to contend with was verbal abuse from a minority of the Guardians and non-co-operation from the overseers in a few of the townships.

But, as soon as they turned from such places to those Unions where the opposition had maintained or improved its 1837 position, the Commissioners encountered determined resistance, and their first choice among these critical Unions, Todmorden,[1] proved to be the worst of all. Yet it was an understandable first choice, for Todmorden was a key Union and a tempting target. As the stronghold of John Fielden, the opposition's chief exponent in Parliament and one of the early backers, first, of the boycott and, later, of the South Lancashire Association, its capture would have undermined him and, very possibly, all the techniques of resistance with which he was associated. Moreover, since the union included townships in both Lancashire and Yorkshire and formed a bridge between the resistance movements in the two counties, a victory for the new law there would have demoralized the opposition throughout the North more perhaps than a victory in any other Union. Such a victory did not seem unobtainable, or even particularly remote. Indeed, the Commissioners were inclined to include Todmorden along with Burnley and Keighley in the doubtful class, for, while the situation there had not changed in the Commissioners' favor as much as in these other two Unions, there had been considerable improvement.

---

[1] For the resistance in Todmorden, the main sources are the files of the P.L.C. (MH 12.6272), supplemented by a number of volumes from the Home Office files (HO 41.43, HO 40.38, HO 73.54). A short account from the P.L.C. point of view can be found in their Fourth Annual Report, 30–1, and Fifth Annual Report, *B.P.P.* 1839, XX, 19–20. See also: T. E. Ashworth, *An Account of the Todmorden Poor Law Riots* (n.p. 1901) and Holden's *Short History of Tormorden.*

The opposition's grip, never strong in four of the Union's six townships, had apparently begun to slip even in Todmorden and Langfield.[1] In 1837, all nominees for the guardianship in both towns had resigned under pressure long before the elections were held. In 1838, on the other hand, two lists of Guardians had been proposed and the opposition had had trouble dealing with both. One candidate on the first list refused to stand down, regardless of pressure, and the overseers were able to rid themselves of the second list only by declaring it void on the basis of a legal technicality. Even so, one candidate remained and only the failure of the overseers to send out voting papers prevented this lone candidate from being returned. Power, who had hoped to break the boycott, was furious and spent much time in the next few months attempting either to get the second list recognized or to have legal action taken against the overseers for contravening the law. Nothing came of these efforts and the boycott stuck, but the fact that it had been so very nearly broken was good cause for optimism. Even more hopeful was the inability of the opposition, however strong in Todmorden, to compel the towns lower down the valley to follow suit. Indeed, far from having spread, anti-Poor Law sentiment in the Todmorden Union seemed to be on the wane, for the non-boycotting townships had elected Guardians in 1838 who were at least willing to give the law a trial. Thus there was a Board of Guardians to work with and, while resistance could be expected from Todmorden and Langfield, the fact that they had boycotted the elections, rather than put forward anti-Poor Law Guardians, meant that the existing Board might prove quite easy to manage. The Todmorden Union was, in short, the prime example of the inherent weakness of a partial boycott, and in the summer of 1838 the Poor Law Commissioners decided to exploit that weakness.

In assessing the situation, however, Power, and therefore the Poor Law Commissioners, seriously under-estimated the opponents' grip on the two refractory townships and also their ability to disrupt the affairs of the Union even from outside the Board of Guardians. No area in all of Lancashire or the West Riding was as united in its opposition to the New Poor Law as Todmorden. In part this was due to its small size—the two townships together had only about 10,000 people—which made organization comparatively

[1] MH 12.6272 Ormerod to P.L.C. 31 March 1838; Power to P.L.C. 23 April 1838.

easy. There was, moreover, the influence of Fielden, by far the largest employer and most important public figure in the area. But pressure from Fielden was only part of it. By skillfully playing on every sort of grievance, the opposition managed to forge an anti-Poor Law alliance which apparently included the overwhelming majority of the local population.

The bulk of the ratepayers were won through appeals to their humanitarian instincts and, above all, by constant emphasis on local loyalty. Throughout the resolutions passed at ratepayers' meetings in early 1837 and again a year later, there were references to self-government, to the traditional liberties of Englishmen, and to the dangers inherent in foreign (i.e. central governmental) interference. 'We are resolved', as one resolution, typical not only of Todmorden but of the North in general, put it,

to make . . . [a] stand for the maintenance of our rights and liberties against the attempt now making by the Poor Law Commissioners to wrest from us the control we have hitherto exercised in relieving our own poor, and to place these poor, whom we love and respect, and who have been guilty of no crime, in a workhouse and under a discipline and restraint more intolerable than is allotted to felons in a gaol.[1]

The local Workingmen's Association, directing its appeal at an entirely different audience, was not particularly concerned with the preservation of local self-government. To the ordinary people of Todmorden the Poor Law was portrayed primarily as a tool of social repression. 'We must warn you', the Workingmen's Association declared in its most colorfully written placard,

to be on your guard. It is no common enemy that you have to deal with. It is a monster that should be seen to have been engendered between the SERPENT and the VAMPIRE; like the one he makes his approach in the night; like the other he crawls, and so deeply hidden under the filth of his hypocrisy, as to be nearly invisible; like both, if he can once sieze his prey his attack is fatal, because the full venom of his malicious work is never brought to light until the body be rendered too feeble for resistance. His tools will ask you to try the law, will tell you that you do not know, until you try, how well it will work; and will add, with a brazen face and a lying heart, that if it does not prove to be good, kind and charitable, he will be the first to assist in destroying it. But recollect, Brother Townsmen, that between the virtuous and the

[1] MH 12.6272 Ormerod to P.L.C. 9 April 1838.

devil there can be no compromise; and if our present enemy be not a child of the Father of Sin, his acts must belie his parentage. God cursed the serpent, and said, 'upon thy belly shalt thou go, and dust shalt thou eat all the rest of thy life'; on his belly would the monster now crawl in amongst us, and on their bellies do his friends crawl after places and salaries.[1]

Such resolutions and placards were not mere bombast. The ratepayers' meetings really did represent the majority of the ratepayers and the Workingmen's Association, though only a few months old at this time, was the direct descendant of local radical associations with roots in the earliest period of the agitation for the reform bill. Moreover, both the ratepayers and the radical workingmen knew that, whatever they might do and whatever pressures might be exerted from London, they would have the backing and protection of John Fielden. It was almost inevitable, then, that, however likely the opposition elsewhere was to back down when actually challenged, in Todmorden the Commissioners would have to fight to impose their authority.

After long consultations with the Board of Guardians and the Home Office, the Poor Law Commission sent its organizational order to the Todmorden Board in June and scheduled the first meeting under the Poor Law Amendment Act for July 6. The opposition countered immediately. Arrangements were made to stage a huge public demonstration at the same time as the first Board meeting and in early July Fielden wrote an open letter to the Guardians calling on them to resign and threatening to close his mills and let his workers loose if the Board proceeded with the New Poor Law. The opposition also appointed delegates to meet individually with each of the Guardians and put pressure on them to resign.[2] The Guardians were terrified. Fearing violence, they met informally on July 5, agreed 'that the New Poor Law cannot be successfully introduced into the Union unless the local influence and opposition of Mr. Fielden can by some means be overcome by the government',[3] and therefore decided to adjourn their meeting scheduled for the following day.

But the victory this represented for the opponents was in no sense conclusive. None of the Guardians resigned, all agreed that

[1] *Ibid.* Taylor to P.L.C. 18 April 1838.
[2] *Ibid.* The anti-Poor Law placards are filed with the July correspondence; *M.S.A.* 14 July 1838.
[3] MH 12.6272 Stansfield to Power 6 July 1838.

they would act if protected, and the adjournment was only for a week. The opposition therefore went ahead with a modified version of their original plan. Fielden closed his mills on July 7 and the great demonstration was adjourned, though only for three days. But a repetition of the events of the first week of July, which the opposition clearly hoped to bring about, did not take place; the government, fearing another Huddersfield, stepped in to prevent it. Such intervention was far easier in Todmorden than it had been the year before in Huddersfield, for a number of the local magistrates were on the government's side and ready to call on it for help at the slightest sign of trouble. The Home Office was therefore not only willing but able to act in anticipation of events. The great public meeting held on July 9, at which Fielden, who came specially from London, was the featured speaker, was attended by a full complement of magistrates backed up by special constables. On the same day, moreover, the government moved a squadron of cavalry into the Todmorden area. Understandably then, the meeting was quiet; an anti-climax, in fact, which marked an end to the tension of the previous week. And nothing which the opposition did in the next few days was sufficient to revive that tension or the fear that it had inspired. Four days later, when the Guardians met at last, Fielden attended with a delegation, hoping, even at this late date, to press them into resignation. The Guardians admitted him and listened to him, but they no longer feared him, and, after he had gone, they simply returned to the business at hand.[1]

The positions of the two sides had been abruptly reversed. The Board of Guardians, once apparently so weak, now appeared strong and resolute, while the opposition's supposedly formidable ratepayer and popular support had melted away at the first sign of counter pressure. The stoppage of Fielden's mills, designed as the final blow in a long campaign of intimidation, resulted instead in a double loss, financial and of popular support, to the Fielden family. Placed in an impossibly exposed position, the opposition had to withdraw. Fielden reopened his factories and, in a letter to the Guardians explaining his actions, admitted the cause of his defeat. 'To oppose with force,' he declared, 'we are not yet prepared.' He was, in consequence, reduced to warnings. He reminded the Guardians that they would not be able to conduct their

[1] HM 12.6272 Taylor to Power 9 July 1838; Power to P.L.C. 12, 14 July 1838.

affairs as they saw fit, but only according to the rules of the Poor Law Commissioners. For a time, he admitted, they might get away with this, 'but, if the people of this and surrounding districts are to be driven to the alternative of [resorting to force] or surrendering their local government into the hands of an unconstitutional Board of lawmakers, the time may not be far distant when the experiment may be tried'.[1] In the circumstances of mid-July, these seemed empty threats, reminiscent far more of the vague predictions of disaster made in southern England in 1834, than of the serious challenge to the new law which Huddersfield and a few other places in the North had presented. Cautiously, but still confidently, the Commissioners counted Todmorden as a victory and, tentatively, as a possible turning point.

But the Poor Law Commissioners, for all their caution, were still too hasty in claiming success. The opposition had another weapon to fall back upon, the one new weapon of the opponents in 1838, the financial boycott. The idea itself was far from new. The nonpayment of taxes or tithes had long been a favorite proposal, though more rarely a practice, of English and, more recently, of Irish protest movements. Within the anti-Poor Law movement it had first been suggested by Oastler and Fielden as far back as the beginning of 1837 when they declared that they, at least, would pay no rates under the Poor Law Amendment Act.[2] But few dared emulate Oastler and Fielden and it was more than a year before the idea received wider official support within the anti-Poor Law movement. The change came as a result of the opposition crisis early in 1838. At the meeting of the South Lancashire Association following the defeat of Fielden's repeal motion in February, a financial boycott was suggested as one of the possible courses of action open to the opponents. Within a month it had been taken up by the *Northern Star*, which endorsed it as the best means of wrecking the law in those Unions where the opposition failed to win a majority on the Board of Guardians.[3] And Fielden, in a postscript to his letter of July 16 to the Todmorden Board, reminded them that 'tithes could not be collected in Ireland' and predicted

---

[1] *Ibid.* Power to P.L.C. 12 July 1838; *N.S.* 21 July 1838.
[2] Oastler, *Damnation! Eternal Damnation to the Fiend Begotten Coarser Food New Poor Law* (London 1837); Fielden at a speech in Oldham reported in the *M.S.A.* 4 Feb. 1837.
[3] *M.S.A.* 17 March; *N.S.* 14 April 1838.

'that if you persevere you may have the satisfaction of knowing that rates cannot be collected in England'. To put such a policy in practice was no easy matter, however. An individual refusal to pay rates was meaningless. Like the boycott of Boards of Guardians elections, it had to be widespread to be effective. In fact, only one method would suffice: defiance by the overseers, who collected and distributed rates.

Overseers' resistance, like the idea of a financial boycott, was anything but new. The Poor Law Commissioners had feared it, though unnecessarily, in southern England in 1834 and again, this time with reason, in the North in 1837. In 1837 overseers' resistance was used to good effect in two ways. It was central to the success of the opposition in Boards of Guardians elections, particularly if a boycott was being attempted. And, as a number of Unions, and in particular Salford, had demonstrated, overseers' resistance could safely be extended to include non-co-operation with the orders of the Poor Law Commissioners.[1] In 1838, as the Poor Law Commissioners began to push ahead with their plans for implementing the new law even in those Unions where a majority of Guardians were opposed to it, control of the overseers or, failing that, of the township vestries assumed even greater importance. In Bury, having failed to maintain the boycott, the opposition's only hope seemed to be to win control of the local vestry. Typically, Fletcher sought to achieve this through the same sort of coercive tactics which had served him so well in 1837, this time by invading, disrupting and seizing control of the annual ratepayers' meeting which nominated vestrymen. As in the Board of Guardians election, however, he failed, largely it would seem because the magistrates and other local officials refused to be cowed.[2]

Elsewhere, and most importantly in Salford, the opposition was more successful.[3] The annual ratepayers' meeting there was as confused and angry as Bury's and as frustrating for the opposition, which failed to get the old anti-Poor Law overseers reappointed or to prevent the nomination of a pro-Poor Law vestry. Luckily for the opponents, they were able to refer the latter decision to a poll of all the ratepayers, which resulted in an overwhelming

---

[1] See above, Chapter V, Note 5. 1838 added a few new cases. See, for example, MH 12.5673 Shaw to P.L.C. 6 April 1838.
[2] *M.S.A.* 7, 14 and 21 April 1838; *M.G.* 11 April 1838.
[3] *M.G.* 31 March–11 July 1838.

victory for a Radical and Tory anti-Poor Law panel of candidates headed by Richardson and including most of the 1837 overseers. Claiming complete legal authority over the overseers, the new vestrymen then proceeded methodically to remove or undermine their power and independence. The new overseers, in turn, ignored the vestry, supplied the Commissioners with the information which had been withheld the previous year, and, when the vestry threatened to take legal action to assert their control, the overseers replied by calling on the Commissioners to support them by introducing the New Poor Law into Salford. Power, now assured of the kind of local co-operation he had been unable to get in 1837, responded immediately and well before the end of August, less than two months after the vestry's threat of legal action, the task was complete. It seemed to the *Manchester Guardian* that the machinations of R. J. Richardson had at long last backfired and to a large extent this was true, but not entirely. With the opposition still in control of the Salford vestry and of a well-organized popular following, obstruction or possibly violent resistance seemed likely. To diminish the risk of this as well as of defeat in the Board of Guardians elections, the local Liberals, apparently on the advice of Alfred Power, withdrew their candidates and allowed the anti-Poor Law coalition to win control of the Board by default.

The lessons of this partial success in Salford were not lost on opposition leaders elsewhere, particularly in Todmorden where Fielden's humiliating defeat at the hands of the Commissioners coincided with the election of a Board of Guardians in Salford. This is not to say that overseers' resistance had not been used in Todmorden prior to July 1838. The initiation of a total boycott in 1837 and still more its preservation in 1838 had been made possible only through the complete co-operation of the overseers and, later in the spring when the Commissioners were preparing to introduce the Poor Law into the Todmorden Union, the overseers of Todmorden township, in emulation of their Salford colleagues, refused to supply the necessary financial information.[1] Resistance of this kind, however, had always played a secondary role to more dramatic activities such as the boycott itself or the use of mass meetings and demonstrations. Only when the Poor Law Commissioners succeeded in outflanking Fielden in his policy of direct confrontation, did Fielden in Todmorden, like Fletcher in Bury, fall back on the township officers as the main line of resistance. But whereas

[1] MH 12.6272 Ormerod to P.L.C. 31 March, 9 April 1838.

the opposition in Bury failed to win control of the local vestry and the opposition in Salford had to settle for something less than complete victory because it lost control of the overseers, opposition control of the overseers and vestry in Todmorden was never endangered. Thus it was possible, if the overseers were willing, to carry resistance one stage further, to the point of actually with-holding funds from the machinery of the New Poor Law.

In theory this was merely the next logical step in overseers' resistance. In practice it was something far more radical and dangerous. Resistance as election officials, even if, as in Tod-morden, it called for circumventing the law, held out few dangers. It was, as Alfred Power soon discovered, difficult to prove any-thing. Non-compliance with requests for information from the Commissioners was riskier, since it involved openly flouting the authority of the Poor Law Commissioners. Even so, the chances of getting away with it were good. The Commissioners were so busy that, rather than press the issue, they would make do with out-of-date averages of township expenditure in assessing the division of Union costs. This, indeed, is what happened in Todmorden and many other places during 1838. But to refuse to hand over the rates to a Board of Guardians was quite another matter. The New Poor Law could function with an incomplete or irregularly elected Board and on the basis of imperfect financial information, but it could not function without funds. Thus, while the Poor Law Commissioners could afford, for a time, to ignore overseers' resistance in certain departments, they would have to react if, by withholding funds, the overseers threatened the very existence of the law.

Understandably, therefore, the Todmorden overseers were reluctant to take this new step, and probably would not have done so at all without the full backing of the ratepayers. Such backing was, however, enthusiastically given. Already in 1837, in order to ensure the full co-operation of the overseers in the election boycott, the ratepayers had agreed 'to indemnify the . . . overseers in any proceedings which may be taken against them'.[1] And in the follow-ing summer, when the Board of Guardians made its first call on the townships for funds, the Todmorden ratepayers proved equally ready to assume responsibility for acts of open defiance. At a ratepayers' meeting, held on August 4 at the request of the overseers, it was resolved 'that the overseers be directed not to

[1] MH 12.6272 Omerod P.L.C. to 9 April 1838.

comply with the order of the Board of Guardians and that the ratepayers present do indemnify the overseers for so doing'.[1]

The effect on the Board of Guardians of this new challenge to their authority was very nearly disastrous. Their hard-won self-confidence melted away and within a few weeks many Guardians were contemplating resignation. Their despondency was not entirely unjustified. A financial boycott was probably potentially the most dangerous form of opposition yet devised and to defeat it could prove difficult and time consuming. Nevertheless, neither the Commissioners nor most of the Guardians doubted that it could and would be done and this sudden collapse of confidence would probably not have taken place, but for the fact that the beginning of the financial boycott in Todmorden was not an isolated event. During the four weeks which separated the two crises there, resistance flared up in other Unions—particularly in Huddersfield and Dewsbury—and threatened to spread and intensify the opposition everywhere in the North. Strictly speaking, it is not quite accurate to talk of Huddersfield re-emerging into prominence at this time.[2] Opposition in other Unions might come and go, playing an important part for a time, but Huddersfield provided the *basso continuo* for the anti-Poor Law movement. It was never really quiet. The election of a clerk in January had solved nothing; if anything, it had made matters worse. The opposition Guardians, still a majority, became recklessly determined to make nonsense of the functioning of the Board and spent a good deal of their time harassing and threatening the new clerk and those unfortunate men who supported him. They soon proved that, even with a clerk in office, there were still plenty of ways of destroying the effectiveness of a Board of Guardians. The proven tactics of moving long adjournments could be tried and, should that fail, the opposition Guardians could always swamp the meetings by bringing in the crowds from outside.

But it was not only the opponents of the law who resorted to illegalities. Angry and desperate, the pro-Poor Law faction began to ape the methods of their opponents. Both sides tried to fix the Board of Guardians election in March, and, in the contest to control the chairmanship which followed, the pro-Poor Law

---

[1] *Ibid.* Power to P.L.C. 11 Aug. 1838.

[2] For Huddersfield in 1838, see: MH 12.15064; HO 73.54; Report of the trial of the Huddersfield Guardians, York Assizes, 1839.

L

candidate was appointed only because of flagrant bias on the part of the clerk and one of the ex-officio Guardians in allowing or disallowing the votes of Guardians whose election had been questioned.[1] When this was brought to the attention of the Commissioners in a memorial from some of the anti-Poor Law Guardians, Power freely, though of course privately, admitted that the proceedings had been illegal. But, he believed, since the result had been to the 'advantage [of] the friends of the law, it is advisable . . . that the answer [of the Commissioners to the memorial] be in favour of the proceeding'.[2]

The Poor Law Commissioners took Power's advice and rejected the complaints of the memorialists. This was a serious error. The opponents now had a legitimate grievance and the supporters of the law immediately lost any claims to righteousness they may once have possessed. The Board of Guardians quickly degenerated into a bear garden. Near chaos, the usual condition of the Huddersfield Board, was replaced by complete chaos and on May 7 the opponents went into open revolt. They seized the minute book, elected their own chairman and set about conducting the business of the Union as if they were legally in control. The takeover had been carefully planned. The opposition leaders gathered at a nearby tavern immediately before the meeting and then marched, along with a few hundred supporters, on the courthouse. With them, apart from the usual local leaders, were Stephens and O'Connor, who purposely played a very conspicuous role in the day's proceedings. The effect on the Board was predictable. The pro-Poor Law faction panicked and began to talk of resignation. Once again, the whole structure seemed about to collapse.[3]

This the Commissioners could not let happen. After having allowed things to drift for nearly six months, much as they had done in the previous year, they could no longer avoid taking action. Even so, they did not act swiftly, for their aim was to break the back of the opposition in Huddersfield once and for all by imposing the Poor Law itself on the Board of Guardians, and to do that would take time and care. Power, in his usual reckless fashion, was all for going further and forcing the issue simultaneously in all the remaining centers of opposition where Boards of Guardians

[1] MH 12.15064 April 1838 correspondence.
[2] *Ibid.* Power to P.L.C. 2 May 1838. (This letter was written on the back of the memorial of the dissenting Guardians to the P.L.C.)
[3] *Ibid.* Hirst to P.L.C. 7 May; Monkhouse to P.L.C. 9 May; Floyd to P.L.C. 9 May. See also *N.S.* 12, 19 May 1838.

existed. But the Poor Law Commissioners refused to go this far; two or at most three Unions were, they believed, enough to contend with at any one time. Even so, they took risks. The decision to go ahead was made in early July, before the outcome at Todmorden was known. Yet it was a risk they had to take, for they dared not let things slide any further. As in January, the Commissioners made elaborate preparations. Legal proceedings were started against the leading opposition Guardians for their part in the tumultuous meeting of May 7, in the hope of deterring them from further resistance. And force was made ready just in case outsiders should attempt a repetition of these events.[1]

Nonetheless, the meeting did not go smoothly and would probably have achieved nothing without the presence of Alfred Power. Realizing that substantial progress was out of the question at this first meeting, he very sensibly concentrated on forcing the Guardians to take action on the one part of the Commissioners' standard order which required immediate action, a clause calling on the Board to set a time and place for regular meetings. 'The opposition Guardians endeavoured to avoid this,' Power wrote, 'and an adjournment of the motion was factiously attempted; on my pointing out, however, the imperative terms of the paragraph, and by dint of great patience and firmness . . . a resolution was at length passed . . . fixing weekly meetings.'[2] This, however, was all that the meeting achieved. The actual reorganization of Poor Law administration was still to come and, just as the election of a clerk half a year before had changed little, so this later victory as well promised to be of little real help. Even Power, who believed that the opposition would now be worn down at weekly meetings, had to admit that genuine progress in Huddersfield would take a very long time to achieve.

Even before the Poor Law Commissioners had won their inconclusive victory in Huddersfield, they were faced with a new crisis elsewhere in the West Riding, in Dewsbury.[3] Dewsbury was an almost ideal Union from the opposition point of view. Remarkably similar to Huddersfield in its geography and social make-up, it was a natural breeding ground for opposition to the new law, and it had the advantage over the Huddersfield Union of being smaller

[1] MH 12.15064 P.L.C. to Floyd 19 May; Power to Frankland Lewis 17 May; Power to P.L.C. 2 July 1838.

[2] *Ibid.* Power to P.L.C. 23 July 1838.

[3] For Dewsbury during 1838, see: MH 12.14830; HO 41.13 Aug.–Sept.; HO 73.54 Aug.–Sept.

and therefore easier to organize. In 1837, even without adequate preparations for the Guardians election, the opponents had managed to win approximately half the seats on the Board. A year later, possessed of a fairly comprehensive organization and sufficient time, they were able to swamp the Board with militantly anti-Poor Law Guardians. So anxious was this new majority to prove its abhorrence of the law, that in April, long before the Commissioners even considered moving on Dewsbury, they pushed through a resolution committing the Board to future non-co-operation.[1] The Commissioners therefore had every reason to expect trouble, but, determined to carry the battle into enemy territory and made confident by their victories elsewhere, they decided, in early July, to challenge the Dewsbury Guardians.

The first meeting under the Poor Law Amendment Act was held on July 23 and, like the meeting held on the same day and for the same purpose in Huddersfield, it was an unpleasant affair. The opposition Guardians, acting in the spirit of their neighbors at Huddersfield, moved delaying and wrecking amendments. The chairman, a local magistrate named Ingham, also using Huddersfield techniques, refused to acknowledge these amendments and, relying entirely on the small pro-Poor Law minority, forced through the initial necessary administrative changes.[2] But this was obviously only the first round. The majority had been defeated by a legal trick, not won over. If backed by a demonstration of popular support, the anti-Poor Law Guardians, though they could not hope to undo what had already been done, might yet be able to wreck the administration of the New Poor Law in Dewsbury. The opposition therefore went all out in a desperate last minute effort to recapture control. A mass meeting was held on August 1 at which anti-Poor Law Guardians railed against the allegedly illegal proceedings of the Board, while Oastler and O'Connor, brought in specially for the occasion, urged the populace to back up the majority on the Board. They did not, as usual, recommend any specific course of action, but the crowd took the hint and, at the second meeting of the Board, there was a serious riot during which the Guardians were stoned and saved from worse only by the opportune arrival of troops.[3]

[1] MH 12.14830 Carr to P.L.C. 26 April 1838.
[2] *Ibid.* Carr to P.L.C. 24 July 1838.
[3] *Ibid.* Carr to P.L.C. 7 Aug., and depositions of Ingham and Greenwood 6 and 7 Aug.; *N.S.* 1 Aug. 1838.

The result was a victory for neither side. Even on the day of the riot, the opposition was not able to prevent further progress in the implementation of the law. Nonetheless, the pro-Poor Law minority had been frightened and the resolve which they and the magistrates had shown at the time of the riot began to weaken in the days which followed. More protection was demanded, but what they really wanted was absolution from responsibility. We 'have received a letter from Lord John Russell', the clerk complained to the Commissioners,

in which he states that if the Guardians continue to meet, they shall have all the support the Government can give them. From this the Magistrates conclude that his Lordship leaves to them the unenviable responsibility of determining whether the New Poor Law shall be enforced in the district or not; and in this position the Magistrates have no wish to be placed. In endeavoring to carry your orders into effect they have merely been doing what, as Magistrates, they conceived to be their bounden duty, and unless the Government is determined to enforce the law and enforce that determination with all its power, the Magistrates have no wish to attempt to enforce the law in defiance of an infuriated mob.[1]

The local authorities, in short, were doing what the government most dreaded in such affairs, they were trying to throw the whole burden of local law enforcement onto the shoulders of the government. Thus, while the Poor Law Commissioners had ostensibly won a victory in Dewsbury, it, like the victory in Huddersfield, was in no sense final, and it had been won at the cost of an alarming falling off in the morale of the law's supporters there and throughout the West Riding. It was in this context that the second and decisive Todmorden crisis arose and developed.

In view of the disturbed condition of the West Riding in early August, the Poor Law Commissioners were understandably anxious to crush the financial boycott as quickly as possible, perhaps within a fortnight, and at first they had every hope of doing so. Legally, at least, there seemed to be no problem; the withholding of rates was clearly punishable under Section 98 of the Poor Law Amendment Act. Thus, when the overseers of Todmorden and Langfield failed to hand over the rates on the appointed day, the Commissioners immediately started proceedings against them. But the legal position of the Commissioners was

[1] MH 12.14830 Carr to P.L.C. 11 Aug. 1838.

not as unassailable as they had imagined, and the opponents were ready with a counter-claim. They argued that the Todmorden Board of Guardians was not competent to act, since it was not, due to the boycott by Todmorden and Langfield, a full Board as defined by Section 38 of the Poor Law Amendment Act. The Commissioners were as confident that they would win this point as they were that the overseers would be convicted, but in the short run this new challenge wrecked the Commissioners' plans. It was enough to prevent the Halifax magistrates from granting a conviction in the Langfield case for more than two months, and it, together with a number of minor legal technicalities, delayed action in the Todmorden case, tried at Rochdale, for an almost equally long period of time.[1]

The Board of Guardians, already demoralized by the events of early August, continued to disintegrate. As in Huddersfield the year before, delay and uncertainty were proving the worst enemies of the Poor Law Commissioners. If anything, the cost of these delays was now even greater, for the future of the Poor Law itself was at stake as it had not been in 1837. With one third of the townships refusing to supply funds, the finances of the Union nearly collapsed and the Guardians, with good reason, began to despair of ever putting the administration of the Poor Law in Todmorden on a workable basis. Outside pressure also took its toll. During the summer, two tradesmen on the Board suffered serious financial losses as a result of a popular boycott of their products and even those Guardians who were not directly affected became less and less inclined to run the risk of incurring popular reprisals by taking action of any sort. 'On the whole,' Power wrote in an uncharacteristically pessimistic letter to London, 'there exists a feeling in the Board that they are called upon to sacrifice too much personally for the enforcement of the law',[2] and it was all that he could do just to keep them all from resigning.

Moreover, there was every prospect that things would get much worse before they got better, for, with the Board of Guardians near collapse, the opponents had every reason to exacerbate the crisis. And they had the means of doing so. Even if the overseers were

[1] The development of this exceedingly complex and confusing legal battle can be followed in MH 12.6272 Power to P.L.C. 11, 14, 20 Aug., 2, 9, 16, 24 Sept., 29 Oct., 8 Nov. 1838. Much of this correspondence, together with additional commentary on legal problems, is also in HO 73.54.
[2] MH 12.6272 Power to P.L.C. 2 Sept. 1838.

convicted, they could refuse to pay their fines. A distress warrant authorizing the seizure and sale of their property would therefore have to be issued, and it was almost certain that this could not be executed without provoking an angry and perhaps violent public reaction. Power was far from confident that, should this happen, the Board of Guardians could be held together. Yet he dared not try to avert it by dropping the prosecution of the overseers, for any further delays in this were bound to end in the complete disintegration of the Board. With some reluctance, therefore, the Poor Law Commissioners headed for the showdown which the opposition so eagerly awaited.

It came, at long last, in late October.[1] The overseers were convicted and, when, as expected, they did not pay their fines, distress warrants were issued, first against Crossley and Robinson, the Todmorden overseers, and soon thereafter against Ingham of Langfield. The first attempt to enforce one of these warrants, in Todmorden on October 21, was a failure. A group of workers from one of Fielden's mills gathered around the auctioneer who was trying to sell some of the goods which had been seized, threatened to assault him and eventually drove him out of town. There was no violence, however, and no special precautions were taken to ensure success later on. This was a serious oversight on the part of the Commissioners, for the second attempt to carry out a warrant, this time in Langfield on November 16, was met with concerted and violent resistance. As soon as the Bradford constables charged with seizing Ingham's goods arrived at his house, a bell was rung there which was answered by the bell at Fielden's factory nearby. This, apparently, was a pre-arranged signal for 'the working people . . . to turn out and fight against the New Poor Law'.[2] Within minutes the constables were surrounded and one of them, the other having escaped, was stripped naked and beaten up. Eventually he was set free and the crowd then marched on the Guardians' meeting place where they broke a few windows before dispersing. During all this time the local magistrates and constables had done nothing to try to bring the crowd under control. Either because they themselves opposed the New Poor Law, as many of them did, or simply through fear, they refused to act and

---

[1] For the Todmorden riots, see: *Ibid.* Power to P.L.C. Oct.–Dec. 1838 correspondence; HO 41.13. Nov.–Dec. 1838; HO 40.38 Nov.–Dec. 1838; Ashworth, *Tormorden Poor Law Riots.*

[2] HO 40.38 Shuttleworth, Holgate and Roberts to Power 17 Nov. 1838.

it was generally agreed, by Power, by the Guardians and by their supporters among the magistrates, that only government intervention could save the situation.

The Home Office, too, agreed and immediately began preparations for intervention on a huge scale. But, before these plans had time to mature, within five days of the attack on the constables in Langfield, the mob acted again. The background to this second outbreak is obscure. It was probably not authorized, as the first almost certainly had been, by Fielden. It may have been planned by the local Workingmen's Association as a last show of force before the introduction of government strength, scheduled to take place in the next few days, made such demonstrations dangerous; but the evidence for this is far from conclusive. Indeed, only one thing is certain, that the crowds gathered in response to a rumor that constables were again coming to levy a distress warrant on the defaulting overseers. This was not true, but in a way that probably made what followed worse. The crowd, once assembled, finding no specific object to attack, attacked at random. It rampaged up and down the valley, sacking the houses of Guardians, relieving officers and pro-Poor Law overseers. About a dozen houses were attacked; in all of them windows were broken, in some furniture was destroyed and one was set on fire.

The government responded immediately. Special constables were sworn in by the hundred, special investigators (a polite term for police spies) were brought north from London, and infantry and cavalry were dispatched to Todmorden and areas nearby. In effect, the Union was placed under military occupation. Arrests of suspected rioters were made under military guard and all officials connected with the New Poor Law were given police or military protection. The effect was much the same as it had been elsewhere when troops were called in; Todmorden quietened down much more quickly than anyone had dared hope.

Though the Commissioners had managed to prevent the opposition from consolidating its control in Todmorden, they were still very far from having control of the situation there themselves. And much the same could be said of the entire Lancashire–Yorkshire textile district late in 1838. In no case had the opposition won in a direct confrontation with the Poor Law Commissioners and, if judged in terms of its stated aim, to prevent the implementation of the Poor Law in the North, the anti-Poor Law movement had failed disastrously. Nevertheless, the Commissioners, too, had fallen very far short of victory and even their minimum goal had not been achieved. Two Unions—Ashton and Oldham—still had no Boards of Guardians and in these two, as well as six others— Manchester, Bury, Bolton, Rochdale, Chorley and Clitheroe—the administration of relief remained entirely in the hands of the township overseers under the old Poor Law. In addition, even in many Unions where a Board of Guardians did exist and had assumed control over poor relief, the system was incomplete. The Todmorden Union, where two townships refused to elect Guardians, refused to hand over their rates to the Board and continued to relieve their own poor, was the most glaring example, but it was not the only one. Few Unions were without at least one township unrepresented on the Board of Guardians and, worse still, there were signs that the success of the financial boycott in Todmorden was inspiring similar resistance in other townships throughout the area.[1]

Nor was resistance limited to those Unions or townships where the old Poor Law had somehow been maintained. Even in Unions which were entirely under the New Poor Law and thus directly subservient to the Commissioners, opposition-controlled Boards of Guardians had developed the means of conducting a war of attrition against the Poor Law Commissioners. The new administrative machinery had to be staffed, and, most important of all, officers had to be chosen to assume the relief functions of the township overseers. The Commissioners' ideal was a small corps of well paid, full time Relieving Officers, but many Boards of Guardians held out for a larger number, most of whom would be responsible for no more than a couple of townships and would therefore be able to and, if they were to be full time employees, have to combine their main function with other duties. This form of resistance was particularly favored in Huddersfield and Dewsbury where the Guardians eagerly seized on the issue of personnel as a means of revenging themselves for past humiliations.[2] But, as in the case of overseers' resistance, the example seemed likely to prove contagious. Many country Guardians,

[1] MH 12.6272 Power to P.L.C. 8 Dec.; and for the effect on other Unions, see: MH 12.14721 Wagstaff to P.L.C. 20 Feb. 1839; MH 12.14830 Carr to P.L.C. 13 Dec. 1838.

[2] MH 12.15064 Correspondence between Floyd and the P.L.C. Oct.– Nov. 1838; MH 12.14830 Mott to Lefebvre. 4 Sept; P.L.C. to Carr 25, 29 Aug. 1838.

anxious to keep the administration of relief on as local a basis as possible, never accepted the principal of large relief districts. In addition there were many Guardians, urban as well as rural, who had quietly accepted the introduction of the new law because the concessions granted by London in 1837 seemed to imply that they would be free to administer relief as they saw fit, and who regarded any sort of outside interference even in the matter of appointments as an infringement of this discretion. Still others had more personal reasons for being obstructive. There were Guardians on every Board who had been or indeed still were overseers, who wanted to be relieving officers themselves or to give these jobs to friends and who understandably did not wish to be restricted in this large new field of patronage.

At first the Poor Law Commissioners were inclined to deal slowly and cautiously with all these problems. In some cases they could do little else. No means of breaking down the total boycott in Ashton and Oldham had yet been devised and for the time being these Unions would have to be left alone. The Todmorden situation also defied a quick solution. The opposition there had taken its case to higher courts and the witholding of rates was bound to continue until the question of the competence of the Board of Guardians could be settled once and for all. The conflicts over the appointment of personnel also proved more intractable than might have been expected. Initiative in local appointments lay with the Guardians, the Commissioners, short of issuing a peremptory order fixing relief districts, could only accept or reject what was suggested to them, and recalcitrant Boards quickly discovered that by digging in their heels they could spin out the process of negotiations for months.

For the moment at least all these problems seemed insoluble, but even where immediate action was possible there were signs late in 1838 that the Commissioners were increasingly inclined towards delay.[1] In the six Unions with Boards of Guardians but still under the Old Poor Law, the New Law could have been introduced at once, but to have done so in four of them would have involved risks that the Commissioners were no longer ready to take. In the highly charged political atmosphere of late 1838 and with the usual heavy wintertime pressure on the rates, the Guardians

[1] For the cautious policy of the P.L.C. at the end of 1838, see: HO 73.54 P.L.C. to Russell 28 Dec. 1838; MH 12.15064 P.L.C. to Floyd Oct.–Dec. 1838; MH 12.14830 Sept. 1838.

and probably the overseers as well in all four of these Unions could be expected to resist, and, in at least three of them, violent resistance was also a distinct possibility. Therefore only two Unions, Chorley and Clitheroe, neither of which had ever given the Commissioners any trouble, were put into operation between September 1838 and March 1839. The Commissioners' caution in late 1838 was even more evident in their handling of those Unions where Boards of Guardians were already in full control. In the long disputes over personnel with the Dewsbury and Huddersfield Boards, the Commissioners backed down far more readily than they need have done, giving way on such important matters as salaries and the size of relief districts in an obvious attempt to buy a little quiet.

This new-found caution on the part of the Poor Law Commissioners is understandable in view of the changing nature of their problems in dealing with the North. With the New Poor Law in effect almost everywhere, their main concern increasingly was with its normal functioning. In the atmosphere of almost perpetual crisis which had existed since early 1837 this was next to impossible, not only in the crisis centers themselves but throughout the district, as the spread of the financial boycott from Todmorden and of obstruction in the appointment of personnel beyond Huddersfield and Dewsbury made clear. Somehow or other the cycle would have to be reversed, even if necessary at the cost of conciliating the opposition in its strongholds. This at any rate was the view of the main architect of this new policy, Charles Mott, who was sent to the North as a new Assistant Commissioner in August 1838 to relieve Power of part of his enormous burden. Though no less committed than Power to the principles of the New Poor Law, he approached the problem of implementing it in an entirely different fashion. Power had never been a good conciliator, though in fairness to him it should be remembered that, as the only Assistant Commissioner in the district until the summer of 1838, he rarely had the time to deal adequately or diplomatically with all the Unions under his care. But the fact remains that he often needlessly antagonized Boards when a little sympathy and encouragement might well have assuaged their fears and doubts.

Mott was particularly critical of the way in which the North had been handled during the summer of 1838. 'It has been a sad oversight', he said, 'to declare these Unions for Poor Law matters without the possibility of attending the meetings of the Guardians.

In a district where the most ridiculous notions and the greatest possible ignorance prevails as to the principles of the New Poor Law, it is desirable of all things that only one Union should be declared at a time and constant attention be given to it until the law is explained and its principles are thoroughly understood.'[1] His role, as he saw it, was to right the damage done through the neglect of adequate preparations and supervision, and for a time his efforts seemed to be successful. Mott's main weapons were patience and an almost incurable optimism. He was always inclined to give even the most troublesome members of the most difficult Boards the benefit of the doubt and he thought nothing of spending four or five hours explaining the intentions of the Commissioners to suspicious and hostile Guardians. This, he believed, together with a willingness on the part of the Commissioners to take account of local feelings, would eventually succeed in creating the conditions for co-operation. He hoped, in short, to kill the opposition through kindness.

Many of Mott's more naïve expectations were short-lived. The opposition Guardians did not hate or insult him as they did Power, but they refused to give him anything concrete in return for the important concessions which he had won for them. Gradually during the winter he lost most of his illusions and, by January at the latest, he had come around to the view which Power had always held, that the Poor Law could be made to function in anything like the fashion envisaged in the 1834 Act only through unremitting pressure from London.[2] Mott did not, however, adopt Power's views on methods. He remained as opposed as ever to a direct assault on a number of Unions simultaneously or without adequate preparation or supervision, and he continued to believe that indirect pressure and persuasion would be far more effective in the long run than the use or threat of force. As a result the means adopted by the Commissioners for what they hoped would be a final attack on the opposition in 1839 were far subtler than anything tried before.

The first priority was to eliminate the remaining exceptions to the rule of the Poor Law in the North but the Commissioners were no longer inclined to be hasty. They decided to start by intro-

[1] MH 12.14830 Mott to P.L.C. 20 Aug 1838; see also his other letters in this file and in MH 12.15064 and MH 32.57, especially for Aug.–Oct. 1838.

[2] For Mott's gradual change of view, see his letters in MH 12.15064–5, MH 12.14830 and MH 12.5593 Dec. 1838–Jan. 1839.

ducing the law into Bolton in the early spring and, should this prove successful, then to move on to Manchester and finally to the two potentially most dangerous Unions, Bury and Rochdale. Their other main task was less straightforward and, for the long-term prospects of the Poor Law in the North, more important. Some means had to be found of ensuring the Commissioners' control in those Unions already, though often only nominally, under the law. Conciliation had failed and was abandoned. The prosecution of the Todmorden rioters and of the Huddersfield Guardians involved in the disturbances of May 1838 could be counted upon to frighten the opposition into inactivity for a while but the effect of this, or indeed of almost any direct pressure, would wear off sooner or later. A lasting change, it was agreed, could only be brought about by altering the balance of power within the Unions.

Two experiments were proposed with this aim in view. The first was an order issued by the Commissioners to a small number of the most troublesome Unions early in 1839 which placed the direction of the entire Board of Guardians election process in the hands of the Union clerk.[1] The other experiment, also limited at this time to a few Unions, involved increasing pressure from London on the Boards of Guardians to appoint a new category of Union official, the Assistant Overseer.[2] Legally such officers would be subordinate to the township overseers but, as Board of Guardians' appointees, they would be subject to orders from the Poor Law Commissioners, and they could be directed to assume the responsibility of collecting the rates. Taken together, the two orders very nearly eliminated the overseers from a major role in the conduct of the Unions' affairs and the election order had the additional advantage of ensuring that, if influence was to play a

[1] For the election order, see: Poor Law Commissioners, Sixth Annual Report, *British Parliamentary Papers*, 1840, XVII, 19 and Appendix A, No. 1. Power had some reservations about the election order, largely on the grounds that many of the Clerks were partisan appointees (MH 32.64 20 Feb. 1839).

[2] The P.L.C. favored the appointment of Assistant Overseers in the industrial districts from the very beginning and made special provision for them in the original orders issued to all northern Unions (P.L.C., Fourth Annual Report, Appendix A, No. 7). At first the Commissioners were motivated almost entirely by the desire for efficient management, but, as resistance grew, the possibility of undermining the overseers became an equally if not more important consideration. For general comments on the problem from the Assistant Commissioners see MH 32.64 17 Dec. 1838; MH 32.57 17 Dec. 1838.

part in the outcome of Boards of Guardians elections, the pre-dominant influence would be that of the Union clerks who were usually supporters of the law.

All in all, this was the most effective attack on the opposition's position yet devised by the Poor Law Commissioners; yet it was never carried out in full. This was not due to any unforeseen imperfections in the Commissioners' plans, for, in so far as they were applied, they were successful. Nor did the Commissioners decide to back away because they met unusually effective resist-ance; on the contrary, opposition to the New Poor Law was less in evidence in 1839 than at any time since before Power first arrived in the North. In part the responsibility lay with the Com-mission's internal problems, with the growing dissension between the Commissioners and their secretary, Chadwick, and with their concern to get their five-year term of office renewed. But the main cause of the Commissioners' sudden about face, as, indeed, of the unexpected absence of resistance, was the transformation of the political situation in the North in late 1838 and early 1839 as a result of the rise of Chartism.

VIII The anti-Poor Law movement and Chartism

The rise of Chartism did not begin to weaken resistance to the New Poor Law until the very end of 1838, but it had posed a serious challenge to the movement at least since May of that year, when the Charter and the National Petition were published. Moreover, even before this—as early, in fact, as the spring of 1837—there were signs of a revival of public interest in radical political reform. The anti-Poor Law movement, in common with other popular movements, was unable, even at its height, to monopolize public attention and support, and, under its shadow, other groups continued to function, if not thrive. Trade unionism, despite its disastrous reverses in 1834, managed to survive in those centers where it had been strongest and most deeply rooted. An even more interesting example of the tenacity of once-dominant movements was the continued activity of the factory reformers. Despite the fact that the anti-Poor Law agitation had siphoned off much of their leadership and, in many cases, taken over their organization as well, neither the leaders nor the old short time committees forgot their origins. Factory reform meetings were held throughout 1837 and there was even some talk of launching a new campaign in support of further legislation.[1]

But, of the issues kept alive during 1837, by far the most vital and popular was electoral reform. The great meeting at Hartshead Moor in May 1837, the culmination of the first phase of public agitation against the Poor Law, was constantly interrupted by calls for universal suffrage, and, when it ended, it was immediately re-convened under a new chairman as a radical reform meeting. But this and similar, though smaller, suffrage meetings at this time were of little immediate importance except as demonstrations of popular feeling. For one thing, the necessary organizational support was lacking. Most local radical associations were the direct descendants of groups which had been created seven or eight years before to fight for the great reform bill and which, having achieved this, had since lost much of their zeal. Many, indeed, were all but moribund and, even when they were still active, their

[1] *L.T.* 11 Nov. 1837.

predominantly middle-class leaders usually placed the extension of the franchise, if they supported it at all, well below other reforms in their list of priorities. There were exceptions. A few radical associations, for example at Bradford, were popularly led, active and ultra-radical, and others, especially in eastern Lancashire, had maintained both their middle class leadership and their commit- ment to a full radical program, including electoral reform. But these were unusual and the great majority of the radical associa- tions in the North were unwilling, at that time and for the future, to associate themselves with a new popular campaign for the extension of the suffrage.[1]

Yet, even had this not been true, it would have been virtually impossible to launch such a campaign early in 1837, for all the important popular leaders, whatever their political beliefs, were agreed that opposition to the Poor Law was and should be the primary object of agitation, and that energy should not be diverted into other channels. Fielden pointed this out to the universal suffrage hecklers at Hartshead Moor and, at the separate radical meeting held later that same day, it was eventually decided to disband in the interests of maintaining a united front. Other suffrage meetings that spring came to much the same conclusion and, since neither the factory reform committees, nor any of the important radical associations questioned the primacy of the anti- Poor Law struggle, there seemed little likelihood of a rival agitation developing in the near future.[2]

There the situation remained until the late summer and early autumn of 1837, when, quite suddenly, there was a great increase in radical political activity in the North. Significantly, the main impetus for this development came from outside the area. Two separate and competing influences were involved. One was the arrival in the North of missionaries from the London Working- men's Association; the other was Feargus O'Connor's drive to establish himself firmly in a position of leadership in the North. The former led very rapidly to the formation of Workingmen's Associations on the London model in most of the major centers of Lancashire, the West Riding and the North-east, while the latter ended in the creation of the *Northern Star* and of an O'Connorite sphere of influence in Leeds. All of this could not have happened,

---

[1] For the active radical associations, see: *L.T.* Aug.–Sept. 1837 (for Bradford); *M.S.A.* 21 July, 23 Sept., 21 Oct. 1837 (for Rochdale, Ashton, Oldham, Bury).   [2] *L.I.*, *L.T.*, *M.S.A.* May–June 1837.

or so it appeared, at a worse time for the anti-Poor Law movement. The Parliamentary elections of 1837 had diverted attention from the Poor Law, there had been no dramatic confrontations with the Commissioners since the June riot at Huddersfield, and there had been almost no public anti-Poor Law meetings during the summer. O'Connor and the Londoners stepped into what therefore seemed to be a political vacuum and, while all of them supported opposition to the New Poor Law, their main interest and the chief purpose of the institutions which they founded at this time, was to further political reform.[1]

It was not yet time, however, for political radicalism to replace the Poor Law as the focus for public agitation in the North. The first attempts of the Poor Law Commissioners to introduce the law itself into the North and, still more, the series of riots at Bradford changed the situation almost overnight. There was an immediate revival of public interest in the Poor Law and of public support for the resistance to it, which very rapidly outstripped what O'Connor and the missionaries from London had achieved for political radicalism in the previous two months. And the emerging radical movement, far from attempting to fight against this tide, voluntarily swam with it. The ultra-radical press, and especially the *Northern Star*, gave far more coverage at this time to Poor Law developments than to any other subject, and the Workingmen's Associations, like the older Radical Associations and Short Time Committees before them, devoted the greater part of their time to aiding the anti-Poor Law movement until well into 1838.[2]

This did not mean that the *Northern Star* or the Workingmen's Associations abandoned the cause which they had been founded primarily to serve; radical activity was not allowed to peter out as it had before its revival in the fall of 1837. But most of the leaders of the new radicalism were still active in opposition to the New Poor Law and many of them held important posts in the anti-Poor Law organization. They did not found the Workingmen's Associations in order to supersede the Anti-Poor Law Associations and they did not regard the two movements as rivals. Over the long run certainly, many, perhaps most, of them believed that political

[1] *L.T.*, *M.S.A.* Aug.–Oct. 1837.
[2] *N.S.*, *M.S.A.* Nov.–Dec. 1837. From December onwards, the *M.S.A.* devoted a separate column in each issue to 'Anti-Poor Law Intelligence'.

reform was the more important cause, but which of the two should be given priority in the short run was another question entirely. And, in the winter of 1837-8, when the Poor Law Commissioners were actually handing over control of the administration of relief to the Boards of Guardians, the argument that resistance to the Poor Law must have priority over all other activities had even more force than in the previous spring. Agitation for universal suffrage, or, indeed, for shorter hours or any other positive reforms, could be undertaken at almost any time and could, therefore, be put off. But, if the Poor Law was not opposed at this stage, the chance of ever doing so effectively would probably be lost. Thus, so long as there was any hope of victory or even of a major advance, the anti-Poor Law organization could count on a continuation of the unanimous backing it had had from every sort of popular group ever since the beginning of 1837.

When, however, the winter campaign failed either to stop the implementation of the Poor Law in the North or to win a respectable showing for Fielden's repeal motion in Parliament, a sharp divergence of opinion emerged almost immediately within the anti-Poor Law movement. Fielden, Stephens, Oastler, Richardson, Fletcher and many others did not regard these setbacks as irreparable. New means, they believed, could be found to keep regional agitation going and, in any case, there were still the local Boards of Guardians elections to be fought. To them, obviously, the need for single-minded concentration on opposition to the Poor Law was as great, if not greater, than ever. But many political radicals within the movement interpreted the situation very differently. On March 24, the *Northern Star* declared editorially that the defeat of Fielden's motion was incontrovertible proof that no amount of popular agitation could save the North from the New Poor Law, that the source of the evil was Parliament, and that only through reforming Parliament could the evil be eradicated. This editorial and resolutions to much the same effect passed at Workingmen's Association meetings held with increasing frequency during March did not advocate abandoning the struggle against the Poor Law. Radical reformism and opposition to the law were still treated as complementary movements and of the two it was, if anything, the latter which retained the advantage in public favor. At least until the end of March, anti-Poor Law meetings were larger and more frequent than radical meetings, the *Northern Star* and the Workingmen's Associations devoted much of their time and energy to helping the anti-Poor Law organization in the Board of Guardians election campaign, and no advocate of universal suffrage omitted to declare that he supported it in large part because it was the only sure means of destroying the New Poor Law.[1]

But soon thereafter the situation began to change rapidly and entirely to the benefit of the growing radical movement. The disappointingly inconclusive results of the Boards of Guardians elections seemed to confirm the radicals' pessimism about the future of the anti-Poor Law movement and during the next three months, when, in any case, there was hardly any activity on the Poor Law front, the attraction of the apparently much more promising universal suffrage campaign became almost irresistible. Inevitably, this process began to affect attitudes not only towards the anti-Poor Law movement but, after a time, towards the Poor Law itself, which, for the first time since the end of 1836 seemed to be losing some of its potency as a great public issue. The successive disappointments of the anti-Poor Law movement and the lack of any dramatic developments during the spring of 1838 were undoubtedly the main reasons why this happened, but, ironically, the limited successes of the movement contributed to the process. The New Poor Law could never of course have lived up to its much advertised horrors, but the watering down of the law in the North and the Poor Law Commissioners' caution in introducing it made its actual administration seem to be very much like the Old Poor Law. In any case, by late June, having already lost its status as the most important single issue in northern popular politics, the Poor Law was no longer necessarily being treated as even the ultimate in arguments for political reform. Increasingly there was a tendency to place it alongside other issues in the standard list of government iniquities which was used to prove the need for a democratic franchise and only the Poor Law's place at the head of this long list attested to its former importance.[2]

This rapid shift in northern opinion did not take place in isolation; as in the case of the first tentative advances towards a new radical movement some eight or nine months before, it was pushed along by outside pressures. And this external influence, though less direct in the spring of 1838, was even harder to ignore than it had been in the fall of 1837. Then the London radicals had sought to

[1] *N.S., M.S.A.* late March–early April 1838.
[2] *Ibid.* late April–June 1838.

affect the course of events in the North through what amounted to missionary activity. Their efforts, measured by the number of Workingmen's Associations that had been founded, had been remarkably successful. But it was a distinctly limited success in that, almost as soon as they had left, the North once again became absorbed in its own affairs. In 1838, on the other hand, the situation was entirely different. There was no need to send envoys to the North in order to influence northern affairs; developments in other regions were of such importance that they demanded attention. In the intervening months the Charter and the National Petition had been published, preparations for a National Convention had been begun and the first of the great Chartist meetings had been held at Glasgow. And all this had been done by London and Birmingham radicals, entirely without reference to northern leaders. The North, not so long ago the unchallenged center of popular unrest, appeared to be in serious danger of being left behind.

For the first time northern leaders were forced to re-assess their activities in the light of national developments and one of the effects of this was to reinforce the already growing tendency to look beyond the anti-Poor Law agitation and put it in perspective. The unpleasant thought that the Poor Law, far from being a central issue, was only a peripheral one occurred to more than one popular leader at this time. Indeed, once they had begun to put it in context, many Northerners became more than a little self-conscious and defensive about how much time and energy they had expended in fighting the law. The *Northern Star*, as usual, very accurately reflected the new attitudes. 'The London Journals', it wrote,

are in error when they suppose that, in the North, all agitation is directed against the New Poor Law Amendment Act. No; but it is the basis of a new constitution, and therefore do we work the battering ram of discontent against it. Its provisions are to give effect to the new system of the political economists and to the new religion of the . . . infidels; and therefore do we denounce it. The auxiliaries to this infernal law are the Factory scheme, the rural police, and the complete destruction of Trades' Associations, which was the last remnant of power in the hands of the working classes by which supply and demand could be wholesomely regulated.[1]

Nonetheless, anxious though the northern Chartists now were to treat the New Poor Law as only one among the evil results of

[1] *N.S.* 23 June 1838.

the 'new constitution', events ensured that for the time being at least it would continue to be considered as by far the most important of these evils, and that organized resistance to it on a regional scale would not be allowed to die away. The near-riot in Todmorden in early July and the riots in Dewsbury a month later gave the anti-Poor Law movement a new lease on life. O'Connor, who had long been moving away from active involvement in Poor Law affairs, re-entered the battle at Dewsbury. Oastler, who had been inactive throughout much of the spring and early summer because of serious illness and a dispute with his employer which was soon to end with Oastler's bankruptcy and the loss of his job as steward of Fixby Hall, made his first public appearance for some time late in July. Newspaper coverage of Poor Law developments, relatively slim since the Board of Guardians elections in late March, was increased again, almost to the point of equalling the space devoted to political radicalism. And the number of meetings held under anti-Poor Law committee auspices rose once more, for the first time since the failure of Fielden's repeal motion in February.[1]

But it did not last. Circumstances and the order of priorities in northern political life had changed too much. Even at the height of the trouble in Huddersfield, Dewsbury and Todmorden, Chartist meetings, the extension of Chartist organization and preparations for the Chartists' autumn campaign still took precedence in the textile districts as a whole. The return of radical leaders to anti-Poor Law activity was at most a side-trip, and particularly so for O'Connor, who had finally achieved his ambition of leading northern Chartism, through the establishment of the Great Northern Union in June. Moreover, the outcome of this sudden flare-up over the Poor Law only served to confirm the already widely held view that resistance to the law was bound to fail. The most that the opposition could claim was that it had prevented the Commissioners from gaining a clear-cut victory in a handful of Poor Law Unions, which was hardly the equal of what Chartism claimed to offer its supporters.

Understandably then, the Poor Law crisis of July and August 1838, far from leading to a lasting revival of the anti-Poor Law movement, as similar circumstances had in the autumn of 1837, was followed by an abrupt and almost complete cessation of anti-Poor

[1] Compare *M.S.A.* and *N.S.* of early July with the same newspapers during August.

Law activity. This decline was no longer merely relative as it had been earlier in the year. Separate anti-Poor Law meetings did not simply decrease; they all but ceased. And, while it is true that the Poor Law was invoked at the mass meetings of late 1838, this was done as a matter of form, almost as a ritual. As a distinct issue, the Poor Law was very nearly dead.

At this point only one step remained in the gradual demotion of the Poor Law from its former position, the castigation of opposition to it as detrimental to the Chartist cause. This was not long in coming. From early September onwards, a new theme began to appear in radical speeches. The people were warned not to let any other issue divert them from the one great goal from which all else would follow, universal suffrage. At first this was put forward entirely by those who had always been political radicals first and anti-Poor Law men second. By the end of the month, however, this was no longer true. Fielden, who had been one of the first to insist on the primacy of the Poor Law in 1837 and stuck to this view well into 1838, perhaps set the seal on the process. At the great meeting on Kersal Moor in Lancashire on September 24 he warned the people that,

All manner of devices will be resorted to, in order to sow divisions amongst you. One will tell you that you should have a factory bill,—a short time bill; another that you should have a repeal of the poor law; another will be for a repeal of the corn laws; another for a minimum of wages for the hand-loom weavers; and another will promise you all you want, if you'll only avoid asking for the suffrage. My advice is, to disregard all applications to you to divert you from your object. Keep to this one single point . . . The suffrage, and the suffrage only, should satisfy the working people of England.[1]

For Fielden and most of those like him who had been deeply committed to fighting the Poor Law in the North, such statements did not mean quite what they implied. They were not ready to abandon opposition to the Poor Law, particularly on a local level in those few Unions where really stiff resistance could easily be mounted. Fielden, for example, continued to play a central role in Todmorden's opposition to the Poor Law long after he made this speech. His intention in speaking as he had at Kersal Moor was to ensure that opposition to the Poor Law, even where it was continued, should not be allowed to detract from the support given to

[1] *M.S.A.* 29 Sept. 1838.

Chartism. There were some, however, even among the top leadership of the anti-Poor Law movement, who went much further than this and demanded the complete abandonment of active resistance, as both futile in itself and likely to distract attention from the all-important Chartist movement. A number of northern radicals adopted this view in the final months of 1838 but by far the most important single defector was R. J. Richardson, the President of the South Lancashire Anti-Poor Law Association.[1] No movement could survive such setbacks and, by early 1839 at the latest, organized resistance to the Poor Law on a regional scale, and to a large extent locally as well, had ceased to be of any importance. Chartism as a cause and as a popular movement at last held the field unchallenged.

Perhaps the most interesting thing about the political changes which led to this conclusion was how very gradual they were. On the basis of past experience, it would have been reasonable to assume that, once the chances of victory in the anti-Poor Law struggle had been reduced almost to the point of being non-existent by the early successes of the Commissioners and the failure of Fielden's repeal motion, there would have been an immediate and wholesale desertion to some other cause. This, after all, is what had happened late in 1836, when the factory reform campaign ran into a dead end. And, just as there had been a new issue, the Poor Law, to turn to then, so, in early 1838, there was an old issue in a new guise, political reform, to fall back upon. Some radicals, led by O'Connor and the *Northern Star*, sought to do so. Yet, in spite of their efforts, it was not until some seven or eight months later that Chartism was able to claim the same sort of hold on northern political life that the anti-Poor Law movement had achieved in a matter of one or two months.

In part the difference can be explained by certain peculiar characteristics of the anti-Poor Law movement. It could not, as other popular movements could, develop at its own pace. Initiative lay with the Poor Law Commissioners and the opposition had to respond at critical moments or not at all. The sudden shift of attention from factory reform to the Poor Law had been as much imposed upon the northern popular leaders by Alfred Power's arrival in the North, as chosen by them because the factory reform campaign was running into trouble. And, once committed to the

[1] Driver, *Tory Radical*, 395–6.

anti-Poor Law movement, these same leaders found abandoning it in favor of Chartism very difficult for much the same reason. On every occasion when a new move by the Commissioners was opposed by a mob or a refractory Board of Guardians, even those, like O'Connor, who would have preferred to concentrate on political reform were honor bound to return to anti-Poor Law activity at least for the moment and would perhaps have risked losing popular support if they had not done so.

Nonetheless, even had these special circumstances not applied, the course of development would very likely have been similar. For, while opposition to the new Poor Law was immediately endorsed by all the groups which had been involved in the factory reform campaign, the rise of Chartism was resisted and to some extent delayed by a few of the most important leaders of the anti-Poor Law movement. Resistance to the Poor Law was always regarded as closely linked to the ten hours agitation and even as an extension of it. One movement sought to enhance, the other to preserve, the security and welfare of the industrial worker, and for both movements the enemy, the *laisser faire* theory of society and the industrial middle class with which such ideas were most closely identified, was the same. Therefore it was possible for the peculiar alliance between renegade Tories and Radical workingmen, which had been founded to fight for factory reform, to carry on intact into the anti-Poor Law agitation. Chartism, on the other hand, introduced the one issue, an extension of the suffrage, on which the alliance was bound to break down, and the Conservative element in the alliance, threatened with exclusion, understandably fought against it. But it was not only politically conservative, anti-Chartist factory reformers and Poor Law opponents who were reluctant in 1838 to abandon the anti-Poor Law movement and with it Radical–Conservative co-operation. Many northern radicals were no less committed to its preservation and many others, who were not, hesitated to speak out openly against it.

The strength of the alliance derived in part simply from age and familiarity. The Short Time Committees of the West Riding had first sought the help of Conservative factory reformers as early as 1830 and, while relations between them had been strained during periods when political reform or trade unionism were dominant issues, the periodic revivals of the factory reform campaign followed by the agitation against the New Poor Law, meant that the alliance was never actually dissolved, only temporarily suspended.

By the end of 1837 it had come to seem one of the permanent and characteristic features of northern political life. There was, moreover, a personal factor which tended to perpetuate the alliance. Oastler, Bull, Sadler, before his death in 1835, and finally Stephens had been able to win a popular following which no political radical before O'Connor could match. In such circumstances, there was a tendency to play down those differences which persisted between them and the rank and file. And, in any case, these differences were far smaller than they had once been, for, in the seven years since the beginning of the decade, the conservatism of the Tory element in the alliance, never orthodox, had changed out of all recognition.[1]

Initially they had assumed that the landed interest was the natural ally of the working classes against the factory owners and their financial allies, and that all that was needed to win it and, for that matter, the bulk of the electorate to factory reform was revelation of the real conditions of industrial employment. But such illusions were soon shattered, first by the long delays that preceded legislation and then by the unsatisfactory nature of the factory act which was eventually passed in 1833. Bad as this was, the New Poor Law, passed less than a year later, was worse, for it seemed to confirm what the failure to pass adequate factory legislation implied, that the propertied classes as a whole were unwilling to assume any responsibility for the welfare of the mass of the population. Indeed, if, as the Conservative opponents of the law, following on Cobbett, assumed, the poor had an historical right through labor or relief to, as they put it, a first mortgage on the land, then the New Poor Law was not merely an act of selfish indifference by the owners of property, but the unilateral abrogation by them of a social contract.

For the Conservative opponents of the law, the implications of this were enormous and frightening. 'Having cancelled this first Mortgage by this Amendment Act,' said Bull, speaking of Lord Brougham who had piloted the bill through the upper house, 'I am at a loss to know, how he can secure the second Mortgagee [the landlord] or any other claimants, to the possession of their right.'[2] In other words, the owners of property could not free themselves from the obligations traditionally and legally imposed on property

---

[1] Perhaps the best general treatment of the origins and nature of this alliance is in Driver, *Tory Radical*, Chs. VIII and XXIX. See also: Cole, *Chartist Portraits*, Chs. II and III.

[2] G. S. Bull, *The Poor Law Act* (Bradford 1834), 1.

without, at the same time, undermining the prerogatives of owner-
ship. And what was true of property could be, and was, extended
to political life as well. By using their power to deprive a portion
of the people of their rights, in this case the right to relief,
the governing classes of England, so Cobbett, Oastler and Bull
believed, forfeited their claim to respect, deference and even perhaps loyalty from the unenfranchised mass of the population. Thus
it was possible for Oastler, a Tory, to declare proudly, 'he will be
the greatest patriot who can produce the greatest dissatisfaction.
And I will strive to be that man.'[1]

Oastler and Bull had arrived at this position as early as 1834, at
the time of the passage of the Poor Law Amendment Act, and only
a reversal of the trend of government policy would have led them
to alter their views. But there was no such reversal of government
policy. New factory legislation was not passed, even the unsatisfactory 1833 factory act was endangered, and the implementation
of the New Poor Law was pushed forward. Bull, Oastler and now
Stephens were therefore led into taking an increasingly extremist
position. The first sign of this was Oastler's threat to resort to
sabotage if the factory act was not enforced but it was the constant
frustrations of the anti-Poor Law agitation which led them to spell
out in detail the often extraordinarily radical practical implications
of their social and political theories. Bull's warning to the propertied classes to look to their obligations was transformed by
Oastler into a threat of social upheaval. 'I do not wish', he said,
'to shake the present title to private property—but it does appear
to me, that, if the poor are to be deprived of their original share of
their natural and legal right in the soil—then that all title to
property must cease, and we must revert to the only original right
of tenure—"Sweating and Tilling".'[2] And Oastler's early promise
to fight the government which passed such a law became, in
Stephens' hands, a declaration of war on all authority.

I have never acknowledged the authority of the New Poor Law, and
so help me God I never will. I have never paid any rates under it,
and so help me God I never will—they may take all but my wife, my
child and my life, but pay one penny I never will . . . I exhort you
and all others to do the same. I do not mean to flinch. I will recommend nothing which I will not do. I will tell you that if they attempt to
carry into effect this damnable law, I MEAN TO FIGHT. I will lay aside

[1] R. Oastler, *Eight Letters to the Duke of Wellington* (London 1835),
102–3.   [2] *N.S.* 16 June 1838.

the black coat for the red, and with the bible in one hand—and a sword in the other—so help me the God that made me—I will fight to the death sooner than that law shall be brought into operation on me, or on others with my consent or through my silence. So help me God, I and the northern men with whom I act will shake England to the center sooner than see this treason established as the law of England. Perish trade and manufacture—perish arts, literature and science—perish palace, throne and altar—if they can only stand upon the dissolution of the marriage tie, the annihilation of every domestic affection, and the violent and most brutal oppression ever yet practised upon the poor of any country in all the world![1]

Yet, extreme though they were in their sentiments, Bull, Oastler and Stephens were not radicals, at least not by the usual definition of that term. They did not believe that political reform could bring any closer the eradication of those evils in society against which they were fighting. At best it seemed irrelevant. '[My] knowledge of the actual conditions of the people', Stephens wrote, 'compared with their acknowledged rights and privileges . . ., brought me to the conclusion, that there was something so radically unsound in the existing state of things, that no abstract theory, no mere change in the framework of our outward institutions, could reach, much less remedy or remove it.'[2] Bull, Oastler and Stephens as well to some extent went even further and dismissed universal suffrage as not only irrelevant but wrong. The people, they believed, were not ready for it and, despite all their talk of social and political upheaval, they had no wish to strike at the roots of English society or government or even to make the propertied and ruling classes of England directly answerable to the mass of the population. On the contrary, they hoped to secure the traditional class and political structure by compelling its wealthier and more powerful elements to assume responsibility for the welfare of the population as a whole. And it was only when persuasion failed to achieve this that they turned to predictions and finally to threats of disaster in the desperate hope of bringing the ruling classes to their senses.

The gulf between these attitudes and the political views of the out and out radicals was, of course, unbridgeable, but this hardly mattered in 1837, or indeed, until well into 1838. As long as political reform was not in itself a major issue, as long, for that

[1] J. R. Stephens, *Three Sermons Preached by the Rev. J. R. Stephens* (London 1839), 16.
[2] *N.S.* 22 Dec. 1838.

matter, as any issue other than universal suffrage took precedence, the area of agreement was so much greater than the area of disagreement, that the latter could safely be ignored. Fielden, in his appeal to radicals not to talk of electoral reform at the Hartshead Moor meeting in May 1837, set the tone for the remainder of the year. As well as urging the primacy of the Poor Law at that time, he noted that to raise the suffrage issue would lead to the alienation of valuable allies. And, at the separate electoral reform meeting which followed, it was agreed to drop the subject on the grounds that, for the time being at least, the Poor Law and unity in opposition to it were of greater importance.

Some radicals believed that the alliance should be carried beyond such negative co-operation and in the 1837 Parliamentary election, for example, the radical workingman of Huddersfield supported Oastler's candidacy. This extension of the alliance into politics was, however, too much for many radicals even in 1837. Peter Bussey wrote an open letter to the Huddersfield radicals castigating them for backing a man 'whose political principles if acted upon would place us in a similar position to that from which we have barely emerged and on which we cannot look back without feelings of abhorrence'.[1] At first the Huddersfield radicals refused to answer Bussey, dismissing his views as merely those of an individual. But Bussey was not alone. He got his local Radical Association to back him up and received the support of the West Riding's leading radical newspaper, the *Leeds Times*. Nevertheless, the Huddersfield radicals almost certainly spoke for a wider public when, eventually, they did answer Bussey's charges. They admitted that Oastler called himself a Tory and that his views on political reform were not their own. But surely, they argued, this was more than outweighed by his opposition to the Poor Law, taxes on newspapers, an uncontrolled factory system and numerous other social evils. In comparison with such a man, how, they asked, could Bussey prefer sham radicals who said all the right things about the suffrage but knew nothing about northern problems and cared less about their solution?

Throughout the remainder of 1837 this was an unanswerable question and, after a few weeks of trying to keep the dispute going, Bussey retired into silence. But the point which Bussey had tried in vain to make in the late summer of 1837 was made for him by

[1] *L.T.* 12 Aug. 1837. For the remainder of the controversy, see succeeding issues through October.

events some six months later. The unwillingness of the Conservative leaders in the North to accept political reform, which had seemed so unimportant as long as resistance to the Poor Law promised to be successful, could no longer be ignored or glossed over once it had become clear that the anti-Poor Law movement, fighting alone, was almost certain to fail. After February 1838, therefore, the advocates of a Radical–Conservative alliance were permanently on the defensive and left with little room for maneuver. They could elect to fall in with those who, like O'Connor and Bussey, had long since come to the conclusion that political reform provided the only answer, and gradually even those radicals who had been most closely associated with Oastler, Bull and Stephens did so. But for the Conservatives this was unthinkable. Indeed, only two alternatives remained open to them: to try to re-invigorate the anti-Poor Law movement, which meant, in practice, moving it even closer to violence, or to retire.

Bull, and with him probably a majority of Conservative opponents of the Poor Law, opted for retirement.[1] In fact, Bull, perhaps foreseeing that the anti-Poor Law movement was bound either to move towards violence or to be diverted into political agitation, had begun to pull out as early as the summer of 1837. He had always been more cautious and less comfortable in the alliance with radicals than either Oastler or Stephens. The Huddersfield riot in June 1837, the revival of political radicalism in the autumn and the reckless speeches of Oastler, Stephens and O'Connor during the winter campaign of 1837–8 probably frightened him in much the same way that the linking of the factory reform movement to trade unionism or Oastler's threats of industrial sabotage some years before had frightened him. This did not mean that he abandoned opposition to the Poor Law, for he continued to appear at anti-Poor Law meetings throughout the winter. But more and more he acted as a restraining influence. He abandoned the leading role he had played earlier in the year in the often turbulent resistance movements at Bradford and Colne and most of his speeches were concerned with emphasizing the need for legality. Clearly he was unwilling to associate himself in any way with a movement which tended towards violence or was even partially politically oriented and, once it became clear that resistance to the Poor Law was moving irretrievably in one or other of these directions, that is by

[1] Gill, *Ten Hours Parson*, Chs. XIII and XVI; MH 12.5673 Power to P.L.C. 5 Dec. 1837.

the early spring of 1838, Bull quietly disassociated himself from any public part in it.

Oastler and Stephens were not quite so squeamish or so ready to allow the leadership of northern protest to slip from their hands. They made every effort to keep the anti-Poor Law movement alive in the gloomy period after the defeat of Fielden's repeal motion. Oastler, backed by Stephens, proposed having northern leaders called to the bar of the House of Commons to plead their cause in person, and the continued resistance in Huddersfield and the riots at Dewsbury were due very largely to their unceasing agitation. But they were fighting a losing battle. Only a decisive victory over the Poor Law Commissioners or, at least, a sign that their confidence was cracking would have been sufficient to revive the anti-Poor Law movement at this late date and resistance along familiar lines was demonstrably incapable of bringing these things about. Only something new and dramatic would suffice and, during the summer of 1838, Oastler and Stephens at last hit upon a device which they believed might work, the arming of the people. They launched their call to arms in July and August, at a time when public interest in the Poor Law had been temporarily renewed by the crises at Todmorden, Salford, Huddersfield and Dewsbury, and the opportunity of reversing the drift away from the anti-Poor Law movement towards Chartism once again seemed open, if only a strong lead could be provided.[1]

But for all the brave talk, there was little of substance in Oastler's and Stephens' advocacy of arming. They never defined their purpose. A rising was impracticable and neither Oastler nor Stephens dared advocate it in any case. They seem to have conceived of arming as a way for the working classes to demonstrate that they would be oppressed no longer and as a warning to the government, but even this is not clear. They were, in short, bluffing and their bluff did not work. The Poor Law Commissioners were not put off even momentarily and the call to arms, far from recouping the mass following of the anti-Poor Law movement, was almost immediately absorbed into the omnivorous program of northern Chartism. To Oastler this came as the final blow, for he was already on the verge of disaster in his personal life. Still suffering from the effects of his illness, he had also fallen out with his employer

---

[1] Stephens seems to have first mentioned arming in late May or early June (*N.S.* 9 June 1838). The campaign reached its height in August (Oastler's 'Letters to the People' in *N.S.* of Aug.).

over the New Poor Law and was about to be thrown out of his home and job and into a long legal dispute about debts incurred during his stewardship of Fixby Hall. In his speeches and articles of August and September 1838 the old jauntiness, confidence and bite flashed through only occasionally; the dominant mood was grim pessimism and self pity. It is hard to escape the conclusion that he turned to arming the people not only because he was now more than half convinced that nothing could deflect England's rulers from their present course but also in one last desperate attempt to salvage something from the wreckage of his public career. When this failed to have any effect, he had neither the faith nor the will to fight on, and soon after leaving Fixby Hall, he left the North as well.[1]

Of the Conservative leaders of the factory reform and anti-Poor Law movements only Stephens now remained active. But he was at the height of his powers and, in any case, far more flexible in his ideas and far more willing to improvise than Oastler. When it became clear, as it had by late August 1838, that the anti-Poor Law movement had no future apart from Chartism, Stephens did not even consider retiring, but adjusted himself accordingly. This did not mean that he became a Chartist in the ordinary sense. He still believed that universal suffrage was of little relevance to a solution of the social problems of the North. What interested him was not the Charter itself but what it symbolized. As he saw it,

The question of Universal Suffrage is a knife and fork question after all. The question of Universal Suffrage is a bread and cheese question, after all. If any man asks me what I mean by Universal Suffrage, I tell him I mean that every workingman in the land has a right to have a good coat upon his back, a good roof for the shelter of his household, a good dinner upon his table, and no more work than will keep him in health, whilst at it and as much wages as will keep him in plenty and in the enjoyment of all the pleasures of life which a reasonable man can desire.[2]

As long as it was possible for him to treat Chartism in these terms, as essentially a continuation, under whatever name, of the social protest movements of the early and middle 1830s, he could go along with it and even play a leading role. Indeed, he felt duty bound not to drop out in order that he might keep northern Chartism close to its origins in the factory reform and anti-Poor

[1] *N.S.* Sept. 1838; Driver, *Tory Radical*, Ch. XXVIII.
[2] *M.S.A.* 29 Sept. 1838.

Law movements. He appeared at every one of the great torchlight meetings held in Lancashire and the West Riding during the winter months of 1838 and he even allowed himself to be appointed as a delegate to the Chartist National Convention, but he never failed to make it clear that his support for Chartism was primarily support for social protest and he always emphasized the need to keep all forms of protest, and especially the anti-Poor Law movement, in being.

How this peculiar relationship with Chartism would have developed during 1839 we do not, unhappily, know, for Stephens was arrested in December 1838, thus becoming the first of the Chartist martyrs. His arrest did not end his public activities. He continued to speak at meetings in the North and elsewhere, and also to write for the radical press. But he gave up his seat in the Chartist Convention and abandoned, permanently as it turned out, a central role in the movement. This might well have happened even had he not been arrested, for, despite his efforts in late 1838, active resistance to the Poor Law even on a local level continued to decline as the focus of Chartist activity shifted away from the North to London, the Convention and the interminable debates over ulterior measures. This was not a change to which Stephens could easily have accommodated himself and throughout 1839 he continued to speak and write of Chartism in the same terms he had used the previous year. 'I don't care about your Charter,' he wrote in June,

it may be all very right; it may be all very good; you have a right to it mind you, and I will stand by you in it; but I don't care about it; and I don't care about a republic . . . I don't care about a monarchy; I don't care about the present, or any other order of things, unless the Charter, the republic, the monarchy, the present order of things, or any other order of things that may be brought to succeed the present, should, first of all, and above all, and through all, secure to every son of the soil, to every living being of the human race . . . a full, a sufficient, and a comfortable maintenance, according to the will and commandment of God.[1]

This might have been acceptable in the North even in 1839, but it would not have been acceptable to the Chartist Convention, and it is very likely that during 1839 Stephens would have been driven, or would himself have elected, to assume the role of outside commentator and critic that had been forced on him by his arrest. This

[1] Quoted from the London Democrat in Cole, *Chartist Portraits*, 73–4.

in fact is what did happen to a number of northern Chartists recruited from the anti-Poor Law movement. One of these, Matthew Fletcher, a member of the Convention, even went so far as to suggest that the agitation for universal suffrage had been got up by the Whigs as a way of diverting the North from the anti-Poor Law campaign.[1] There is no reason to believe that Stephens accepted this far-fetched theory, but unquestionably he did share Fletcher's disillusionment with Chartism and his regret that the rise of Chartism had meant the extinction of a cause which they both believed was far more representative of the real interests of the North.

The last direct links between Chartism and the radical Tories of the North had finally been broken, but, though Bull, Oastler, Stephens, Fletcher and a few others had failed to preserve the anti-Poor Law movement against or even within Chartism, their efforts had not been wasted. They had managed to keep popular agitation against the Poor Law going far longer than would otherwise have been the case and in the process they had profoundly influenced the nature of northern Chartism. In many respects, to be sure, the influence of the anti-Poor Law movement on Chartism would have been much the same with or without the intervention of Bull, Oastler and Stephens. All the northern delegates to the Chartist Convention—O'Connor, Pitkeithly, Bussey, Fletcher, Richardson, James Taylor—and all the important local leaders of northern Chartism as well came out of the anti-Poor Law movement.

This alone would probably be enough to account for the obvious links between the two movements in organization and tactics, and there is no reason to suppose that these links would have been any weaker if active resistance to the Poor Law had been abandoned at the beginning instead of at the end of 1838. What the persistence of the anti-Poor Law movement into late 1838 contributed was something less tangible but no less important, a political climate. The mass demonstrations and riots or near riots which broke out or threatened to break out throughout the year ensured that northern Chartism, unlike southern or midland Chartism, would grow up in an atmosphere of perpetual crisis and potential violence. At the same time Oastler's and Stephens' constant search for new and ever more dramatic ways of keeping the anti-Poor Law movement alive opened the way for the early adoption of extremist

[1] *N.S.* 19 Oct. 1839.

N

opinions by all the northern radical leaders. Without this precedent it is unlikely that O'Connor would have introduced the subject of arming to national Chartist audiences as early as August 1838 or that the northern delegates to the Chartist Convention would have arrived in London in February 1839 already talking of ulterior measures. This speeding up of the radicalization of northern Chartism meant that, from the moment that the various local varieties of Chartism came together in one national movement early in 1839, northern Chartism, and to some extent through its influence the movement as a whole, was identified with physical force. For this the anti-Poor Law movement and above all, ironically, its two greatest, and anti-Chartist, leaders were largely responsible.

IX The Commissioners mark time

The rise of Chartism did not have an appreciable effect on the activities of either side in the Poor Law controversy until the beginning of 1839. The survival of organized resistance right through 1838 was paralleled by an almost complete lack of concern on the part of the Poor Law Commissioners with the possible effect of Chartism on their plans. If anything, the Commissioners initially welcomed the rise of this new movement. It diverted public attention from the Poor Law and led to the retirement of a number of their most troublesome opponents. With increasing conviction, the Commissioners began to look upon the elaborate plans devised by them in late 1838 and early 1839, not merely as preparations for yet another round in the familiar struggle, but as the prelude to a final victory in the North.[1]

To some extent their optimism was justified. The Bolton Union was put into operation in March and, though this was resisted by a hard core of anti-Poor Law Guardians, their efforts were not echoed or supported from outside, as would almost certainly have been the case a year or more before.[2] Later in the same month the Commissioners made an even more substantial advance in the Boards of Guardians elections. A number of the most recalcitrant Unions, including both Huddersfield and Dewsbury, returned pro-Poor Law majorities and in townships throughout the area, though not in Ashton, Oldham and Todmorden, boycotts were abandoned or broken. How much these successes were due to the new election procedure, it is impossible to say. Mott was enthusiastic about its effects and, in a number of cases, particularly in the most important one of all, Huddersfield, his enthusiasm was almost certainly justified. But the election order applied in only a handful of Unions, while the Commissioners made gains throughout the area, and in the textile districts as a whole the most important single factor behind this dramatic change of fortune was the almost complete absence of an organized opposition election campaign.

[1] MH 12.5593 Mott to P.L.C. 19 March 1839.
[2] *Ibid.* March 1839 correspondence.

The anti-Poor Law committee structure was already beginning to disintegrate by the time of the elections and the leaders of the movement had long since moved on to other questions and other places. Oastler and Bull were in semi-retirement, Stephens was soon to follow and O'Connor, Pitkeithly, Bussey, Richardson and Fletcher were all in London attending the Chartist National Convention. Public interest had also waned. There seem to have been fewer contests for seats on the Boards than in previous years and the press devoted comparatively little space to the elections. For the first time, the Boards of Guardians in the textile districts had been chosen in normal conditions.[1] In effect, the machinery of the New Poor Law had at long last been accepted in the North and the way now appeared to be open for the Poor Law Commissioners to clear away the remaining anomalies and start on the far more difficult task of introducing their relief policies.

But the Commissioners did not follow up their successes. Bolton, far from being the first of a number of Unions placed under the Poor Law in 1839, was also the last and the Commissioners' substantial victories in the Board of Guardians elections did not lead to the expected rapid changes in relief policy. Probably the main reason for this was the political situation in the North. The torchlight meetings and the arming and drilling of Chartist units late in 1838 led many in the North to expect a popular rising at some time in the following year and a series of crises in 1839 kept these expectations alive until the early months of 1840. Trouble was first anticipated for May, on the date when the Charter was originally to have been submitted to Parliament. May passed quietly but fears were again aroused by the prospect of a general strike in support of the Charter in August. Once again little happened. The Chartists themselves called off the general strike and, though there were a number of stoppages and a few attempts to widen their scope, the strike movement of 1839 did not come near to getting out of hand. No sooner was this cause for panic passed, however, than another took its place, this time in the form of rumors of a national rising scheduled for the end of the year. As before, anticipation proved to be far worse than the event itself. The Newport rising was echoed only feebly in the North. Sheffield alone among northern cities experienced a period of

---

[1] On the 1839 elections, see: HO 73.55 Mott to P.L.C. 11 April; MH 12.15065 Mott to P.L.C. 1 April; *N.S.* and *M.S.A.* late March–early April.

violence; the rest of the area remained peaceful, if not exactly quiet, as indeed had been the case throughout the year.

This relatively happy outcome surprised a great many in the North, though by no means everyone. The nearly hysterical reaction of many local citizens, including magistrates, was rarely shared by the army officers, Home Office representatives and Assistant Poor Law Commissioners. Even at the worst of times they never abandoned the view, correct as it turned out, that nothing disastrous would happen. Even so, despite their optimism, they emphasized that it was only the leadership and organization necessary for a successful revolt, and not the frame of mind and social conditions which could produce serious disturbances, that were lacking. Therefore they tended to agree with the often panic-stricken local citizenry at least to the extent that they advised against any policies which might seem provocative.[1]

Possibly this need not have affected the Poor Law very much. It played only a small role in the great Chartist meetings of May and June, the strikers in August rarely directed their attention to workhouses or Boards of Guardians, and the unrest at the end of the year seems to have had little direct connection with anti-Poor Law agitation. But the Commissioners and the government were not inclined to take risks. Anti-Poor Law meetings and anti-Poor Law speeches at Chartist meetings never died off completely; Indeed they were given a fillip in 1839 by the wide distribution of a pamphlet, written under the pseudonym 'Marcus', on the subject of the possibility of limiting populousness. This extraordinary document, the main theme of which was the possible ways of getting rid of surplus population, was almost certainly intended as a bitter parody of Malthusianism, but many anti-Poor Law leaders, including Stephens, took it seriously and even attributed it to one of the three Commissioners or their secretary, Chadwick.[2]

Quite apart from the popular outcry against the 'Book of Murder', there was the problem of dealing with the Boards of Guardians. From the Poor Law Commissioners' point of view, one of the most damaging effects of the anti-Poor Law disturbances of 1837 and 1838 had been that many respectable northerners refused to serve as Guardians, or, that if they did agree to serve, they

[1] P.L.C., Sixth Annual Report, 4; HO 73.55 passim; W. Napier, *The Life and Opinions of General Sir Charles James Napier* (London 1857), II, 1–112.
[2] *On the Possibility of Limiting Populousness*, by Marcus (London 1839); *The Times* 10, 15 Jan. 1839.

refused to carry out unpopular policies, or, alternatively, tried to thrust the responsibility for such policies entirely on the Commissioners. In the hyper-tense atmosphere of 1839 this was likely to be even more rather than less the case than in the two previous years. At best, the Commissioners would have had an uphill fight in trying to advance their position in 1839; at worst they might have been faced with mass resignations from the Boards or a virtual strike of Guardians. Thus, despite their gains in March, the Commissioners began to have second thoughts in April and, when Mott advised London that it would not be possible to hand over the administration of relief in Bury to the Board of Guardians without a show of force, the Commissioners, despite Mott's desire to go ahead, decided to wait.[1] Similarly, fundamental changes in relief policy were also put off and the Boards of Guardians throughout the North were left with the same wide discretion that they had originally been given.

Such delays were initially intended by the Poor Law Commissioners to be only tactical and of short duration, but the loss of momentum involved in making them proved hard to reverse. Admittedly there was a slight increase in the activities of the Commissioners in the North in 1840. Two Unions, Bury and Manchester, were put into operation during the year.[2] But the boycotting Unions, as well as Rochdale, were left entirely to their own devices and no attempt was made to bring the northern Unions into line with the rest of the country on relief policy. This continued passivity on the part of the Poor Law Commissioners is difficult to explain, since few of the justifications, or excuses, for delay and caution which had existed in 1839 had much potency in 1840 or early 1841. Chartism, and with it all forms of popular protest in the North, appeared to be dead. The North was quieter than at any time since 1836 and it was generally believed that this state of affairs would continue for some time.

Moreover, the Commissioners were probably freer to act without public notice than ever before. There was, to be sure, some opposition to the Poor Law even in these years, but it was nothing as compared to what the Commissioners had had to deal with in 1837 and 1838, and it was, as well, opposition of a type which could be turned to the Commissioners' advantage. Popular agita-

[1] HO 73.55 Power to P.L.C. 21 Sept. 1839.
[2] MH 12.6039 Mott to P.L.C. Aug.–Nov. 1839.

tion against the Poor Law did not die away completely. Anti-Poor Law meetings were still held, reference to Marcus on *Populousness* was still a sure way to rouse the audience at any northern public meeting and Baxter's *Book of the Bastilles*, a vast anthology of anti-Poor Law information, found a large audience when it was published in 1841. But the most characteristic form of opposition in the North at this time came, not from the general public, but, in emulation of Todmorden in 1838, from the overseers. It was a serious problem. At one time, for example, no less than ten of the twelve townships in the Bury Union were withholding rates and, while this was an extreme case, it was paralleled on a smaller scale in nearly every Union in the textile districts. As Todmorden had shown, this was by no means an easy problem to deal with. Legal proceedings took time, the scale of fines under the Poor Law Amendment Act was small and a group of anti-Poor Law rate-payers could almost always be found to indemnify the overseers.[1]

Troublesome as this form of resistance was, however, it was, as far as the Commissioners were concerned, a great improvement over the popular opposition of two and three years before. Both could partially, or even wholly, immobilize a Board of Guardians, the one through the threat of violence, the other through starving it of funds. But popular resistance was worse, for it also had the effect of turning a Board, whose only wish when under severe pressure was to retreat, against the Poor Law Commissioners, whose main interest necessarily was to prevent such a retreat. When, however, resistance came from the overseers and was un-accompanied by the threat of mob action or popular reprisals, the effect on the Boards of Guardians was usually the opposite. There were, to be sure, a few Unions where a majority of the Guardians, like the non-paying townships, hoped to undermine or destroy the New Poor Law. In most Unions however only a few Guardians were committed to total obstruction whatever the cost. For the bulk of Guardians the natural desire that their affairs should work smoothly made them regard overseers' opposition as an annoyance rather than a danger, at least so long as it was not backed up by popular pressure, and the Commissioners found that they were increasingly able to get the co-operation of the northern Boards in reducing the authority of the overseers. Indeed, throughout most

[1] On ratepayers' and overseers' resistance, see: MH 12.5593 March 1840 correspondence; MH 12.14721 Wagstaff to P.L.C. 20 Feb. 1840; PUB 1/2 Nov.–Dec. 1840, April 1841.

of 1839 and for a year or more thereafter the Commissioners were able to establish and maintain good working relations with a majority of Guardians.[1] Yet, strangely, the Commissioners did not use their new-found influence as a lever for implementing their relief policies. Intervention was almost always limited to dealing with immediate problems, which in practice usually meant overseers' resistance. In this they were quite successful. The election order, first tried out in 1839, was extended to all the northern Unions during the next two years and the great majority of Unions in the textile districts were pressed into appointing, or agreed to appoint, Assistant Overseers during the same period. Beyond that, however, the Poor Law Commissioners rarely ventured.

This caution on the part of the Commissioners is all the more inexplicable in that, quite apart from the fact that dangerous opposition was unlikely to arise, the economic condition of the North was more conducive to a major change in relief policy than at any time since early 1836. It is far from easy to summarize economic conditions at this time; there were too many contradictory trends between industries and even within single industries. Nonetheless, it can be said that, after the worst of the recession of 1837–8, there was a slow and uneven recovery which lasted at least until the middle of 1841.[2] Admittedly, a qualified recovery of this sort did not provide the Commissioners with ideal conditions in which to make far-reaching changes in the administration of poor relief; the economic levels of the mid-1830s were not regained, profits remained low and distress, particularly in handloom weaving and other domestic industries, continued to be severe. But the economic situation was far better than it had been in 1837 and 1838, and the Commissioners would probably have done well to act at this time.

That they did not do so may have been due in part to an expectation that the gradual improvement in the economic and political situation in the North would continue. Other factors,

[1] The Commissioners' difficulties were not limited entirely to overseers' resistance. Other issues, especially workhouses and the payment of Union officers, were sources of friction with a number of Unions. But, significantly, these were in every case Unions with long histories of resistance. Huddersfield: MH 12.15065 Nov. 1839–April 1840; Bolton: MH 12.5593–4 Oct. 1839–Dec. 1840; Todmorden: MH 12.6272 passim.

[2] Gayer, Rostow and Schwartz, *Growth and Fluctuation of the British Economy*, Ch. V, Part II; Matthews, *Trade Cycle History*, Ch. XII, Part 4.

primarily of a political nature, were, however, of more immediate importance in determining the Commissioners' essentially passive policy in 1840 and 1841. First of all there was Parliament to be considered. This was a new problem, since it is probably fair to say that up until this time the Parliamentary opposition to the New Poor Law had done as much if not more harm than good to their cause. Certainly they had been totally unable to make an impression on either front bench or even a significant number of backbenchers in either party. In 1839 however a new avenue of attack was opened up by the coming to an end of the Commissioners' first five-year term of office. Renewal, admittedly, was inevitable but there was at least the possibility of imposing restrictions on the Commissioners and changes in their policy as conditions of renewal. From the point of view of the government and all supporters of a stringent relief policy the question could not have arisen at a worse time. The government's position in the House of Commons was precarious, Chartism was at its most threatening and many supporters of the law had begun to have doubts about how it should be administered in future. A growing number of M.P.s of all parties, oversimplifying the relationship between Chartism and resistance to the Poor Law, tended to look upon the physical force school of Chartism as little more than an extension of the anti-Poor Law movement and from this drew the conclusion that, whatever the merits of the Poor Law in theory, it ought to be softened in practice as the best means of disarming the Chartists.[1]

Understandably, the government was inclined to side step the issue and to this end it combined a promise of future reforms in the law with a proposal to extend the term of the Commissioners for one year only. This was not enough, however, to satisfy the vociferous minority of M.P.s who believed that the law had to be watered down immediately and who managed at one point to win a small majority in a thin House for the principle of local discretion in the granting of out-relief to the able-bodied. At first Russell seemed inclined to capitulate under this pressure but, given the full backing of the Conservative leadership, his attitude stiffened, a clause incorporating the proposed change in relief policy was

[1] The best statement of this view, which also cropped up frequently in the Parliamentary debates on the renewal bills (for which see below), is in an article on 'The People's Charter', usually attributed to Edward Bulwer Lytton, in the *Monthly Chronicle*, Oct. 1838.

rejected in the committee stage of the renewal bill and the dispute
was deferred for a year.[1]

Much the same thing happened, with variations, in the two
following years. In 1840, the cabinet, hardpressed by both the
supporters and opponents of a stringent poor law, extricated itself
from an increasingly difficult situation by once again putting off
reforms in the law and limiting the extension of the Commission's
life to a year. In 1841, the government started off more cour-
ageously by proposing a bill which combined a number of
administrative changes with a ten-year extension of the Commissioners' powers. But this was met with bitter opposition from
anti-Poor Law newspapers and M.P.s as well as a petitioning campaign reminiscent of the 1830s, and the government, already very
much on its last legs, abandoned the bill in favor of yet another
short term extension of the Commission's existence. There was
little excuse for the Liberal government's timidity over the Poor
Law between 1839 and 1841. In 1842, Peel's government encountered no difficulties in extending the Commission's life for a
further five years, despite the fact that many Conservatives had
been elected at least in part because of the unpopularity of the
New Poor Law.[2] The delays had certainly not served to abate
opposition; probably the reverse was true. Worse still, by avoiding

---

[1] Hansard, op. cit., XLVIII, 218–20; XLIX, 353–68, 551–85, 965–72;
L, 97–113, 339–53.
[2] For the intricacies of this long-drawn-out dispute, see: Finer, Chadwick, 188–93; Hansard, op. cit., LV, 582–9, 860–8; LVI, 155–74, 375–
453; LVII, 9–11, 400–52, 460–82. The controversy produced a large
crop of more than ordinarily interesting pamphlets. The Commissioners
defended their record in their Report on the Continuance of the Poor
Law Commission, B.P.P., 1840, XVII. Nassau Senior gave his support
(though anonomously) in the following year: Remarks on the Opposition
to the Poor Law Amendment Bill, by a Guardian (London 1841); 'The
English Poor Laws', Edinburgh Review, Oct. 1841. There were many
other pro-poor law pamphlets, of which perhaps the most interesting are:
J. H. Gurney, The New Poor Law Explained and Vindicated (London
1841); J. L. Latey, Letters to the Working People on the New Poor Law,
by a Working Man (London 1841); Rev. G. Sandby, Discretionary Power
(London 1841); and a series by the Rev. Thomas Spencer, the radical
parson of Hinton Charterhouse, of which the two best are The Outcry
Against The New Poor Law (London 1841) and The New Poor Law;
Its Evils and Their Remedies (London 1841). The anti-poor law literature
of this period was, by contrast, very mediocre stuff. Apart from Baxter's
Book of the Bastilles, which was published at this time, typical examples
are: Rev. E. Duncombe, Gilbertise the New Poor Law (York 1841) and
a series of pamphlets by Charles Brooker, including An Appeal to the
British Nation (Brighton 1840) and The Rejoinder (Brighton 1842).

a decision, the government had weakened the authority of the Commissioners and undermined their willingness to act.

This indecisiveness was not, however, the fault of the government alone. Government vacillation was as much a convenient excuse for the Commissioners' inactivity as a cause of it, for, had the Commissioners given a firm lead, the government would almost certainly have acted more forthrightly. But the Commission was in no position to give such a lead. Two of its three members shared many of the more moderate opponents' misgivings about the law and in consequence the Commission was as deeply divided on fundamental policy issues as was the government.[1] The first signs of this dated back at least to 1837, when the Commissioners and the government had bowed to the northern opposition by giving the Boards of Guardians in industrial areas almost complete discretion in the administration of relief. Nor was this the only indication that the resolve of the Commissioners was weakening. Twice, once in 1837 and again in 1840, the Commissioners sought to mollify the opposition in Parliament by proposing liberalizations of the restrictions on out-relief, on the latter occasion quite extensive ones.

On both occasions, Chadwick, with the support of his one ally on the Commission, Nicholls, and the great majority of the Assistant Commissioners, was able to convince the government that such changes were inimical to the principles of the Poor Law Amendment Act. But Chadwick's victories over his employers were meaningless, for, while he might be able to prevent the government from sponsoring a watering down of the law, he could not prevent the Commissioners from watering it down in the course of day to day administration, let alone impose his own policy views. The only way in which he could have hoped to keep the Commissioners close to the principles of the 1834 report was by persuasion and a willingness to compromise in small things for a time. Instead, he refused any compromise, whatever the political or economic circumstances, and tried to bludgeon the Commissioners into administering the law as he interpreted it. They could not fire him, as they must have wished to do, but they could and did contrive to exclude him gradually from a central role in the formation of policy. By 1842 he was completely powerless and

[1] The main source for these divisions within the Commission is Finer, *Chadwick*, Books III–IV.

even before that he, and with him the policies he represented, had lost much of their influence.

Perhaps the decisive event in this process was the last of Chadwick's major quarrels with his arch-enemy on the Commission, George Cornewall Lewis. The issue between them was the most important on which they had yet clashed, the future of Poor Law policy in the North. In late 1840 and early 1841, as we have seen, the northern Unions as a whole were relatively quiet. Most Boards of Guardians were reasonably co-operative. They administered relief with care, rarely abused their discretion by supplementing wages or paying rents and acquiesced in the appointment of Assistant Overseers and other special officers. In return, the Assistant Commissioners and the Poor Law Commissioners in London left them alone. There were exceptions, however. In a handful of Unions the Boards of Guardians were lax in the administration of relief, the Assistant Commissioners felt obliged to interfere constantly and the Boards of Guardians responded by refusing to co-operate in even the most insignificant changes.

By far the worst examples were Macclesfield in Cheshire and Bolton in Lancashire.[1] Three Assistant Commissioners had had responsibility for them at one time or another since 1839 and none of them had been able to make the slightest headway. The existing workhouses were dangerous, insanitary and unclassifiable but the Boards of Guardians in both Unions had refused to undertake the necessary repairs, let alone build new workhouses. Relief was administered with few checks, often by small subcommittees of the Boards, and, worst of all, there was a growing tendency in both Unions to grant relief in aid of wages to able-bodied men in partial employment. 'Within my experience,' Mott informed the Commissioners in April 1841, 'I have seen few instances in which the discretionary power vested by the legislature in the Board of Guardians has been exercised with more mischievous tendencies than in these two unions.'[2]

At this point Chadwick, on the advice of Nicholls, who had recently passed through the district and discussed the problem with Gilbert and Mott, decided to intervene personally. He went North, investigated the situation, consulted Gilbert and Mott, and helped Mott prepare a full report for submission to the Commis-

---

[1] Macclesfield: MH 12.968 May 1840–March 1841 correspondence; Bolton: MH 12.5593–4 Oct. 1839–April 1841 correspondence.
[2] MH 12.5594 Mott to P.L.C. 30 April 1841.

sioners. It was an uncompromising document. Nothing less than putting an immediate end to the discretionary powers of the Guardians, the building of new workhouses or at least the extensive repair of the old ones, and the rapid extension of the strictest regulations, preparatory to the introduction of the workhouse test could, they asserted, stop the rot.[1]

Lewis flatly rejected Chadwick's and the Assistant Commissioners' advice. Recalling the situation some years later, he noted that

There was great difficulty even in inducing some of the Boards of Guardians in that part of the country to carry on the administration of the law in any form whatever; and propositions were made at that period to prohibit the Commissioners from interfering in the manufacturing districts . . . Certainly there was great indisposition to acquiesce in the interference of the Commissioners, either by regulation or by the Assistant Commissioners, in the towns of the manufacturing districts . . . It was impossible for the Commissioners to eradicate the allowance system . . . at that time, and I was not prepared to take any active measures in the manufacturing towns for that purpose.[2]

In many respects, Lewis's justifications of the Commissioners' cautious policy in the North were legitimate. The vacillations of the government had placed the Commissioners in an invidious position and the developments in Bolton and Macclesfield were ominous. These had been the only Unions in the North where considerable pressure for major reforms had been put on the Boards of Guardians and they were also almost the only Unions where any sort of resistance from the Boards had been encountered. It could well be argued that similar pressure for changes elsewhere would have led to a revival of resistance on a large scale, that the relative quiet in the North was illusory and depended on the area's being left to itself, and that economic conditions in the North were such that it would be courting political disaster to try to impose even the ordinary minimum restrictions on out-relief to the able-bodied. These, certainly, were the implications of Lewis's argument.

But generalization on the basis of Bolton and Macclesfield was by no means entirely justified in 1840 or 1841. In both Unions the Boards of Guardians had been factious for years; resistance, rather

[1] Copy of a Report Relative to the Bolton and Macclesfield Unions, B.P.P., 1846, XXXVI.
[2] Minutes of Evidence Taken by the Select Committee on the Andover Union, B.P.P., 1846, Vol. V, Part II, Questions 21560 and 21831.

than coming in response to pressure from the Poor Law Commissioners, had preceded it and even been a cause of it. Moreover,
as Mott pointed out, economic distress was unusually severe in
both Unions. Elsewhere, probably in well over half the Unions in
the textile districts, where pressure on the rates was considerably
less and the Boards of Guardians were at least neutral if not
friendly, modest advances could probably have been made. Had
Chadwick and the Assistant Commissioners in the North been
more astute, they might have suggested such a course of action.
But Chadwick in particular was interested in nothing less than
sweeping change throughout the entire district and this, quite
rightly, the Commissioners dismissed as impracticable. In rejecting
Chadwick's views, however, the Commissioners went too far in the
other direction. A middling policy of limited and gradual reform in
selected Unions was not adopted and the northern Unions were
left in 1841 in much the same position, as far as the regulation of
relief was concerned, that they had occupied three or four years
before. The Commissioners' opportunity—the last such opportunity, as it turned out, before the beginning of the great depression of the 1840s—to build the foundations of a new system of
relief had been wasted.

Yet, even had they been willing and able to lay these foundations,
the Commissioners would have been very hard pressed by the
depression which began in the second half of 1841. It was far
worse than the recession of the late 1830s, largely because virtually
every sector of the economy began to contract sharply within a
very short time.[1] In some cases this was the result of the winding
up of commitments undertaken during the prosperous mid-1830s.
The most important example of this was railway building which
continued on a large scale into 1840 and fell away sharply only in
the following year when the major lines projected four or more
years back had been built. In manufacturing industries the problem was different, though the result was much the same. Early in
1841 there was a sharp decline in the demand for cottons and soon

[1] Matthews, *Trade Cycle History*, Chs. VIII (Part 2); IX (Parts 5–7);
X, XII (Part 5); Gayer, Rostow and Schwartz, *Growth and Fluctuation
of the British Economy*, Vol. I, Ch. VI. For the advent and effects of the
depression in the textile districts, see the reports to the P.L.C. on the
state of Rochdale, Bolton and Stockport in *B.P.P.*, 1842, XXXV; and
the files of the P.L.C. for late 1841 and early 1842, especially: Blackburn:
MH 12.5529; Burnley: MH 12.5673; Halifax: MH 12.14975; Keighley:
MH 12.15158.

thereafter in most other textiles as well. Prices fell, stocks accumu-
lated, the slim profits which had been maintained even at the worst
of times during the 1830s disappeared and production, which had
also been maintained and even increased during the earlier recession, had to be cut back. In many cases, after a brief period of part
time working, mills were closed completely and very often this was
followed by bankruptcy.

The effects of this on the working population of the North
cannot be summarized easily, for between Lancashire and Yorkshire and within the two counties there were significant local
differences. Generally speaking, the more backward an area was
economically, and the smaller a town or city was in population,
the more likely it was to suffer. Districts with a high proportion of
recently built factories often managed to escape large-scale closures
and mass unemployment. The desire to get some return on a large
capital investment operated, as it had in the late 1830s, as an incentive to keeping the mills working, and it often proved possible
to do this with the newer, more efficient factories and still make a
small profit. But in the older centers of factory production, such,
for example, as Stockport in Cheshire, where many of the mills
were out of date, they could not be worked except at a loss, and
closures, bankruptcies and mass unemployment followed almost
inevitably. Still worse hit were those districts where domestic industry remained predominant or of considerable importance. No
Union in the area was without a sizeable population of handloom
weavers, and in the worsted districts of Yorkshire of woolcombers
as well, but the great majority of outworkers were concentrated in
a few areas, primarily in the northern half of the textile district.

Next to economic development, probably the most important
factor in determining a community's ability to withstand a depression was its size. The larger the town or city, the more varied it
was economically, and the more likely it was therefore to be able
to escape widespread distress. But many of the lesser towns, some
of them by no means small, were virtually one industry towns and,
as such, peculiarly vulnerable. In Lancashire, most of the larger
towns to the north and east of Manchester had between 50 and 60
per cent of their working population employed directly in the
cotton industry, whereas, in the Manchester–Salford region,
though the proportion was still high at about 25 per cent, the local
economy was far less dependent on the prosperity of one industry.
Much the same was true of the woollen and worsted industries in

the central West Riding. In Leeds, not much more than 20 per cent of the work force was employed in textiles, while, in the smaller cities and still more the towns, the figure could rise to more than 50 per cent.[1] What is more, in the smaller centers this over-dependence on one source of employment was further aggravated by special conditions. All too frequently, a small industrial town derived its livelihood primarily, not merely from one industry, but from one or two employers. In the recession of the 1830s, when, by and large, mills stayed open, such towns managed to come through fairly well, but the mill closures which accompanied the depression of the early 1840s could destroy the economy of such a town overnight. This in itself was bad enough, but where, as often happened, such overdependence was combined with economic backwardness, the results could prove very nearly disastrous. In such areas the administration of relief, no matter how efficient, and no matter what the policies followed, was bound to be subjected to unprecedented strains.

The Poor Law Commissioners were aware of this. They were given a foretaste of the difficulties they were likely to encounter in the North in 1842 by earlier developments in a number of industrialized Unions where the recession of the late-1830s had continued or worsened in 1839 and 1840. In Bolton and Macclesfield, the Boards of Guardians had responded to economic distress by relaxing the administration of relief and, when the Assistant Commissioners had attempted to intervene, the Guardians became, if anything, more intransigent. There was, however, good reason to believe that these were special cases, unlikely to be imitated by less traditionally fractious boards. More ominous was the case of Nottingham, which had always been considered an ideal industrial Union, but in which, nevertheless, the situation deteriorated in the early 1840s almost as seriously as it had in Bolton and Macclesfield.[2]

Nottingham never really came out of the recession of the late 1830s and the first signs of a very severe depression were felt there as early as the autumn of 1839, nearly two years before the northern textile districts experienced a similar downturn in trade.

[1] These figures are based on the Abstract of Answers and Returns under the Population Act: Occupation Abstract, *B.P.P.* 1844, XXVII, 9–13, 68–97, 222–37.
[2] The main sources on Nottingham during this period are: MH 12.9445 and W. Roworth, *Observations on the Administration of the New Poor Law in Nottingham* (London 1840).

The Poor Law Commissioners were not particularly worried by this, for the Nottingham Union seemed to be especially well prepared to handle such an emergency. The pattern established during the relief crisis of 1837 could, it was hoped, be repeated. The prohibitory order would be maintained until it was no longer possible to do so, a supplementary labor test would then be introduced, and finally, when the need for this had passed, the prohibition of out-relief to the able-bodied in any form would be returned to. Since this policy had already been successfully tried out, the supporters of a stringent Poor Law naturally assumed that it could be used a second time, perhaps with even less difficulty.

In their optimistic assessment of the situation in Nottingham the supporters of a strict interpretation of the law failed entirely to take into account substantial changes in attitudes both in Nottingham itself and within the Poor Law Commission in London. Largely because of the unpopularity of the policies pursued in the 1830s, the Board of Guardians elected in 1839 was much more evenly divided between pro- and anti-Poor Law forces than the 1837 board and it was not willing, as it turned out, to face the public opprobrium meted out to the earlier Boards as a result of their long delays in seeking and getting a relaxation of the workhouse test. Timing was also of considerable importance. The revival of severe pressure came in November and December 1839, when a Chartist rising seemed likely at any moment. The unemployed marched through the streets, begging in large groups and, according to the Union clerk, Barnett, attempting to intimidate the wealthier classes in general and the Guardians in particular into giving out-relief on a large scale.[1]

Understandably then, the Guardians began to back away from the prohibitory order at the first signs of pressure. They made plans for granting relief in return for labor even before applying to the Poor Law Commissioners for permission to do so. Barnett, at first inclined to delay any relaxation, realized that the Guardians were determined and abandoned his opposition. When the Board asked for a suspension of the prohibitory order, he seconded their request, as he had not done two years before. The Poor Law Commissioners, for their part, were no more inclined to prevaricate than Barnett. They did not even question the need for relaxation at this time and issued a suspending order in December 1839.[2]

[1] MH 12.9445 Barnett to P.L.C. 6, 26 Nov., 3, 10 Dec. 1839.
[2] Ibid. Barnett to P.L.C. 21, 26 Nov. 1839.

o

In the circumstances there was little else that Barnett and the Commissioners could do. They had no wish to repeat the very unpopular expedients of overcrowding the workhouse and renting additional space which they had resorted to in 1837. Yet this was the only alternative open to them, since the building of a large new workhouse for which they had pressed after the worst of the earlier recession was over had been delayed and then shelved because of dissension on the Board and political pressures from outside. The immediate concession on relief policy was therefore made; but it was accompanied by increased pressure on the Board of Guardians to move ahead with the building of a new workhouse. This reopening of the workhouse issue in Nottingham coincided with Mott's attempts to impose major reforms on Bolton and Macclesfield, but, whereas Mott was almost bound to fail, the prospects of the Commissioners in Nottingham seemed bright. Admittedly, the building of a new house had been a subject of bitter controversy and there was an influential anti-Poor Law faction on the Board; nonetheless the majority of the Guardians were still co-operative and Nottingham did not have a tradition of out-and-out resistance. Thus, in June 1840, Barnett and Assistant Commissioner Senior had little difficulty in persuading the Board to agree on plans for a new workhouse.[1]

Once again, however, the advocates of a stringent Poor Law had failed to take into account the strength of local opposition to their views, especially in a time of acute distress. The Board had been pressed and cajoled into agreement but public opinion outside had not. The mayor of Nottingham, William Roworth, was an ardent opponent of the Poor Law and it was primarily through his efforts that a campaign of counter pressures on the Board of Guardians was launched. A series of public meetings was held in July and August at which he tried to organize ratepayer resistance and he even went so far as to promise official backing for any move to sabotage the plans for a new house. The arguments put forward by the opposition in Nottingham were familiar. The use of the workhouse to test the able-bodied unemployed in times of mass unemployment was derided as inhuman, impractical and unnecessarily expensive. A labor test, it was argued, would be a sufficient check of the genuineness of a man's need for relief. Moreover, to build a new house would in itself be terribly costly and there

[1] MH 12.9445 Senior to P.L.C. 23 June 1840; Barnett to P.L.C. 7 July 1840.

was always the danger that, once built, it would be used not only to test the able-bodied, but the old and the sick as well. There was also considerable opposition to the concept of a general mixed workhouse. Much better, it was argued, to place each class of pauper in a house designed and run to cater for his special needs and circumstances. Since there was already a workhouse in each of the three parishes of the Nottingham Union, such a policy would have the additional attraction of saving a good deal of money. Indeed, perhaps the most characteristic feature of rate-payer resistance in Nottingham was the way in which policies advocated on humanitarian grounds were always found to coincide precisely with those advocated for reasons of economy.

There was nothing new in all this; what was new were the weapons which the opposition, since it controlled the city government, could make use of. Land was in short supply in Nottingham and, when the Board tried to get hold of some public land, the town council refused. In much the same spirit, considerable pressure was put on local banks in the hope of starving the Board of Guardians of the necessary funds to build a workhouse. And finally, Roworth, in the hope of undercutting the Guardians' local influence still further, started a public subscription to provide relief in return for labor.[1] Naturally enough, the Guardians backed down when faced with opposition on this scale and the conditions for obtaining outdoor relief were still further relaxed. But, surprisingly, this willingness to make concessions did not extend to the most important issue of all, the workhouse. The Guardians, once committed to it, did not lose courage and with help and prodding from London made extraordinarily rapid progress.

Foiled in their attempt to get land within the Union, they searched for and found a suitable site in an adjacent Union, and, having met long delays in their attempts to get loans locally, they turned successfully to the central government for financial assistance. Thus, despite the opposition campaign, they were able to start building before the end of 1840. The price paid for this speed was considerable. The cost of the workhouse was almost certainly higher than was necessary and the plans were by no means entirely satisfactory to the Poor Law Commissioners, but speed, as far as the Commissioners were concerned, was all important. They feared that the next Board of Guardians election

[1] On the opposition's techniques, see: *Ibid*. Senior to P.L.C. 28 July, 23 Aug. 1840; Roworth, *Observations*, 7–55.

would result in an anti-Poor Law majority and they hoped to get so much of the building completed by that time that there could be no turning back. In this they succeeded. The overwhelmingly anti-Poor Law Board elected in March 1841 stopped work for a time and wasted some months in investigating the proceedings of its predecessor, but the workhouse was very nearly finished and in the end the Guardians had to go ahead with it.[1]

But the Poor Law Commissioners paid dearly for this victory. They won the enmity and distrust not only of the 1841 Board of Guardians but of every succeeding Board for the next four or five years as well. The Guardians did not mince their words. They accused the Commissioners of having forced the ratepayers of Nottingham against their will into building a workhouse which was far too large for the needs of the city. In retaliation the Guardians made it quite clear that, though they would obey the letter of the law, they would do no more, and not even that if they could find any loopholes. The spirit of co-operation that had existed between the Commissioners and the Nottingham Board ever since 1837 had been totally destroyed.[2] The implications of this for other industrialized Unions were alarming. Nottingham had long been thought of by the Commissioners as a model for other districts. It had been used in the early days of the New Poor Law as a testing ground for the urban policies of the Commissioners and the results had been almost uniformly successful. Yet, when, during a time of depression, the Commissioners had attempted to complete the structure of the new law, the effect had been to turn Nottingham into a center of dogged resistance hardly distinguishable from the worst of the northern Unions.

If this could happen in Nottingham, what on earth would happen in similar circumstances in the North itself, where the Poor Law had never won acceptance? In Nottingham the law had made sufficient headway that the Commissioners, under pressure, could make a tactical withdrawal. The prohibitory order could be suspended and the Commissioners could fall back on the labor test. But in the North neither the workhouse test, nor the labor test, nor, for that matter, any fixed body of rules governing the administration of relief was in force. Thus, when the depression of the early 1840s struck the North, the Poor Law Commissioners found themselves with virtually no room for maneuver. Faced

[1] MH 12.9445 Aug. 1840–Aug. 1841 correspondence.
[2] *Ibid.* Brewster to P.L.C. 1 Feb. 1842; Butler to P.L.C. 31 May 1842.

with anything approaching the opposition shown at this time in Nottingham, their position was likely to prove exceedingly precarious.

In some ways to be sure the Commissioners were better situated in the North in the early 1840s than they had been four or five years before. For one thing, as a result of their experiences in the 1830s they now had much greater respect for the strength of northern prejudices against the New Poor Law, if not for the actual prejudices themselves. This together with their difficulties in Bolton, Macclesfield and above all Nottingham, their troubles with Parliament, their own growing predilection for gradualism and the removal of Chadwick's influence all tended to make the Commissioners more circumspect and diplomatic in their later dealings with the textile districts. At no time in the 1840s, for example, was the subject of the workhouse test raised in the North, despite the fact that at least one of the Commissioners and many of the Assistant Commissioners still believed it to be applicable to industrial areas. Largely because of this, but due also to the continued primacy of Chartism in 1842 and the revival of other working-class movements in the years that followed, there was little violent popular opposition to the Poor Law throughout this period. Popular antipathy to the law was translated into action only once, during the great waves of strikes in the summer of 1842. Roving bands of strikers intimidated relieving officers and in a number of Unions workhouses were attacked, but compared with the importance that the Charter assumed in the strike movement the role of the Poor Law was insignificant. Thus, even in 1842 and certainly thereafter, the Commissioners were able to discount what had once been their major problem. What is more, their second greatest obstacle, overseers' resistance, had also largely been removed by late 1841 as a result of the Commissioners' election order and the extension of the practice of appointing Assistant Overseers. Only the ratepayers and their representatives on the Boards of Guardians remained to be considered and, since almost no Board had offered resistance or begun to disintegrate unless spurred on or undermined by popular or overseers' opposition, the Commissioners appeared to have good reasons for feeling confident about the future, at least as long as they continued to move with caution.

On the other hand the unpleasant fact remained that, because the Commissioners had accompanied the introduction of the New

Poor Law with very extensive concessions, the extent of northern antipathy to the law and the willingness of the Boards of Guardians to act upon it had never really been tested. Nor was there any reason to believe that the arguments advanced against the relief policies of the Poor Law Commissioners in the 1830s were any less compelling half a decade later.[1] If anything the depression of the early 1840s reinforced these arguments and added new ones. In face of the actuality of mass unemployment, the familiar case against a workhouse test on the grounds of expense, of the impossibility of its universal application, of the indignity it would impose of people out of work through no fault of their own and of the burden in unused resources it would impose on the ratepayers once prosperity returned, appeared unanswerable.

The exigencies of a depression led many northerners to go even further and argue that, as well as being unnecessary, the application of a workhouse test might actually worsen the situation it was supposed to hold in check. To refuse relief except in a workhouse might well drive the unemployed into selling all their possessions, falling behind on rent payments, running up debts and even perhaps, in desperation, leaving their own towns in search of work or relief on easier terms elsewhere. This process, if widespread and extended over a long period of time, could ruin not only the unemployed but whole communities as well. Retailers and property owners, particularly the owners of houses for rent, had an obvious interest in preventing such a complete pauperization of the unemployed, and so, for quite different reasons, did the large employers of labor.

The prosperity of the mid-1830s had resulted in an acute labor shortage and steeply rising labor costs. To allow an adequate work force, once assembled, to disperse could put potential employers at a serious disadvantage when prosperity returned, and it was in their interest, therefore, to maintain a workforce at hand, ready for re-employment, even if to do so meant spending considerable sums on relief to keep it solvent when unemployed. Needless to say, the unemployed themselves and those whose employment or

[1] The following assessment of northern attitudes is based on communications from the Assistant Commissioners and the Boards of Guardians to the P.L.C., written between late-1841 and mid-1844. The great majority of these documents, to most of which specific references are given in the next two chapters, are in the files on Blackburn, Bolton, Bradford, Burnley, Dewsbury, Halifax, Huddersfield, Keighley, Todmorden and Wakefield.

full wages were threatened, who were not without a voice in local policy since many of them had been or were still ratepayers, agreed. Indeed, it is difficult to find anyone in the North at this time who did not agree.

This unanimity did not, however, extend to other forms of test. Many ratepayers accepted the need for some restrictions on the kind of out-relief that should be given, agreeing with the Poor Law Commissioners, for example, in objecting to allowances in aid of wages or the payment of rents, and favored a test of some sort, such as a labor test. But there were a great many northerners, and by no means only the unemployed or those whose employment or wages were threatened, who objected to any form of universally applied restrictions, either because they feared that the Poor Law Commissioners would use them as an opening wedge for the introduction of the workhouse test, or because they genuinely opposed uniform regulations as such. The latter maintained that most of the arguments against the workhouse test could be applied with equal validity to any form of test, including a labor test, if it was universally enforced, and they defended such practices as the payment of rents or of allowances in aid of wages as justifiable in cases where, otherwise, homes would be broken up or the parish would be forced to undertake the entire cost of keeping a family.

Nothing could have been further from the views of the Poor Law Commissioners, let alone the Chadwickians. Far from regarding the depression as a situation which threatened to sink the administration of poor relief in a sea of abuses and therefore required the strictest enforcement of uniform relief policies, the out-and-out opponents of the New Poor Law saw the depression as a temporary crisis which had to be dealt with as flexibly and as economically as possible, even if this meant making selective use of practices which in ordinary times would rightly have been considered abuses. In other words, they argued, each case had to be decided on its merits and from this it followed that local discretion, rather than being cut back at a time of economic crisis, ought, if anything, to be enhanced.

None of these views could be called extreme, at least in comparison with those advanced by the popular opposition leaders of the 1830s. The Radical or Tory–Radical view of the New Poor Law as an attempt to subvert local autonomy in England or as part of a conspiracy to deprive the workingman of his economic and social independence played little or no role in the thinking of those who were to resist the application of its principles in the North in the 1840s. On the other hand, the more moderate and practical objections to the New Poor Law developed during the 1830s were not only reinforced as a result of the depression but were probably more widely and generally accepted as well. Precisely how widely accepted it is difficult to say. There were many individual examples of prominent northerners, such as the Ashworth family of Bolton, who qualified or abandoned their earlier support of the Poor Law during the depression. The Assistant Commissioners' reports back to London also indicate that, if there had been a softening of northern opinion during the years of relative inactivity following the disintegration of the popular anti-Poor Law movement, the trend was reversed in the early 1840s.

The only measurable indicator of northern opinion, however, was the composition of the Boards of Guardians, but unfortunately it is by no means easy to discover the attitudes of Guardians. The elections reveal less than might be expected, less in fact than they do for the 1830s. There were occasional pro- versus anti-Poor Law contests but the number of these and of contested elections in general declined as time went by. In addition after 1841 the equation of political allegiance with attitudes towards the Poor Law was even less certain than it had been in 1837 and 1838. Self declared Radicals could still be counted on to oppose the New Law at every turn. The same was true of a new element in the Boards of Guardians elections, the Chartist candidates, who, if the Assistant Commissioners are to be believed, were often quite successful, especially in the West Riding. But with Peel in office in London, many Conservatives appear to have moderated their opposition while at least a few Liberals reversed their earlier stand for equally partisan reasons.[1]

In such circumstances, a better index of Guardians' attitudes is how they reacted to pressure from London. But here too there are difficulties. The amount of pressure the Poor Law Commissioners exerted on different Boards varied enormously and a few Unions were left almost entirely to themselves throughout the 1840s. This

[1] Local politics and the Boards of Guardians elections in the 1840s. A decline in the number of contested elections was noted in all the Manchester and Leeds papers (late March–early April 1841–5), as was a swing to the Tories, especially in Lancashire, in 1841. For evidence of a change in partisan views of the Poor Law see: *Halifax Guardian*, 25 March 1843. On alleged Chartist influence on the Yorkshire Boards see: MH 32.57. 30 June 1842.

did not necessarily mean that such Boards were favorable to the Poor Law or the Commissioners, or that they administered the law well. A number of Unions were co-operative only because they were generally left alone, as the Commissioners discovered a number of times when belatedly they began to interfere.[1] Therefore it is impossible to speak with certainty of the balance of opinion within about a quarter of the approximately two dozen Boards in the district. The situation is clearer, however, in the remainder, where the Commissioners intervened fairly frequently throughout the first half of the decade. The intensity of the reaction to such pressure varied of course, from year to year and from Board to Board, but, as will be seen from the following chapters, a majority of Guardians in a majority of the Unions were uncooperative and suspicious throughout the period.

To some extent this is misleading. A small number of Unions were genuinely co-operative, even when hard-pressed from London, and even on the most uncooperative Boards the uncooperative majority was rarely a large one. Opponents of the law may well have been a minority among the Guardians of the textile districts as a whole and they almost certainly represented areas with a smaller population than did the Guardians who by and large supported the Poor Law Commissioners. Had the opposition been evenly spread throughout the district and represented on the Boards strictly in accordance with its strength, it would, very possibly, have been little more than a constant but ultimately ineffectual nuisance to the Poor Law Commissioners.

What made the opposition so effective in the 1840s was that, far from being widely spread over the entire area, it was heavily concentrated in particular types of locality. In general, the smaller the town the more likely it was to be a center of opposition.[2] The larger cities, on the other hand, usually remained co-operative. There

---

[1] The best example of a Union which erupted under pressure after a long period of quiet was Huddersfield (MH 12.15068 Aug.–Sept. 1846 correspondence). Other Unions which the P.L.C. ignored during the early 1840s, apart from those still entirely outside the New Poor Law (Ashton, Rochdale, Oldham), were Chorlton, Haslingden, Leigh and Wigan.

[2] The contrast between the larger centers and the out-townships was one of the recurrent themes of the Assistant Commissioners' reports to London. There are references to the problem in almost all the P.L.C. files on the northern Unions, but for general comments, see: MH 12.5593 Mott to P.L.C. 27 March 1839; MH 12.6039 Mott to P.L.C. 8 Feb. 1839.

were a number of reasons for this difference. In the first place, local resentment against outside interference was usually stronger in the smaller centers. The local city or large town was always the center of the Union, the place where the Guardians met, the location of the workhouse should a workhouse be built. In many Unions the central town was inconveniently far from many of the out-townships and, even where it was not, there remained considerable opposition to a system of paying money into a central Union fund which would then be spent very largely in the central town or city. The out-townships were, in short, terrified of being swallowed up and forced to administer and pay for policies designed, so they believed, not to meet their needs, but those of larger towns. It was not merely control from London they opposed, but control from anywhere outside their own boundaries.

On relief policy, too, strong anti-Poor Law opinions were more likely to be prevalent in the out-townships than in the larger towns and cities, for, in addition to the fact that it was the smaller centers, so much more likely than the larger towns to be over-dependent on one industry, which were hardest hit by mass unemployment, it was, by and large, in the smaller centers that the problem of the persistence of domestic industry was most acute. An exact estimate of the number of towns and villages where this was a serious problem or of how large a percentage of the population in such places was made up of domestic workers is impossible. The census reports did not distinguish between handloom and factory weavers; indeed the occupation data in the censuses of the period are frustratingly inadequate. It is necessary therefore to fall back on the reports of Assistant Commissioners and of the Royal Commission on the Handloom Weavers according to which towns and villages where domestic workers formed a high proportion of the population were depressingly common in the hills and small valleys on which most of the great textile towns backed. In many towns entire families were wholly dependent on handloom weaving, while in the surrounding countryside small farmers frequently supplemented their inadequate income from agriculture by weaving. Though most frequent in the northern half of the textile districts, such concentrations of weavers were present in almost every Union and, in all such places, as in the small one industry towns threatened with mass unemployment, any attempt to restrict relief was bound to meet with stiff resistance.[1]

[1] Reports of the Assistant Commissioners to H.M. Commission on the

Had the influence of these out-townships on the northern Boards of Guardians been more or less in proportion to their size, their intransigent opposition to the Poor Law would have been more of an inconvenience than the major stumbling block it was in the 1840s. In most Unions the headquarters township and its immediate suburbs had at least a quarter and, in many cases, a near majority of the population of the Union. With the larger cities usually reasonably receptive to the law and the smaller cities more or less evenly divided, most Boards could probably have been pressed into functioning fairly well, but for the fact that the smaller towns and villages were heavily over-represented on the Boards. The number of townships varied greatly from Union to Union, but very few had less than ten and more than a third had twenty or more. Since each township had to be represented on the Board, and it was necessary for efficiency to keep the number of Guardians small, the representation of the larger towns and cities was never in proportion to population. Collectively, the out-townships had an artificially large voice in the management of a system against which many of them were already predisposed. It was almost as if the Poor Law structure had been designed to crack under stress and that all that was needed to start the process off was some sort of crisis, such as was more than amply provided by the great depression of the early 1840s.

Handloom Weavers, *B.P.P.*, 1839, XLII. Extended comments on the problem in different parts of the textile districts can be found in: MH 12.5673 Mott to P.L.C. 4 Dec. 1841; MH 12.5594 Mott to P.L.C. 3 March 1841; MH 12.1139 Power and Twistleton to P.L.C. 9 Feb. 1842; MH 12.15158 B.G. to P.L.C. 27 June 1842; and the reports on the condition of Rochdale, Bolton and Stockport cited above (note 1, page 198).

X National uniformity and local discretion

The first signs of renewed trouble in the North came at the end of 1841 when the Poor Law Commissioners began once again to interfere in the local administration of poor relief throughout the textile districts. This rather sudden departure from their usual practice of selective intervention was due in part to considerations of national policy and in part to circumstances beyond their control. Starting in May 1841 the Commissioners drew up a number of General Rules governing almost every aspect of Poor Law administration which they intended to introduce throughout the country in place of the regulations previously issued to individual Unions. In most Unions these new rules involved little change since similar orders were usually already in force. The Commissioners' main purpose was to rationalize their dealings with the approximately 600 local Boards by creating a measure of national uniformity.[1] In the North, however, where no regulations even remotely resembling the Commissioners' General Rules governing relief were in force, the introduction of these rules would involve a dramatic departure from established policy and, therefore, elaborate preparatory investigation and almost constant supervision thereafter. It was this process that Charles Mott began in the autumn of 1841.

Even had the Commissioners not hoped to bring the North into greater conformity with the rest of the country, there can be no doubt that interference in the day to day administration of relief in the North would have increased at this time. On those few occasions when the Poor Law Commissioners did intervene in local affairs between 1839 and 1841 they usually did so in response to reports that a Union was in financial difficulties or to accusations of mismanagement or neglect on the part of local authorities. With the onset of mass unemployment late in 1841 both problems were seriously aggravated. Like the crisis itself the increase in poor rates was unprecedented and many individual ratepayers and in some cases whole townships found it impossible to meet the larger

[1] P.L.C., Eighth Annual Report, *B.P.P.*, 1842, XIX, 1–3 and Appendix A.

and more frequent calls for funds. In addition, the enormously increased burden on relieving officers and Guardians led inevitably
to an increase in cases of individual neglect as well as to emergency
expedients such as the overcrowding of workhouses, the reduction
of relief scales and the payment of rents and relief in aid of wages.[1]
There was in short at least the possibility of a serious breakdown in
the system of relief in the North and, as reports of this began to
flood into Somerset House in the late months of 1841, the extent
of central intervention in local management was bound to grow.
From the winter of 1841–2 onwards the practice of closely and
constantly scrutinizing the affairs of individual Unions, limited for
so long to a handful of places such as Macclesfield and Bolton, was
gradually extended. Over a period of little more than a year Mott,
joined in mid-1842 by a new Assistant Commissioner Charles
Clements, investigated almost all of the Unions in the textile
district.

Most of the northern Unions were singularly ill-prepared for
such visits, for the practices which the Commissioners had censured in Bolton and Macclesfield were found on investigation to be
very widespread.[2] Financial chaos was common. Long delays in
the payment of rates were characteristic of some townships in
nearly every northern Union, bookkeeping practices were rarely
either efficient or accurate, and the auditing of accounts, good in
those areas where the Commissioners had been able to prevail
upon the Guardians to accept district auditors, was appalling elsewhere. These conditions were not new—in many cases they dated
back to the foundation of the Union—and they could not be
blamed on the depression. The depression simply made them
worse and, to complicate the problem further, added a few new
abuses. Having failed to raise sufficient funds through the rates,
many Boards of Guardians had begun to rely on loans, pledging
future rates as security and adding the interest charges onto the
debts of the defaulting townships.

[1] MH 12.5529 Ellingthorpe to P.L.C. 19 Aug. 1842.
[2] The most important of the Assistant Commissioners' reports are:
Blackburn: MH 12.5529 Mott to P.L.C. 27 Aug., 13 Sept. 1842; Bolton:
MH 12.5595 Clements to P.L.C. 9 Jan. 1843; Bradford: MH 12.14722
Mott to P.L.C. 24 Sept. 1842: Chorley: PUX 1/1 14 Dec. 1841; Clitheroe:
MH 12.5752 Mott to P.L.C. 26 Jan. 1842; Dewsbury: MH 12.14831
Clements to P.L.C. 29 Dec. 1842; Halifax: MH 12.14975 Mott to
P.L.C. 14 Feb. 1842; Keighley: MH 12.15158 Mott to P.L.C. 23 April
1842; Preston: PUT 1/8 27 Sept. 1842; Todmorden: MH 12.6272 Mott
to P.L.C. 28 Sept. 1842; Warrington: PUV 1/1 22 June 1842.

Bad as the financial situation was, the management of workhouses was, in Mott's and Clements' view, if anything, even worse. Only four Unions in the area had built or were planning to build new workhouses; the rest had rejected the Commissioners' advice that they do so or had refused even to consider the question. Some Unions had gone even further in their resistance to the Commissioners' concept of workhouses and continued to administer them as if the New Poor Law had never been passed. Though theoretically under Board of Guardians' control, the workhouses in such Unions were used in practice only for the reception of paupers from the townships in which they were situated and all the costs were borne by the town rather than being paid out of Union funds. This practice was comparatively rare, but the situation was little better in the majority of Unions, for, whether administered directly by the Board of Guardians or not, almost all existing workhouses were totally inadequate to the purposes of the New Poor Law. Northern workhouses had traditionally been used as places of refuge for the aged, infirm or orphaned poor and they were usually too small to be used as a test for the able-bodied. Moreover, being both old and small, these buildings were rarely suited to rearrangement for purposes of classification. Often there was no classification at all, and paupers of all types and both sexes mixed freely.

The administration of outdoor relief was open to very much the same sort of objections. The northern view of the workhouse as a refuge and a last resort meant that in practice relief was given where possible out of doors. Only the homeless and the sick, those in short for whom the workhouse was a necessity and not a test, were offered indoor relief. The remainder were given outdoor relief and that, as often as not, in money rather than goods. This was true, by and large, of all classes of paupers and while, up to a point, the Commissioners accepted this as not too dangerous in the case of the aged and infirm, they believed it to be intolerable in dealing with the able-bodied. Admittedly, perhaps the worst abuse of all, the giving of relief in aid of wages, was comparatively rare in the North and, insofar as it was limited to handloom weavers, the Assistant Commissioners were inclined to overlook it as a special case. But there were signs that such relief was being extended throughout the area to workers in partial employment and, even where this was not true and only the unemployed among the able-bodied were given outdoor relief, the Commissioners had good reason to be concerned. With few exceptions the unemployed were given relief without a test of any sort, outdoor let alone indoor, and even without adequate investigation of their claims.

Mott and Clements regarded the situation revealed in these reports as a complete vindication of their and Chadwick's objections to the wide discretionary powers that the northern Boards had enjoyed for so long. The depression, they asserted, had not caused the existing crisis, but only revealed the weaknesses which had been allowed to develop through years of lax administration and constant deviation from the letter of the Poor Law Amendment Act. Only substantial reforms, they concluded, could correct the situation and they ended every one of their reports at this time with a strongly worded plea for immediate action from London. The problem was where to start, which of the Commissioners' many General Rules regulating relief to introduce first. For obvious reasons, political and practical, the order prohibiting out-relief to the able-bodied was not even considered; Mott and Clements appear to have considered it still as the ultimate solution but realized that it would have been impossible to introduce it in 1842. The imposition of a labor test on the able-bodied throughout the North was also rejected for the time being. This is more surprising in that the Commissioners officially regarded the labor test as ideally suited to urban areas in times of acute distress. There were a number of very good reasons for the Commissioners' reluctance to press the issue, however.

The main difficulty was timing. Any attempt to place conditions on the granting of out-relief at the height of the crisis would certainly have produced an explosion and probably have run into stiff resistance from the overworked Guardians as well. Another important consideration was the always delicate issue of local autonomy. Any or all of the General Rules threatened that autonomy and the Commissioners wisely recognized that if they wished to extend the principle of national uniformity in the administration of relief to the North, it would be better to do so in an area less controversial in itself than outdoor relief to the able-bodied. By process of elimination then the Commissioners decided to press first for the introduction and enforcement of two hopefully less contentious General Rules, those relating to medical relief and to the regulation of workhouses.

These and particularly the latter promised to be difficult enough

to impose in any case. Mott's and Clements' investigations revealed not only an absence of workhouse discipline and classification, but, in many cases, appalling neglect as well. Most workhouses were overcrowded and the squalid conditions which had
been allowed to develop in the worst of them amply fulfilled the
descriptions of workhouses found in the propaganda which had
been directed a few years back against the old poor law. Workhouse masters were often underpaid, corrupt, lazy and incom-
petent; sanitary facilities were frequently primitive; food was
sometimes bad (though sometimes, according to Mott, it was
much too good); the inmates often had no work to do or they were
allowed to go out to work, using the house in effect as a hotel;
moral standards were low or were not enforced; children received
little or no instruction; and so on.

In combating such conditions the Commissioners had a wide
range of powers.[1] They could review all Board of Guardians' appointments, including those of workhouse master, workhouse
porter and schoolmaster to the pauper children. The Workhouse
Regulation Order covered everything from discipline and sanitary
arrangements to classification, the fixing of diet tables, and the
regulation of the number and type of paupers allowed in a given
house; and regulations in accordance with this order could,
theoretically, have been imposed on any Union at any time without
prior consultation. Should a workhouse be unsuited to such reforms, the Commissioners had the power to compel a Board of
Guardians to spend up to £50 or 10 per cent of the annual rates,
whichever was less, on improving or enlarging existing accommodation. And finally, if even this should prove fruitless, the Commissioners could close a workhouse. Indeed, about the only power
which the Commissioners did not have was to force a Board against
its will to build a new workhouse and, while this restriction meant
that they could not solve the problem once and for all, the authority they did possess appeared to be more than sufficient to deal
with the inadequacies in the existing system.

Spurred on by the almost constant flow of reports, the Poor Law
Commissioners began to press the worst offenders among the
Northern Boards on this issue early in 1842. A number of ap-
proaches were used. In some Unions, the Assistant Commissioner
himself took the initiative, but, more often than not, he worked in-

[1] Clauses 15, 21, 23–6 and 42 of the P.L.A.A. The workhouse regulations are in P.L.C., Eighth Annual Report, Appendix A, Nos. 3 and 4.

directly through the Poor Law Commissioners. In such cases the usual procedure was to send a summary of the Assistant Commissioner's report to the Guardians, who were asked for comment. This usually resulted in a reply from the Guardians filled with feeble excuses and pious resolutions to do better in future. It was at this point that the Commissioners really began to move. The Guardians' reply was sent to Mott for a detailed gloss and this, plus a fuller version of the original indictments, was flung back at the Guardians along with a statement of the Commissioners' intention to impose the workhouse regulations immediately and in full. On a few Boards these shock tactics had the desired effect; they resigned themselves to making the required changes. But most Boards were a good deal less tractable.[1] While, at least in most cases, acknowledging that the Commissioners' workhouse regulations were acceptable as an ideal, they argued that 1842 was the worst possible year in which to push through such reforms. Throughout the year they feared that any new restrictions on poor relief might provoke violent popular reaction and the plug plot strikes and riots in mid-summer served to confirm the Boards in their fears.

In addition, the workhouse regulations were assailed by the Guardians as being unrealistic in existing economic circumstances. In dealing with the depression they had found that it was often necessary to resort to unpleasant expedients such as the temporary overcrowding of workhouses. To attempt to reorganize the houses in accordance with a set of uniform principles would, they argued, be foolish and self-defeating, for, far from leading to desired economies and smoother operation, it would involve the expenditure of additional funds, when funds were desperately short, and mean the dislocation of established relief procedures, when these procedures were already stretched to capacity and could often be made to work at all only through rapid improvisation. If the whole of northern objections to the new regulations had been contained in such arguments, the Commissioners need not have worried. A

---

[1] Very few Boards reacted favorably: Bradford: MH 12.14722 Mott to P.L.C. 24 Sept. 1842; Burnley: MH 12.5673 Jan.–May 1842 correspondence; Preston: PUT 1/8 Sept.–Oct. 1842 correspondence. Much more typical were: Blackburn: MH 12.5529 Ellingthorpe to P.L.C. 6 Sept. 1842; Bolton: MH 12.5595 Jan.–Feb. 1843 correspondence; Chorley: PUX 1/2 Jan. 1842; Dewsbury: MH 12.14832 Jan.–Feb. 1843 correspondence; Keighley: MH 12.15158 B.G. to P.L.C. 28 June 1842; Warrington: PUV 1/2.

slight delay together with a bit more pressure would have been sufficient to bring the Guardians into line. But this was not the case. Behind all the talk of the need for reconsideration in the light of temporary difficulties was bitter local resentment at interference from London, which had nothing at all to do with the rights and wrongs of this particular proposal.

'The Guardians and ex-officio Guardians of this Union', the clerk of the Blackburn Board wrote to London, 'have, since its commencement, expressed the greatest desire to give the new law a fair trial, and as the Commissioners have not unduly interfered with their arrangements, the result of their arrangements has been so far successful as to give the greatest satisfaction and effect a material saving in the Poor Rate.' And more than that, he noted, 'In all the tumults and electioneering contests which have occurred in this town, not a single voice has been raised against the poor law, or the generally obnoxious regulations of the Commissioners.' But such harmony was exceedingly precarious. 'I need not inform you', he continued, 'of the difficulty and impolicy, I may say the utter impossibility in disturbed times like the present, of suddenly urging any severe regulations, with the hope of benefit or advantage, in a large Manufacturing District.' The result of any attempt to do so would, he assured the Commissioners, be a popular revulsion against the law, one of the effects of which would be the resignation of most of the present Board. And 'should the more respectable of the Guardians refuse to act in consequence of their measures and proceedings being, as they might consider, unduly interfered with by the Commissioners, a course which I am not without doubt they would adopt, we should be left entirely without Guardians, or the management would fall into hands whose measures would defeat the objects of the enactment, and bring upon it a portion of the odium which attaches to the law in neighboring Unions'.[1]

Such letters would have come as no surprise to the Poor Law Commissioners if sent by the Boards of Huddersfield or Dewsbury, or the overseers of Ashton, Oldham or Todmorden. But Blackburn, as the clerk pointed out, had never directly defied the Poor Law Commissioners and, though not a model Union on the lines of Stockport or Chorlton, had been remarkably free from attempts, even on the part of a minority, to wreck the law by boycotting or rigging elections, holding back on rates or organizing popular

[1] MH 12.5529 Ellingthorpe to P.L.C. 6 Sept. 1842.

resistance. It now appeared, however, if the clerk of the Board was to be believed, that the failure of the Blackburn Guardians to emulate the root and branch resistance shown by some Unions in the 1830s indicated nothing more than that they had been willing, as the root and branch opponents had not, to gamble that administrative reforms would not be followed by a complete overhaul of relief policy dictated from London. If, however, it became clear that this was not to be the case, then, they threatened, the Commissioners would soon discover how little separated the apparently co-operative Unions from the intractable trouble spots of 1837 and 1838.

Few Boards were as outspoken as Blackburn's in their condemnation of the Commissioners' new turn of policy. Even while seeking delays and expressing their resentment of outside interference, they refrained from openly declaring war on the Commissioners and they continued, as, indeed, did Blackburn, to pay lip service to the principles of workhouse management outlined in the proposed regulations. But in many, perhaps most cases it was only lip service. The reaction from Blackburn implied, as, even more strongly, did the reaction from other Unions, notably Dewsbury, Bolton and Todmorden, a rejection of the workhouse regulations as alien to the North, and not only in the peculiar conditions of 1842. Many Guardians feared that the workhouse regulations would be used to lay the foundations for a workhouse test, certainly for the able-bodied, and perhaps for all classes of paupers. Such fears were largely groundless. The Commissioners had probably already begun to doubt the applicability of the workhouse test to able-bodied paupers in urban areas and the extension of the prohibitory order to other classes, if it had ever been seriously contemplated, had long since been abandoned. Nonetheless, many Guardians unquestionably believed that this was official government policy and resisted the workhouse regulations because they seemed to be a first indispensable step towards a universally applied abolition of outdoor relief.

There were short run and more practical reasons for die hard resistance as well. A repetitive subsistence diet, drab workhouse uniforms, the separation of all inmates, including families, according to age and sex, strict isolation of the inmates from the outside world, and rigid internal discipline, all of which were envisaged in the Commissioners' rules, would have made impossible the sort of workhouse, so characteristic of the North, which served primarily as a haven for those who, because of illness or financial difficulties could no longer live from their own labor or on outdoor relief. In the eyes of the Commissioners, of course, such workhouses were not workhouses at all, but 'mere receptacles for the aged, harmless idiots and children'.[1] Yet, try as they might, Clements, Mott, Power and the other Assistant Commissioners who worked in the area were unable to get the Guardians to see it in this way, and furious at these obdurate Boards, they dismissed their objections as flimsy excuses for not spending money, pointing to the most run-down workhouses as proof. 'If expense is not the real cause of opposition', wrote one of the Assistant Commissioners after visiting a particularly horrible example, 'why are not the unfortunate inmates of these miserable workhouses properly clothed and adequately provided with bedding and other conveniences . . . instead of being left in rags and filth?'[2]

This was an understandable reaction, but it blinded the Assistant Commissioners and their employers to the complexities of the situation. The motives of the Guardians were mixed. Admittedly niggardliness, even to the point of neglecting the workhouses and their inmates, was a factor. So was stubborn, unreasoning resistance to any sort of outside interference. And fear of the popular reaction which the new workhouse rules might bring also played a part. But so too did the Guardians' rejection of the Commissioners' concept of what a workhouse should be and their adherence to their own very different concept. That there could be a genuine alternative to which the northern Guardians might be committed for other than pecuniary reasons never really dawned on the Assistant Commissioners, and from this failing much of the trouble they experienced in the 1840s derived. In attributing only the basest of motives to their opponents, the Commissioners underestimated their dedication and staying power. Much the same thing had happened in 1837, when the early protests against the new law had been dismissed as the work of a rabble led by minor demagogues. The result then had been the emergence of a popular clamor against the law for which the Commissioners were wholly unprepared. The result of a similar underestimation of Guardians' opposition after 1841 was a less dramatic but hardly less effective war of attrition against the Poor Law Commissioners by the northern Boards.

[1] MH 12.14831 Clements to P.L.C. 29 Dec. 1842.
[2] MH 12.6273 Clements to P.L.C. 26 Jan. 1844.

At first, to be sure, the battle seemed to be going all one way. On the issue which had raised the storm, the subject of workhouse management, the Commissioners held most of the cards and there was apparently very little that the Guardians could do. In a number of Unions the Commissioners quashed the practice of using the workhouses for parish rather than Union purposes and also compelled a measure of classification by closing a number of houses and limiting admissions in each of those that remained to one or two classes of paupers. Similarly, in cases where negotiations broke down over the question of the number of inmates to be allowed in a workhouse or on diet tables, the Commissioners used their power to fix maximums or set out diet tables over the heads of the Guardians. The implementation of the full regulations governing the actual administration of workhouses presented greater difficulties, since the usual procedure of the Poor Law Commissioners had been to bring the management of workhouses more or less in line with the regulations before issuing them to a particular Union. But a few months' experience of the dilatory tactics of the average Board led the Commissioners to reverse the process in cases where no progress seemed likely. By issuing the order first, the Commissioners found that they could then force the Guardians in most cases to come at least part way towards living up to them.

This was, as might be imagined, a long slow process.[1] Mott's first major tour of inspection started in late 1841 and it was more than a year before he, later joined by Clements, was able to get around to all of the Unions in the area. Much time was lost in attempting to cajole rather than push the northern Unions into acquiescence. The objections and pleas for delay made by each Union were answered in long memoranda from London and the Assistant Commissioners made repeated visits to the Boards of Guardians in order to explain the proposed rules. Even the adoption by the Commissioners of the procedure of issuing the rules first and answering questions later did not speed things up very much. Most Boards proved quite willing to stretch and even ignore the rules unless some representative of the Commissioners was near at hand to enforce them. More important still, it soon became apparent that, while the Commissioners held most of the

---

[1] Developments in the following Unions are representative: Blackburn: MH 12.5530 1843 correspondence; Bolton: MH 12.5595 1843 correspondence; Chorley: PUX 1/2 1842; Dewsbury: MH 12.14832 1843

cards, the Boards of Guardians had trumps. It was all very well to issue orders governing the management of workhouses so long as the workhouses were capable of reorganization in accordance with the rules. In many Unions this was out of the question. The buildings used as workhouses had often been built for other purposes and then converted. 'Workhouses', Clements wrote of the buildings in use in Dewsbury, 'they never can be made. Nor indeed', he added, 'does anything of the kind appear to be thought of.'[1] Much the same could have been said of the great majority of Unions in the textile districts. Apart from the four Unions which built new workhouses during this period, only a handful of places had what the Commissioners would have accepted as satisfactory workhouse accommodation. The rest were left with a miscellaneous collection of old buildings which could not be made to meet the minimum requirements of the Poor Law Commissioners, or, if they could, then only with the greatest ingenuity.

This was the case in so many of the northern Unions that the real battle between the Commissioners and the local Boards often developed not over the advisability or workability of the rules themselves but over the more basic issue of making the physical changes in existing workhouses that would have allowed the rules to be introduced at all. At this level the Commissioners had little advantage over a determined opponent. They could order repairs or alterations to be made within certain financial limits but it was the Guardians who drew up and submitted the plans which the Commissioners could then accept, reject or try to amend. A Board determined to make no changes or only changes unacceptable to London could spin out the process of negotiations almost endlessly and be reasonably certain that in the end the Commissioners would settle for a compromise which fell far short of what they hoped for. A number of Boards of Guardians did precisely this with the result that many of the most important goals of the Commissioners such as rigid classification and the provision of work for the inmates remained all but unrealizable in perhaps half of the Unions in the textile districts. In such cases, though the regulations were issued, this was done more as a matter of form than in the hope that they could or would be implemented. It is hardly surprising therefore that the complaints which were the substance of the first

correspondence; Warrington: PUV 1/2 1843; Preston: *Preston Chronicle*, 1842.
[1] MH 12.14831 Clements to P.L.C. 29 Dec. 1842.

series of reports on workhouses in 1841, reappeared in similar reports written four or five years later.[1]

The gap between the Commissioners' real and apparent power to effect substantial reforms in workhouse management was often not very clear; it was usually obscured by the flurry of directives on this or that detail of management which issued constantly from Somerset House, or was bridged over by makeshift compromises between opponents who were mutually sick of wrangling. But there were occasions when unyielding resistance by a particularly fractious board revealed in full the limits on the Commissioners' authority. Perhaps the best example was the feud over workhouses between the Commissioners and the Todmorden Board of Guardians in 1844–5.[2] The usual report on the ghastly state of the local workhouses was answered by the equally familiar evasive reply from the Guardians, and this, in turn, drew from the Commissioners a stern ultimatum to begin needed reforms. But the Todmorden Board, instead of embarking on the few minor changes, which were all that the Commissioners could realistically hope for, and which, in most other cases, had been enough to divert their attention, went on the offensive. As in so many Unions, the workhouses in the various townships were only nominally under Board of Guardians' control; in practice they received only the paupers, and therefore all classes of paupers, from the townships in which they were located. Clearly it was this system which the Poor Law Commissioners had first to seek to change, but the Todmorden Guardians were unwilling to make concessions even on this point. They informed the Commissioners that they

do not think it expedient to use the workhouses in the several townships for union purposes . . . and that if the Poor Law Commissioners should consider it incumbent on them not to allow the workhouses to be used as heretofor, the Board will abandon them altogether with a view to dispense with any workhouse system whatever.[3]

Undoubtedly the Guardians expected an equally firm response from London and it is probable that their ultimatum was written

[1] Blackburn: MH 12.5530 Clements to P.L.C. 27 June 1845; Burnley: MH 12.5674 Clements to P.L.C. 13 March 1844; Dewsbury: MH 12.14832 Clements to P.L.C. 19 March 1844; Huddersfield: MH 12.15063 Austin to P.L.C. 23 Dec. 1846; Keighley: MH 12.15159 Austin to P.L.C. 25 May 1846.

[2] For Todmorden during this period, see: MH 12.6273 Jan.–April 1844 correspondence.

[3] *Ibid.* Stansfield to P.L.C. 6 March 1844.

primarily in order to put them in a strong position for the coming battle. But the Commissioners chose to avoid further conflict. Perhaps tired of years of inconclusive struggle over the workhouse issue, and, in any case, advised by their Assistant Commissioners that the workhouses of the Todmorden Union could never be used efficiently for New Poor Law purposes, the Commissioners gave in. The Guardians were authorized to sell all their houses, which they did, and Todmorden thereby found itself in the unique position of being a Poor Law Union without workhouses, a situation which must have been as surprising to the Guardians as it would have been to the framers of the Poor Law Amendment Act.

Admittedly Todmorden was an extreme case; no Union attempted to match its reputation as the most troublesome in England and Wales. Still, what had happened in Todmorden was in many respects the logical extension of a situation which was general in the North, despite the fact that the workhouse regulations had been issued to every one of the northern Unions except Todmorden well before the end of the 1840s. The almost universal refusal to build new workhouses in the North meant that in many Unions the houses were little if any better than those which had been closed in Todmorden. Elsewhere, even in many Unions with satisfactory workhouses, the tendency of the Guardians to interpret the Commissioners' regulations as they saw fit, made the regulation order as often as not a dead letter. Even more symptomatic of the situation in the North was the Commissioners' failure to win acceptance for the basic promise that workhouses must serve Union purposes and be financed out of Union funds.

In the early 1840s the Commissioners made some progress towards this goal. The workhouse used for the reception of all classes of paupers from a single township was replaced almost everywhere by the house receiving one or two classes of pauper from all the townships in a Union. But a number of Boards soon found a way around this. Instead of treating workhouse costs as Union charges to which each town contributed a percentage based on its average Poor Law expenditure over the last three years, they charged each town according to the number of its paupers in the Union workhouses.[1] This was done largely at the instigation of the out-

---

[1] As this particular form of resistance was legally suspect, it had to be carried out in semi-secrecy, and evidence is therefore scanty. There are a few clear-cut cases, however. See, for example, Keighley: MH 12.15159 May–July 1844 correspondence; Huddersfield: MH 12.15067 Dec. 1843 correspondence.

townships, which felt that they would be unfairly burdened if work-house costs were paid for on a Union basis, and the Commissioners, in order to avoid yet another source of friction, usually acquiesced in this procedure. But it had serious implications for the New Poor Law. By pinpointing the costs of workhouse relief, it fortified the Guardians' normal preference for outdoor over indoor relief and made even less likely the acceptance of any changes which might increase the costs of administering indoor relief. Moreover, by allowing the Guardians to get out of the system of Union charges, it encouraged them to continue to think of the Poor Law Union as an often inconvenient federation of individual townships, forced on them against their will from London.

The persistence of this intense parochialism was perhaps the most discouraging aspect of the workhouse controversy from the point of view of the Poor Law Commissioners, for it demonstrated more clearly than anything else just how far they were from getting not only compliance with but even a basic comprehension of the principles of the Poor Law Amendment Act. Prior to the summer of 1842 the Commissioners consoled themselves with the thought that their failure to convince the northern Guardians of the benefits of Union-wide organization could be attributed to the belief so prevalent in the North 'that the Poor Law Commission will be discontinued, and that the relief of the Poor will fall again into the hands of the officers of the separate townships'.[1] The Assistant Commissioners, underestimating their opponents as usual, hoped that the renewal of the Commissioners' term of office for another five years in 1842 might win the Boards over or, at the very least, lead them to resign themselves to their fate. If anything, however, the reverse was true. Not only did the workhouse controversy remain as intractable as before but resistance along similar lines began to flare up in other areas and in particular over the issue of the appointment and control of personnel.

Personnel had of course been a subject of dispute before and it always remained potentially one of the most explosive issues between the Commissioners and the northern Boards of Guardians, since it involved such sensitive questions as the control of patronage and the extent of local administrative autonomy. To these familiar bones of contention the depression of the early 1840s added another equally delicate problem. As pressure on the rates

[1] MH 12.5673 Mott to P.L.C. 4 Dec. 1841.

mounted, Boards of Guardians began to search desperately for ways of making economies in local administration. The most likely target because it was the most obvious and the easiest to attack was the salaries of the permanent Union staff, many of whom, however, the Commissioners considered to be already underpaid.

Taken together these factors may have been enough to explain the sudden re-emergence of disputes over personnel, but, in view of the earlier history of such disputes, it seems unlikely. Important as the subject of personnel was, it rarely arose independently as an issue or became the greatest source of friction. Perhaps because the authority of the Poor Law Commissioners in this area was so great and that of the Boards of Guardians so small, or because the Commissioners' case for a professional well paid corps of officers was essentially unanswerable, opposition Guardians rarely challenged the Commissioners over personnel unless they had already fallen out with them over some other issue. This had certainly been the case in the 1830s when serious differences with the Commissioners over the appointment of Relieving Officers began in and remained largely confined to Unions such as Dewsbury and Huddersfield. Later on between 1839 and 1841, when the Commissioners by and large let the northern Boards alone, the appointment of personnel caused very little trouble, even though it was one of the few areas where the Commissioners did interfere with local discretion. Only when the Commissioners began to intervene across the board in northern affairs late in 1841 did co-operation in many fields including personnel cease abruptly and many of the hitherto co-operative Unions begin to emulate the tactics of the die hards of four or five years before.

This could not have happened at a more unfortunate time for the Poor Law Commissioners, who were about to introduce another of their General Rules, the order regulating medical relief.[1] This order like most of the General Rules was a codification of earlier regulations many of which applied already even in the scarcely regulated North. In two respects, however, it was much more stringent than any earlier regulations. It defined maximum areas and populations for medical relief districts which were a good deal smaller than most of those already in existence and it required higher medical qualifications than had previously been the case. Ostensibly there was little that even a determined Board of Guardians could do to thwart the implementation of this order since the

[1] P.L.C., Eighth Annual Report, Appendix A, Nos. 5 and 6.

Commissioners had almost unlimited powers over the administration of relief including medical relief. The division of a Union into districts for any purpose could be dictated from London and, though the Commissioners did not have the power to appoint an individual to a local post, they could refuse to sanction any appointment of a Board of Guardians.

In practice this rarely happened. Only in those few cases where existing medical districts or the qualifications and pay scales of doctors were very far from meeting the Commissioners' standards, and the Boards of Guardians refused to make concessions voluntarily, did the Commissioners step in and dictate terms. In most Unions the Guardians acted more subtly.[1] The usual reply to the Commissioners' order was an offer of minor changes in the size of medical relief districts, slight increases in doctors' salaries, the addition of one or two highly qualified men, or some combination of the three which the Commissioners would accept as evidence of good faith in preference to declaring open warfare or embarking on long and complicated negotiations. If the Guardians were then able to maintain the right combination of determination and flexibility, they could usually retain the substance of what they wanted. After an initial interchange of correspondence and a few reprimands from London the Commissioners tended to give way much as they had in the disputes over Relieving Officers in 1838 and 1839, and for much the same reasons.

If the Commissioners hoped that a conciliatory policy would lead to greater co-operation in the future, they were sorely mistaken, for, unlike the disputes over the appointment of the first relieving officers, the medical relief battle was not fought out in isolation, or in a period of improving economic conditions, or in a few Unions only. It ran parallel with and was exacerbated by the much more serious workhouse controversy, it was protracted by continuing heavy pressure on the rates which continued well into 1844, and, since many Unions were involved, there was a tendency for each one to vie with its neighbors in spinning out the

[1] The controversy lasted for a number of years and involved almost all the northern Unions at one time or another. The following places and times are, however, perhaps the most important: Blackburn: MH 12.5530 Nov. 1843; Bolton: MH 12.5594–5 April 1842, Feb., June 1843; Burnley: MH 12.5674 Aug. 1843–Jan. 1844; Clitheroe: MH 12.5752 Nov. 1843–July 1844; Dewsbury: MH 12.14831 June 1842–May 1843; Keighley: MH 12.15159 April–July 1843; Todmorden: MH 12.6273 Aug.–Oct. 1844; Preston: *Preston Chronicle* Jan.–Sept. 1843.

endless game of proposal and counter proposal. As if this were not enough, a few Boards, having wrung concessions from London in the battles over workhouses or medical relief, began to try to undo some of the Commissioners' earlier achievements. The most extraordinary instance of this was the Bolton Board of Guardians' systematic destruction of the office of Assistant Overseer.[1] Having fought with the Commissioners ever since 1840, first over the initial appointment of Assistant Overseers which was forced on the Board by order of the Commissioners, and then in an inconclusive dispute over workhouse management, the Guardians went into open revolt when the Commissioners ordered them to give a raise in salary to the Assistant Overseers. The chairman of the Board took it upon himself to stop the increases and even, for a time, the entire salaries of the Assistant Overseers.

He dared do this only because of a series of recent court decisions that called into question the legal authority of the Poor Law Commissioners to compel the appointment of Assistant Overseers and, understandably in view of these decisions, the Commissioners' first reaction to this new act of defiance was defensive. Gradually however they regained their composure and, advised by the Assistant Commissioners that indecisiveness in this field could lead to a general revolt against their authority, they decided to bring as much pressure as they could to bear on the Bolton Guardians, however weak the legal backing for such pressure might be. The Bolton Board, no surer of the legal position than were the Commissioners, but far more vulnerable should they be proved wrong, therefore began to back down. But retreat on the matter of salaries was not the end of the business, for simultaneously the Board hit on another means of resistance which turned out to be absolutely foolproof. The Guardians demanded, as they had every right to do, that the Assistant Overseers should hand over the rate books for their districts. The books were given to the township overseers who then resumed the function they had performed under the Old Poor Law. The Commissioners were dumbfounded and completely helpless. They pleaded with the Guardians not to abuse their authority, but the Guardians, having at long last found a way of getting back at the Commissioners for years of interference in their affairs, turned a deaf ear.

[1] For developments in Bolton, see: MH 12.5593 passim, but especially Nov. 1841, Jan., April, July, Sept.–Oct. 1842, June 1845 correspondence.

Like the Todmorden workhouse affair, what happened in Bolton was an extreme case. But again like Todmorden, it was representative, if not in its results, at least of prevailing attitudes in the North. In Union after Union further progress by the Poor Law Commissioners in standardizing the requirements for local officers and bringing control of local administration more into central hands ceased;[1] the Commissioners were kept so busy preventing a deterioration of the existing situation that they had little time or opportunity to plan for further advances. Many Boards, using the pressure of unemployment as an excuse, attempted to re-introduce the old overseers as supplementary relieving officers or to resurrect the idea of a relieving officer for each township. Almost no Board at this time would even consider raising salaries and many pressed to have them lowered. The Commissioners, of course, resisted all these suggestions, but, with a dozen or more Unions simultaneously making the same complaints and the same demands, they found it increasingly difficult to keep abreast of the situation. Correspondence piled up and adequate supervision of each and every Union by the Assistant Commissioners proved impossible to maintain.

The Boards of Guardians soon learned how to take advantage of this. They carved out new relief or medical districts or appointed new men without the prior agreement of the Commissioners and then relied upon the usual long delays in correspondence and the cursory nature of the Assistant Commissioners' infrequent visits to endow their provisional arrangements with permanence. Even if, by chance, the Commissioners did react swiftly and decisively, the Guardians did not back down easily. Their favorite and least risky weapon was procrastination. Delays of some months were not uncommon in answering the Commissioners' letters and, even when an answer could no longer be avoided, it was possible to leave out vital information and thereby start the whole process over again. Should even this fail, or should a pro-Poor Law clerk or group of Guardians attempt to defeat an anti-Poor Law majority by feeding information to the Commissioners, a number of Boards

[1] Like the medical relief controversy, the disputes over other Union personnel, districts and salaries were both long lasting and very nearly universal. The following is a selection of the most important places and times: Blackburn: MH 12.5530 Dec. 1843; Bradford: MH 12.14721 Feb., April 1842; Chorley: PUX 1/2 Jan.–June 1843; Dewsbury: MH 12.14832 Aug.–Oct. 1843, Aug.–Oct. 1844; Huddersfield: MH 12.15067 Nov. 1843–March 1844; Wakefield: MH 12.15566 Oct.–Dec. 1842.

were not above conducting their affairs in secret and imposing a ban on all unofficial communications with London.

That this was illegal and that, for that matter, many of their tactics bordered on illegality, rarely troubled the really determined Boards. The Commissioners could, of course, have invoked the penalty clauses of the Poor Law Amendment Act and taken the offending Guardians to court as they had in Huddersfield in 1838. But the situations were hardly comparable. The prosecutions in 1838 had come only after months of sometimes violent resistance to the law in all its aspects, while in the 1840s the recalcitrant Boards confined themselves to pecking away at the edifice in an undramatic, if nonetheless effective, fashion. The opposition Guardians rightly judged that the Commissioners would not take the issue to the courts so long as opposition was subtler and less openly defiant than it had been at its worst in 1837 and 1838. It was necessary, therefore, to keep opposition within bounds, and this the Guardians did. If every one of the devious weapons in their arsenal failed, they did not move on to more direct defiance, except in very unusual cases, but backed down. The Commissioners had the authority and, if they chose to use it, no Board was willing to risk the consequence of non-compliance. Thus the opposition rarely was able to bring the Commissioners to a complete stand-still, as happened so often in the workhouse controversy where the relative powers of local and national authority were so well defined. Still, as a result of the special conditions prevailing in the North during the early 1840s and because of the Commissioners' un-willingness to impose their views on fractious Boards, the opposition did manage to gain a remarkable degree of control in a field where, theoretically, they should have had little.

The long-drawn-out struggles over personnel and workhouse management would each alone have been more than enough for the Commissioners to cope with, but they were not the only or even the most important problems which had to be faced in the North. The economic crisis of the early 1840s overshadowed them both and was to a large extent responsible for bringing them to the surface and for ensuring that they would remain a constant source of friction between the Poor Law Commissioners and the northern Boards. It was the prospect of the collapse of the relief system under the pressure of unemployment that led some Boards to seek the Commissioners' help and led from that to the investigations and revelations from which sprung the bitter controversies of 1842 and later years. Also it was the economic crisis which induced the Boards to seek the economies in relief costs, the overcrowding of workhouses and the keeping of salaries low, which were the main bones of contention between the Boards and the Commissioners. But, quite apart from its contribution to disputes in other areas, the depression itself was a source of controversy, at first rather less important than either personnel or workhouse management, but later on of much greater significance than both. These other issues remained and did much to poison the atmosphere in which an attempt was made to find a way of dealing with the burden of mass unemployment, but it was the failure to arrive at an agreed solution to this particular problem that led to an irrevocable breach between the Poor Law Commissioners and the northern opponents of the law.

XI Relieving the unemployed

Throughout the early months of 1842, while the Commissioners were absorbed in the controversy over workhouse management, they studiously avoided a confrontation with the northern Boards of Guardians on the most important issue of all, the relief of the able-bodied. It mattered little whether a Union was well- or ill-managed. As long as unemployment was kept within certain limits and the ability of most townships to keep up with rate payments was maintained, as long, in other words, as a margin for error still existed and the average Board felt able to cope, the Poor Law Commissioners were willing to let it do so without looking too closely at the means it employed. A number of explanations for the Commissioners' adoption of this approach to the problem have already been suggested, but it is possible that they had other, more devious motives as well.

The workhouse problem seemed to demand interference from London, since most Boards appeared to be quite content to go on forever treating them as laxly administered places of refuge rather than strictly disciplined tests of pauperism. Out-relief for the able-bodied was another matter, however, about which the Commissioners hoped the northern Boards might learn much from experience. For years the Commissioners had tried to convince the northern Guardians that out-relief given without a test or even proper supervision could lead only to disaster in times of severe distress, but most Boards, accustomed to prosperity and low rates, had refused to listen. In the early 1840s, however, it seemed possible that where the Commissioners had failed to convince, the depression might succeed. Given complete freedom to follow their own course, the Boards would, so the Commissioners believed, inevitably flounder and be forced to adopt the very restrictions which they had resisted for so long.

Allowing the northern opponents of the Law to stew in their own juice for a while did not mean that the Commissioners abdicated their responsibilities, for, while they did not attempt to dictate policy to the northern Boards of Guardians, the Commissioners constantly issued stern admonitions to the worst offenders and kept in touch and gave advice through occasional visits by the

Assistant Commissioners. Moreover, in those few cases where a Board of Guardians did seem to be approaching disaster and did turn to London for help, the Commissioners readily intervened, even to the point of assuming control. There were a number of Unions in which this happened to some extent but two, Stockport[1] and Burnley,[2] are particularly interesting.

No two industrialized Unions could have been less alike. The Burnley Union stretched out along the upper Calder valley at the northern end of the Lancashire textile district and its population was clustered, not around one center, but in a series of towns and villages strung out along the length of the Union. This was one of its problems, in some ways its worst problem, for it probably should have been two Unions. The upper part of the valley—the Colne district—had always resented its inclusion in a Union with Burnley. At first by boycotting the Board of Guardians elections and later on by electing Guardians pledged to the disruption of the affairs of the Union, it had always sought with considerable success to prevent the Burnley Board from functioning as a unit. The other half of the Union—Burnley and the area around it—had been comparatively co-operative and, in the early years when the Colne area had been unrepresented, some progress had been made. The Union was divided into large but workable relief districts, the salaries of permanent officers were low but adequate and the workhouses, though still rather carelessly administered, had been reduced in number and were used for Union purposes.

But even these modest attainments were peculiarly vulnerable in the Burnley Union. None of the problems of the Colne district which had made it so intractable on the 1830s had been solved. It was still economically backward with one of the highest concentrations of handloom weavers in the textile districts. It was chronically depressed and very nearly as prone to disorder as it had been seven or eight years before. Moreover, local resentment at having been included in the Burnley Union had not died out. Its Guardians constituted an unshakable permanent anti-Poor Law minority which only needed the defection of a handful of ordinarily pro-Poor Law Guardians from other townships to become a majority.

[1] For Stockport during this period, see: MH 12.1139; Report of Commission for Inquiring into the State of the Population of Stockport, *British Parliamentary Papers*, 1842, XXXV.

[2] For Burnley during this period, see: MH 12.5673.

Stockport, by contrast, was an almost perfect Union, at least as far as any Union in the industrial North could be called perfect. It was small in area and reasonably compact. It included most of the industrial townships to the south of Manchester, and Stockport was the natural center for the entire district. Like most of the Unions in that part of the North, it had always had an overwhelmingly pro-Poor Law Board of Guardians and, in the four years since it had first been formed, its progress had been remarkable. The Board had adopted what were, from the Commissioners' point of view, almost ideal standards in appointing and fixing the salaries of the permanent Union officials and in carving up the Union into relief and collection districts. Without pressure from London, the Guardians had established a system of safeguards on out-relief, which, short of accepting the prohibitory order, was all the Commissioners could ask for. Finally, the Stockport Board was one of the very few anywhere in the North which had agreed to build a workhouse. But Stockport was also an almost perfect example of a Union which, however well managed, was still dangerously vulnerable to economic crises. It was not economically backward like Colne; on the contrary, it was one of the greatest and longest established of the Lancashire–Cheshire mill towns. But because of this, many of its factories were out of date, comparatively inefficient and therefore more likely to close down during the depression than were more recently built plants in the newer centers of factory production.

Despite the extraordinary differences between these two Unions, they found themselves suffering in much the same way from the depression. In Burnley the main cause of the breakdown was the increasing pauperization of an already hard-pressed population, while in Stockport it came suddenly as the result of a few large factory closures, but the effect on the rates and on the Board of Guardians was identical. Similarly, while the lax control of the Burnley Board may have hastened the crisis, and the efficient procedures adopted in Stockport perhaps delayed it, the difference was at most a matter of weeks. In both Unions the relief system, however managed, was simply unable to cope.

At first the Commissioners were reluctant to admit this and started off by treating the two Unions very differently. The first reports of an impending crisis in Stockport brought an immediate and sympathetic response from London.[1] The Commissioners dis-

[1] MH 12.1139 Nov.–Dec. 1841 correspondence.

patched a special investigator and promised to give aid as quickly as possible. Almost identical reports of distress at Burnley were treated quite differently, however.[1] The Commissioners assumed, as they had in dealing with despairing reports from Burnley's neighbors, that most of the Union's troubles were due to lax administration. The Guardians' pleas for help were therefore used, as they had been so often elsewhere, as a pretext for administering a severe reprimand to the Board of Guardians. Mott spent much of his next visit to Burnley berating the Guardians and, while he did not neglect to investigate the peculiar hardships to which the Union was subject, these were given far less emphasis in his report to London than were his strictures on the general conduct of the Board.

The Commissioners, taking their cue from Mott, therefore followed their usual practice in dealing with the uncooperative northern Boards at this time and began to press the Guardians on the subject of workhouse management, rather than following up the evidence that Burnley's situation was particularly critical. Indeed, it required the sending of a special deputation from Burnley to convince the Commissioners that this was perhaps an exceptional case, worthy of the kind of special consideration which was being accorded automatically to Stockport. Sir John Walsham, who was about to set off for Stockport, was requested to extend his investigations to Burnley and, within little more than a fortnight after the visit of the deputation, he was in the North, first at Burnley, then at Stockport, directing a reorganization of the relief system and preparing a series of detailed reports on the situation.

The condition of both Unions as revealed in these reports was incredibly bleak.[2] In Stockport, for example, Mott estimated that in January 1842 the unemployed numbered at least 3,000, or 10 per cent of the entire population. The figures in Burnley were complicated by the large number of handloom weavers, many of whom were still partially employed, but, if anything, the position there was even worse. The relief roles were huge in both

[1] MH 12.5673 Nov. 1841–May 1842 correspondence.
[2] MH 12.1139 Mott to P.L.C. 9 March 1842; Power and Twistleton to P.L.C. 9 Feb. 1842; Report on the State of the Population of Stockport; MH 12.5673 Walsham to P.L.C. 19, 20, 21, 23, 26 May 1842. On the subject of unemployment rates in these and other Lancashire towns at this time see: E. J. Hobsbawm, *Labouring Men* (London 1964), Ch. V, Part III B.

Unions and there was every reason to believe that they would grow far larger unless economic conditions improved rapidly. Many who were already unemployed were kept off public relief only because they could draw funds from the many workers' provident societies—Stockport apparently had more than one hundred—which existed all over the North. And many others refrained from seeking public assistance only because they came from other areas of the country and feared being sent back to their Union of settlement. Should the depression persist, it was inevitable that unemployed in both categories would eventually seek public help.

Yet, even while these special limiting factors still operated, and even after relief scales had been cut to the bone, the Guardians found it impossible to meet the demands for relief. Both Unions, in their entirety, were in the dangerous position which a few townships in almost every northern Union had also reached. No matter how often the rates were levied, they did not bring in enough to pay the costs of relief and the levying of rates in itself was worsening the situation. Mott estimated that in 1842 a rate levied on the same scale as in 1838 would bring in only half as much money. The number defaulting on rate payments had risen alarmingly and of those taken to court because of this a majority were excused by the magistrates on the grounds of poverty.

In Stockport there seemed to be no escape from the downward spiral. Neither Mott, nor Walsham, nor any of the other special investigators sent from London could find much to complain about in the way the Guardians were handling the crisis. Relief payments in money, common until mid-1841, had been stopped, as had the payment of rents and even the supplying of clothing. All relief was now in foodstuffs and the amount dispensed was pitifully small even by Mott's exacting standards. The Stockport Guardians did not, to be sure, make use of a workhouse test, but, as Mott admitted, the prohibitory order, if it had been in force, would have to have been suspended in any case. The recommended alternative, a labor test, was also not in force in Stockport and one of the few suggestions which the Commissioners believed could usefully be made to the Guardians was that they should put the able-bodied unemployed to work breaking stones. The Guardians complied but this failed to have the deterrent effect that was hoped for. Only a small proportion of those on out-relief could be employed at any one time and, even so, the Guardians soon found themselves burdened with a large supply of broken stones for which no buyers could be found.[1]

Burnley was less frustrating for the Commissioners, at least at first. The administration of relief and the conduct of the Union's finances had been so inefficient for so long that it was possible to hope that a major overhaul would reduce the crisis to manageable proportions. With the full co-operation of the Guardians, united for the moment by the prospect of disaster, Walsham set out to transform Burnley into a model Union.[2] The immediate crisis was met by appointing supplementary Relieving Officers in each of the relief districts and by abolishing all relief in money in favor of relief in food only. A more efficient system of processing applicants was made possible by setting up separate district relief committees composed of Guardians, Relieving Officers and Overseers, whose findings would then be brought back to the full Board of Guardians for final approval. Progress towards more substantial reforms was ensured by the creation of special subcommittees of the Board to deal with Union finance, workhouse relief and a proposed labor test. All these changes had immediate and substantial results. The Union's finances were put on an orderly basis, the per capita cost of relief was reduced, a workhouse test was applied on a limited scale to single, able-bodied, unemployed males and a labor test was imposed on able-bodied unemployed heads of families. By mid-summer, according to Walsham, the Burnley Union had become the equal of Stockport as a model of efficiency and sound policy in the North.

The Commissioners' handling of the crisis in Stockport and, at least after an initial misunderstanding, in Burnley as well fully vindicated the caution (or timidity) with which they had approached the explosive question of relief to the able-bodied in the winter of 1841–2. In neither Union had the Commissioners intervened unasked, nor had they issued or threatened to issue any regulations restricting the granting of out-relief. On the contrary, the Guardians of Stockport and Burnley under the pressure of mass unemployment had themselves seen the need for and voluntarily adopted such restrictions, and had moreover invited

[1] MH 12.1139 Power and Twistleton to P.L.C. 9 Feb.; Forster to Power 24 May 1842.
[2] MH 12.5673 Walsham to P.L.C. 23, 26 May, 20 June; Walsham to Hyett 28 May, 2, 13 June 1842.

the Poor Law Commissioners to aid them in implementing these measures. Yet in late April when the Stockport and Burnley Boards were on the verge of throwing themselves on the mercy of Somerset House, reports of an impending crisis of a similar nature in the Keighley Union met with a very different response.[1] In accordance with the by-now-familiar procedure in such cases, Mott visited the Union, unearthed the expected examples of gross mismanagement, lectured the recalcitrant Guardians in scathing terms and recommended to London that the workhouse regulations be issued immediately. But, contrary to normal procedure, he did not stop at this point. He also recommended that a labor test be imposed on all able-bodied male applicants for relief, despite the fact that this was opposed almost unanimously by the Keighley Board of Guardians.

This abrupt about-face was due in part to special conditions in the Keighley Union itself. The Board of Guardians election in March resulted in an overwhelming victory for an anti-Poor Law slate of candidates which then embarked on a wholesale review of Poor Law policy that appeared to be leading to open defiance of the authority of the Poor Law Commissioners. Hence Mott's tough response, which, however risky, seemed necessary if discipline was to be maintained. At the same time, there is good reason to believe that there were more general considerations behind Mott's treatment of Keighley. During the early months of 1842 Mott's views on the whole question of out-relief to the able-bodied hardened discernably, largely because of the extensive use of privately subscribed relief funds to supplement relief given under the New Poor Law.[2] Such funds dated back to late 1841 and had quickly become an integral part of the relief system. At the time of Mott's visit to Keighley a new campaign to expand and multiply private sources of relief was just getting under way and, as it turned out, the money raised was to prove indispensable in the efforts of Burnley and Stockport to bring the crisis under control. The relief of Stockport required no less than three massive appeals, the last of them coinciding with Walsham's arrival there, and in the case of Burnley the backbone of the reformed relief

[1] On developments in Keighley early in 1842 see: MH 12.15158 Ellis to P.L.C. 6 April 1842; Mott to P.L.C. 23 April and 21 June 1842; Walsham to P.L.C. 9 June 1842; Board of Guardians to P.L.C. 27 June 1842.

[2] For the gradual hardening of Mott's views see: MH 12.1139 9 March, 1 April and 30 May 1842.

system, the labor test, was financed entirely from public subscription. There can be little doubt that left to itself the New Poor Law in these Unions would have collapsed.

Walsham, who had no permanent responsibilities in the area and had come to the textile districts primarily to administer the funds raised by the largest of the private groups, the Manufacturer's Relief Committee, quite freely admitted this and saw in the situation no criticism of the New Poor Law.[1] A depression of this magnitude was an extraordinary occurrence and Burnley and Stockport were extreme cases in an extraordinary situation. It was no reflection on the normal system of relief to admit that it could not cope with the abnormal. In such circumstances, Walsham maintained, an emergency relief fund was as sensible as it was necessary and, so long as its life was not extended into normal times and its benefits were restricted to those who were suffering directly from the depression, there was no danger in making use of such a fund. Mott disagreed. At one time or another during the first half of 1842 he put forward any number of different explanations of the relief crisis rather than accept the proposition that the New Poor Law was not adequate to the task. He blamed the privately raised relief funds and especially the early ones, which, he asserted, had been dispersed in such a way as to create a hard core of free-loaders. He even blamed the poor themselves, whom he dismissed in one of his unguarded moments as for the most part vicious, dishonest and unworthy of being helped.

More fundamentally he blamed the Guardians, who, he believed, could have prevented the creation of a large class of semi-dependent paupers and managed without the intervention of private charity. As proof of this he cited the case of Halliwell in the Bolton Union.[2] There, in the spring of 1841, approximately 1,000 men had been thrown out of work by factory closures. In many, perhaps most northern townships this would have led to a huge increase in the relief roles, but the poor of Halliwell, as Mott observed, had not been taught dependence and were not now given the chance to learn it. Large-scale relief was not forthcoming and the unemployed of Halliwell scattered in search of work. Forty per cent found it in similar jobs in the Bolton Union. Another 10 per cent also remained in the Bolton area by getting

[1] MH 12.5673 Walsham to Hyett 14 June 1842; Walsham to P.L.C. 26 May 1842.
[2] MH 12.5594 Mott to P.L.C. 30 April 1841.

jobs in different trades. But 30 per cent were forced to leave in order to find work and some of these had to go as far as forty miles before they were successful. A few died (from what causes we do not know) and the remainder, just over 200 men, remained either totally or partially unemployed. Mott was convinced, probably correctly, that had relief been offered immediately this last group would have been far larger and, while he admitted that not every town could do as well especially as the crisis deepened in 1842, he nonetheless believed that the contrast between what Halliwell had done and what the great majority of northern Boards of Guardians were doing was decisive.

This was perhaps obvious in the case of badly mismanaged Boards such as Burnley's, but Mott was now convinced that even the Stockport Guardians were almost equally deserving of censure. Their honesty, efficiency and co-operativeness could not be denied but it was Mott's contention that in the most important quality of all, the understanding of and readiness to adopt the strictest preventive measures, they were little less deficient than the worst of the northern Boards. All of the restrictions on relief that the Commissioners could have hoped for—the cutting back of relief scales, a labor test, a limited workhouse test—had been adopted, but in no case had they been used to avert a crisis and encourage people to seek an alternative to relief. Instead they had been resorted to in a succession of desperate attempts to hold down spiralling costs and persuade people already on relief to seek an alternative. Used in this way, Mott argued, such restrictions, however well administered, were bound to be less effective than the same measures used earlier, because in the interim the number on relief and habituated to relief had been allowed to grow to the point where local financial and administrative resources could no longer cope and private charity, which itself tended to aggravate the situation, had had to be called in. To implement restrictive measures effectively under these conditions was bound to be far more costly, not only in money, the reorganizational effort involved and time, but also in terms of the credibility of the New Poor Law.

The practical conclusions were obvious. Since, as Mott was now certain, deterrence as a cure was not and could not be made the equal of deterrence as a preventive measure, the earlier optimistic assumption that the northern Boards of Guardians could and should be allowed to learn from bitter experience had to be abandoned. If this was true even in Stockport, how much more the case in a Union like Keighley. There Mott foresaw the possibility that the Union might sink into a nearly irretrievable state of chronic mismanagement and ingrained pauperism before the Guardians realized their errors. To gamble that this would not happen rather than compel an unwilling Board to take preventive action was a risk Mott was no longer willing to take. Hence his unprecedented recommendation that the Labour Test Order be imposed on the fractious Guardians of Keighley in the depths of a serious recession.

Whether Mott intended this experiment in compulsion to be the first step in a new and tougher policy throughout the North we do not know, for if Keighley was the victim of a new view of general policy, Mott's plans were in turn the victim of Parliamentary politics.[1] Unfortunately for the Commissioners Peel's Poor Law renewal bill was being debated in Parliament at just this time and one of the anti-Poor Law Tory M.P.s elected in 1841, William Busfeild Ferrand, happened also to be the chairman of the Keighley Board of Guardians. Inevitably therefore the problems of Keighley quickly became a subject of Parliamentary debate. As so often with the Parliamentary opponents of the Poor Law, Ferrand got some of his facts wrong. He accused the Commissioners of having introduced the Prohibitory Order rather than the Labour Test Order into Keighley, a mistake the Home Secretary, Sir James Graham, made good use of when he rose to answer Ferrand's charges. Ferrand therefore shifted his attack from the general problem of relief policy in the North to the specific issue of the character and conduct of Charles Mott, whom he accused of being overbearing in his handling of the northern Guardians and of having maligned and misrepresented the conduct of the Keighley Board. In order to defend Mott and the Commissioners, Graham produced Mott's reports on Keighley and later proposed the appointment of a Select Committee to investigate the whole affair.

These moves were intended, of course, to vindicate both Mott and his employers but the effects were quite the opposite. The main achievement of the debates and the Select Committee was to bring Mott's private and often vituperative comments on the

[1] Hansard, *op. cit.*, LXIV, 133–60, 259–70; Returns Relating to the Keighley Union, *B.P.P.*, 1842, XXXV; MH 12.15158 August 1842 correspondence.

Keighley Union out into the open with the result that he soon found himself distrusted by almost all the northern Boards. It was probably because of this that Mott was relieved of his post as an Assistant Commissioner early in 1843. The effects on Keighley were hardly less discomfiting to the Commissioners, who now had not only to deal with an aroused Board of Guardians but had to do so with Parliament peering over their shoulders. Though they did not admit that this was their reason for doing so, the Commissioners beat a hasty retreat from what was becoming an embarrassingly exposed position by suspending the Labour Test Order in Keighley for the remainder of the parochial year. In addition the Commissioners abandoned whatever plans they may have had for using Keighley as an opening wedge; in the one other Union, Warrington, to which the Test Order had been issued, a suspending order followed almost immediately, well before any steps could be taken to implement the labor test.

The Commissioners had in effect been forced back to their earlier policy of waiting until economic conditions improved before dealing directly with the question of out-relief to the able-bodied poor. They were not inclined to wait very long, however, and as soon as the winter of 1842–3 was over and it had become clear that the economic situation was not as bad as it had been the year before, Assistant Commissioner Clements returned to the attack with the full backing of Somerset House. But it was to be an altogether more cautious attack than Mott had begun to mount nine months earlier. Unemployment was still great enough that the introduction of a labor test was bound to entail very substantial changes, and what had happened in Keighley had proven just how unpleasant the repercussions of attempting to force such changes on a factious Board could be. Therefore the Commissioners moved far more cautiously in 1843. They attempted to introduce the labor test into three Unions only and, while each of these suffered from serious economic pressures and none could have been called a model of efficient management, all of them had been reasonably co-operative ever since their formation.

Unfortunately for the Commissioners, one of these three was Warrington[1] where the Guardians had narrowly escaped having to

---

[1] For Warrington during this period we are entirely dependent on the Board of Guardians minute books (PUV 1/2–3) which are often far from adequate.

introduce a labor test in 1842 and knew that they were unlikely to escape it much longer. Thus forewarned, the opposition Guardians had begun to prepare themselves for a war of attrition with Somerset House.[1] Some time before the reactivation of the Test Order in April 1843 the Board directed one of the Relieving Officers to investigate the administration of labor tests in other similar Unions, and, on the excuse that the report was not yet complete, the Board requested a further delay which the Commissioners reluctantly granted. Two months later, with the report in hand and Clements applying pressure, the opposition changed its tactics. A number of Guardians suggested that a new workhouse might prove an acceptable alternative to the labor test and the Board voted to consider the possibility. To some extent this vote reflected a genuine division of opinion on relief policy within the Warrington Board but many, perhaps most Guardians had no intention of seriously considering a workhouse and were simply maneuvering for a further delay. This at any rate was the only result. Months of debate and correspondence followed and, though nothing was decided or seemed likely to be decided, it was not until the end of the year that the Commissioners woke up to the fact that the Warrington Board was playing games with them.

Once they did realize this, the Commissioners began for the first time to apply severe and constant pressure on the Board.[2] By this time, however, the Warrington Guardians were jealous of their independence and had little respect for the Commissioners' determination. As a result it was nearly a year before the situation was brought under control. When Clements finally forced the Guardians to decide between a new workhouse and the labor test, they decisively rejected the former but then proceeded to try to worm their way out of the latter by interpreting its provisions in a way that would have made them almost meaningless. This of course was rejected by the Commissioners, who immediately directed the auditor to disallow all relief granted in violation of the letter of the Test Order, and threatened the Guardians with legal action if they refused compliance. Even these threats did not have the desired effect, however. The Guardians voted overwhelmingly to ignore the Labour Test Order and began drawing up memorials and petitions demanding an end to the labor test,

[1] For the early delaying tactics of the Warrington Guardians see: PUV 1/2 29 March, 28 June and 19 July 1843.
[2] *Ibid.* Dec. 1843–July 1844.

greater local autonomy and the breaking up of the Warrington Union.

With this move to extend their opposition from the labor test to the New Poor Law as a whole, the Warrington Guardians became overnight a danger rather than an annoyance. Already their successful resistance was having a disquieting effect on neighboring Unions[1] and the Commissioners must have been haunted by the parallel between this situation and role of Huddersfield in the West Riding seven years before. With major concessions therefore out of the question and threats having proved worse than useless, the Commissioners appear to have decided on yet another change in tactics. Open warfare with the Warrington Board gave way to private pressure and negotiations which resulted eventually in the implementation of the Labour Test Order.[2] Precisely how the Commissioners finally won the battle is not clear since information on its last phase is totally inadequate; but that the Commissioners' victory, however won, was hollow is certain. A superintendent of outdoor labor was not appointed and work was not begun until December 1844, twenty-eight months after the Labour Test Order was first issued to Warrington. In the interim the Commissioners had suffered a serious loss of respect and confidence throughout the northern textile districts. And, in any case, by the time it was put into effect the Labour Test Order was of greater symbolic than real importance, since returning prosperity had very largely solved the problem of the unemployed male able-bodied poor.

The Commissioners' handling of the labor test dispute in Warrington had been disastrous almost from start to finish. In Bradford and Halifax,[3] the other two Unions where the Labour Test Order was tried out at this time, the Commissioners had better luck, at least at first. In both cases the order was issued early in 1843 in the wake of reports of mismanagement and an impending financial crisis. In both cases groups of opposition Guardians began immediately to devise methods of delaying or defeating the Order. Yet in neither case were they able to circumvent the Poor Law Commissioners. Divided among themselves and taken completely by surprise by the Commissioners' action, the opposition Guardians were unable to organize effective resistance before they found

[1] MH 12.14724 Clements to P.L.C. 27 May 1844.
[2] PUV 1/2 16 Oct. 1844; PUV 1/3 Nov.–Dec. 1844.
[3] For the labor test controversy in these two Unions, see: Bradford: MH 12.14723; Halifax: MH 12.14976. Newspaper coverage is also helpful, especially that of the *Halifax Guardian*.

themselves pressed into implementing the Order. Clements attended one or the other of the Boards' meetings almost every week, the Commissioners allowed the Guardians only a few weeks in which to make preparations, every request for an extension was carefully scrutinized, and when the Bradford Board showed signs of moving from dilatoriness to outright opposition the Commissioners replied with a sharply worded ultimatum demanding immediate compliance. Faced as they now were with the choice between open defiance and at least nominal compliance, both Boards caved in and did what was necessary. The able-bodied male paupers of Bradford were set to work filling in a quarry and converting this into useful agricultural land, while the Halifax Guardians undertook to have their paupers reclaim waste moorland for agricultural use. Both tasks won the immediate approval of the Commissioners as being useful while at the same time not likely to compete with private industry or to promote private gain. Both Boards, moreover, appointed supervisory staff of good quality, rather than political friends of the Guardians, as was so often the case with Union officials.[1]

Because of the haste with which it had been implemented the labor test did not work smoothly in either Union at first. Nonetheless the Commissioners were reasonably satisfied. At least the principle of a labor test had been established and this in itself seemed likely to make the later ironing out of anomalies a good deal easier. Such an approach appeared infinitely preferable to the endless delays involved in the probably fruitless attempt to establish a perfectly working labor test. Much the same reasoning lay behind the Commissioners' policy, adopted at about the same time, of issuing the workhouse regulations even to Unions where the workhouses were well below the standards envisaged in the regulations. This approach to the problem of workhouses was already proving partially successful and would have been even more so, but for the legal restrictions on the powers of the Commissioners with regard to workhouses. There was, therefore, every reason to suppose that the use of similar tactics in promoting a labor test would have even better results, for there were no comparable restrictions on the authority of the Commissioners in regulating out-relief.

The Commissioners' satisfaction at the results of their firmness

[1] MH 12.14723 Jan.–April 1843 correspondence; MH 12.14976 Jan.–March 1843 correspondence.

in Bradford and Halifax was short lived, however. Furious at having been rushed into providing a labor test, the Guardians began to oppose the Commissioners in almost everything else.[1] Nor did it prove as easy as the Commissioners had hoped to win more than nominal compliance with the Labour Test Order. Indeed the search for loopholes which the Guardians had not had time to make before the Order came into effect was now begun in earnest.[2] There were, for example, a number of clauses in the Labour Test Order allowing relief without a test in cases of great urgency, illness and other unusual circumstances. Every such case had to be reported to London for final approval but the Guardians judged correctly that, so long as they did not blatantly abuse their dispensing powers, few of their decisions, once taken, would be reversed, and steadily throughout the year the list of these exceptional cases grew. The Bradford Board, which had always been the more difficult of the two, went even further. It interpreted the Commissioners' assurance that the labor test would be administered flexibly as a license to apply the test selectively. The Guardians never even attempted to put to work all the able-bodied male paupers receiving relief. They counted on the exemplary management of their limited labor test to provide cover for what they were doing until renewed prosperity would absorb the unemployed and eliminate the problem.

Such double dealing, Assistant Commissioner Clements observed when he discovered what was going on, was only to be expected from the Bradford Board of Guardians, but, within a month, it was revealed that the heretofore docile Halifax Guardians were not above resorting to similar tactics. At the beginning of November the Board decided to suspend the operation of the labor test on the grounds of the difficulty of carrying it out in the winter months. They did not, however, ask the Commissioners' approval or even inform them of their decision until four weeks later. Clements was furious:

It appears to me that here, as in Bradford, it has become a question, not whether the order can be satisfactorily carried out, but whether your Board are or are not to have any control over the mode of administering relief. To concede the point will be to acknowledge that you cannot establish that control for which the Commission appears to

---

[1] *Halifax Guardian*, 18 Feb., 15 April 1844.
[2] MH 12.14723 Oct.-Nov. 1843 correspondence; MH 12.14976 Nov. 1843 correspondence.

have been especially created. I recommend therefore that the same course be adopted here as has lately been done in Bradford, that the Guardians be informed that the provisions of the order must be carried out and that after a certain day named the attention of the Auditor will be called to the necessity of disallowing all relief granted to the able bodied contrary to its provisions.[1]

The Commissioners responded immediately, though their ultimatum was couched in milder terms than Clements would have liked.[2] The auditor of the Bradford Union was ordered in mid-November to disallow all relief payments made in violation of the labor test. The Halifax Board was treated somewhat more leniently, perhaps in the hope that a spirit of co-operation could be restored. Rather than order the auditor to disallow certain payments after a given date, the Commissioners informed the Board that they would be compelled to do this if the order was not carried out. This threat was sufficient to force the Guardians into renewing the labor test but it also led to a rapid deterioration in the relations between the Board and the Poor Law Commissioners. From early 1844 until the time when returning prosperity made relief to the unemployed an issue of little practical importance, the Halifax Guardians outdid even their neighbors in Bradford in devising ways of wrecking the labor test. If the weather was bad, work was suspended, men in partial employ were taken on and the number of those relieved without a test in accordance with the various escape clauses was extended to include as many applicants as possible.[3]

As in the long struggle over workhouse management, the Commissioners tended to assume that Board of Guardians' resistance to the labor test sprang from the basest of motives, and, in particular, from a short-sighted desire to save money. Unquestionably pecuniary motives did play a part. Every Board which was threatened with a labor test complained about the cost of administering it and, in addition, there was the even more difficult problem of working out an equitable distribution of the costs among the various townships in the Union. There were any number of variations on this theme, but in every case it boiled down to the fear on the part of each township that it would be

[1] MH 12.14976 Clements to P.L.C. 30 Nov. 1843.
[2] MH 12.14723 P.L.C. to Clough 16 Nov. 1843; MH 12.14976 P.L.C. to Barstow 5 Dec. 1843, 22 Jan. 1844.
[3] MH 12.14724 and MH 12.14976 Feb.–March 1844 correspondence.

paying for labor performed in other towns by the paupers of other towns.

In at least one Union, Warrington, this seems to have been far and away the most important reason for resistance to the labor test. In late 1844 the Guardians came up with a scheme to spread the work to be done over all the townships of the Union in direct proportion to the amount each township paid into the relief fund, and, within a few weeks of the adoption of this formula, almost all signs of Board of Guardians' opposition had died away.[1] The issues of principle on which the Warrington Board had based its case against the labor test were shelved. Nothing more was heard of the inapplicability of the labor test or of the need to keep the administration of the law in local hands. Admittedly, there were other factors, in particular the tremendous pressure which the Commissioners exerted on the Guardians in the late months of 1844. But they had resisted equally strong pressures before and it is hard to see any reason for the complete lack even of an attempt to resist at this time other than that the Guardians had at last solved the financial problem to their satisfaction.

The same, however, cannot be said of the opposition to the labor test in other Unions.[2] No Board, to be sure, was unconcerned with this aspect of the question. In every Union where the test was proposed the Board sooner or later began to agitate for the breaking up of the Union, always a sign that the out-townships were dissatisfied, usually over financial matters. But there were other objections as well, which, though they often touched on the financial problem, existed independently of it. Divided though they were on the principle of a labor test and its efficacy as a deterrent, the Bradford and Halifax Guardians were almost unanimously agreed on one point, that a uniformly and universally applied labor test was bound to be both unjust and inefficient. Starting from the assumption that the great majority of the unemployed would work if work were available, the Guardians were unable to see why the Commissioners sought to treat all able-bodied paupers in the same way. In the interest of justice as well as economy they believed that some distinction had to be made between the honest and dishonest poor as well as between those

---

[1] PUV 1/3 13 Nov. 1844.
[2] On B.G. attitudes towards the labor test, see: MH 12.14723 Wagstaff to P.L.C. 25 April 1843; MH 12.15158 B.G. to P.L.C. 27 June 1842; *Halifax Guardian* 19 and 28 Jan., 9, 11 and 18 Feb., 25 Nov. 1843.

wholly unemployed and those who were temporarily under-employed. In addition the Guardians doubted whether even the most elaborately organized labor test would be able to cope with mass unemployment in times of severe depression and, should this prove possible, there was the alternative problem of what to do about unfinished tasks and redundant supervisory staff when prosperity and full employment returned. The parallel with the Guardians' complaints against workhouses is obvious and the dispute over the labor test only served to confirm the view, already so widely held, that the New Poor Law was inapplicable in the industrial North of England.

The Commissioners were no more willing to listen to this point of view in 1844 than they had been eight years before. Whether or not they still believed that the workhouse test was suited to urban industrial areas, there can be no question that the Commissioners regarded a labor test as not only applicable but indispensable. Thus, when unemployment in those Unions where a labor test was in force fell to insignificant proportions, the Commissioners were placed in a quandary. To revoke the test order was unthinkable, and suspension, which was the sensible course, had its dangers. 'If the Guardians were reasonable people', Clements wrote of the Bradford Board when the issue of suspension was raised, 'one would say suspend it. But if that is done, we shall have no end of difficulty getting it into operation again at some future time.'[1] So the Commissioners delayed as long as possible and, when finally suspension became unavoidable, they arranged it in such a way that the Guardians would have no doubt about its provisional character. Each individual case of out-relief to the able-bodied had to be reported to London for approval and, whenever the number of such cases began to grow significantly, the Commissioners took care to warn the Guardians that any further increase would lead to a re-imposition of the labor test.[2]

Accompanied as it was by safeguards and warnings, the suspension of the Labour Test Order in Bradford and Halifax involved no diminution of the Commissioners' authority, nor did it necessarily imply any slackening in their resolve. If anything it should have made the extension of the Labour Test Order throughout the textile

[1] MH 12.14724 Clements to P.L.C. 27 May 1844.
[2] MH 12.14724 July 1844 correspondence; MH 12.14725 Nov. 1846 correspondence; MH 12.14976 July–Aug. 1844 correspondence.

R

districts more rather than less likely. The introduction of the order in a suspended form would have established the principle of uniform administration of a test to the able-bodied, as well as a constant check on the number and type of able-bodied paupers seeking relief, without at the same time forcing a major change in the actual day to day administration of relief which might have aroused public excitement and destructive opposition from the Boards of Guardians. In view of what Mott and Clements had been saying since 1842, this should, logically, have been the Commissioners' next step. Indeed, unless it was their intention to extend the labor test throughout the area, the long battle with those few Unions where it had been introduced made little sense. Yet, despite the fact that conditions were favorable—the North was more prosperous and peaceful than it had been for years—no such action was taken nor apparently even contemplated. The suspension of the Labour Test Order in Bradford and Halifax, far from opening a new and more subtle phase in the Commissioners' campaign to establish some measure of uniformity in the North, marked the effective abandonment of that campaign. The Labour Test Order was introduced in only one additional Union in the area during the remaining years of the Commissioners' term of office and it was not until eight years later that the Commissioners' successors reopened the question.

The Commissioners' disengagement from the battle over a labor test was not an isolated event. The suspensions of the Test Order in Bradford and Halifax in July and August 1844 were only two among many indications that year that the Commissioners were growing tired of the struggle in the North and becoming reconciled, in practice if not yet in theory, to the idea that some sort of compromise was inevitable. The process was hardly dramatic. In most cases it was simply a matter of reducing pressure on those Unions with which the Commissioners had been almost constantly at war for two years or more, and of being more amenable to compromise when new issues arose. Most of the familiar subjects of dispute such as personnel and workhouse management were handled in just this way from mid- or late-1844 onwards.[1] In some cases the Commissioners went even further,

---

[1] Typical examples of this new relationship between the northern B.G. and the P.L.C. could be taken from almost any Union. The following subjects, places and times are only a selection. Workhouses: Blackburn: MH 12.5530 June–Dec. 1845; Bury PUB 1/3 April–Oct. 1844. Medical

actually withdrawing from exposed and, at least for the moment, untenable positions. The most interesting examples, because their potential implications for relief policy throughout industrial England were so great, were the Commissioners' failure to renew the Prohibitory Order in Nottingham and the permission given to Todmorden in 1844 to abandon its workhouses completely. But there were other instances of the Commissioners' reluctance to engage in combat which involved scarcely less important issues of principle.

In the winter of 1845–6 Keighley experienced a minor relief crisis. Since the Union was subject to the Outdoor Labour Test Order, the Guardians, as well as being obliged to provide a labor test, which they did, were prohibited from paying the rents of any pauper. This was all very well in theory, but it soon proved enormously troublesome in practice. As the unemployed fell behind in rent payments, many landlords began to resort to the practice of distraining and selling the personal possessions of their tenants in lieu of rent. There seemed to be no way of checking this within the terms laid down by the Labour Test Order and in the early spring of 1846 Assistant Commissioner Austin wrote to London urgently requesting advice and help. In reply the Commissioners reiterated their view that 'rents cannot be paid as such', but then went on to provide a large loophole. 'The Guardians', they noted, 'are without doubt bound to make such allowance to a pauper destitute of lodging as will enable that pauper to procure lodging during such time as the allowance is intended to cover.'[1] This distinction may perhaps have meant something to the Commissioners; to the Guardians of the Keighley Union it meant simply that indirect payment of rents through the paupers would now replace the traditional practice of direct payments to the landlords.

Another problem from which the Commissioners backed away during these years was the perennial question of non-resident relief. They had skirted this issue from the beginning in the North

Relief: Clitheroe: MH 12.5752 Jan.–July 1845; Dewsbury: MH 12.14832 Feb.–March 1844. Assistant Overseers: Bolton: MH 12.5597 March–May 1845; Haslingden: MH 12.5840 June–Sept. 1845. B.G. procedure: Dewsbury: MH 12.14832 May–June 1845; Wakefield: MH 12.15568 July 1845. Relief policy: Huddersfield: MH 12.15068 Aug.–Sept. 1846; Keighley: MH 12.15159 May 1846.

[1] MH 12.15149 P.L.C. to Spencer 23 May 1846, in reply to Spencer to P.L.C. 7 May and Austin to P.L.C. 13 May.

on the grounds that, because such a large percentage of the working population of the textile districts lived outside its area of legal settlement, any sudden prohibition of non-resident relief would cause severe hardship and enormous administrative difficulties. Nonetheless the Commissioners remained committed to its abolition or at least its reform, and with some reason since it was subject to a variety of abuses. In some cases Relieving Officers from the paupers' Union of settlement actually visited and relieved them in their Union of residence. More often, the Relieving Officers processed all applicants, whether settled or not, in their Union of residence, and then periodically squared accounts with the Relieving Officers of neighboring Unions. In either case adequate supervision of the granting of relief and of the use of funds was difficult, so that the potential for lax administration, fraud and the unequal treatment of paupers was enormous, as, indeed, was recognized by all the Assistant Commissioners and many Boards of Guardians.

Even so, most Boards believed that this was the only way the problem could be handled and, as might be expected, preferred bi-lateral agreements between Unions to outside interference as a means of improving the situation. None of the Assistant Commissioners believed that this would suffice; the only remedy, they argued, short of repealing the law of settlement, was to tighten central control over the settlement of accounts for non-resident relief between the northern Unions. Yet, at the end of 1843, when a particularly glaring example of the inefficiency inherent in the system was revealed, Assistant Commissioner Clements rather wearily advised London that, 'As a question of policy I am persuaded that we shall do no good in trying to impede non-resident relief by creating difficulties in the settlement of accounts. The Guardians will only consider this as an additional example of the inapplicability of the law to their district.'[1] The Commissioners agreed. The most that they were willing to do at this stage was issue an order tightening up bookkeeping procedures and placing responsibility more firmly in the hands of the Boards of Guardians, in the hope of reducing the danger of fraud. No restrictions, as the Commissioners were very careful to point out,

---

[1] MH 12.14976 Clements to P.L.C. 5 Dec. 1843. For a more general discussion of the whole problem see: MH 32.1128 Feb. 1844. The non-resident relief order is in P.L.C., Eleventh Annual Report, *B.P.P.*, 1845, XXVII, 9–10, 39–44.

were placed on non-resident relief itself or on the freedom of the Boards of Guardians to transfer funds from Union to Union for that purpose.

Almost the only exception to the growing caution with which the Commissioners handled nearly every issue affecting the North after 1843 was their treatment of Rochdale, Oldham and Ashton.[1] Of these three Unions only Rochdale yet had a Board of Guardians and it, like the two boycotting Unions, was as free from outside interference as it had been seven years before. In every year since 1839 the Assistant Commissioner for the district, first Power, then Mott and finally Clements, had reminded the Commissioners of this and urged immediate action. But always the Commissioners had deferred the problem on the grounds that political unrest or economic recession made it inadvisable. In 1844, however, the North was calmer and economically healthier than it had been since 1836 and the Commissioners decided to take the plunge. Even so, their determination was not nearly so impressive as the opposition's proved to be, at least initially.

An order of October 1844 requiring the Board of Guardians of Rochdale to assume the relief of the poor was received with a public outcry uncomfortably reminiscent of 1837. Huge petitions were drawn up, mass meetings were held, deputations were sent off to Parliament and the Board of Guardians refused to comply. The Commissioners responded by taking legal proceedings against the Guardians but this led, as had similar action against the Todmorden overseers six years before, to appeals and a long legal dispute, which meant, in practice, that the whole question was deferred until the following year. At the same time the Commissioners quietly abandoned their plans for bringing Oldham and Ashton into line.

In 1845 the Commissioners had far better luck. In Rochdale a boycott of the usual March Board of Guardians election was overcome by means of an extraordinary election held under the auspices of the ex-officio Guardians, and the handful of Guardians produced at this election was prevailed upon to put the law into effect. In the last quarter of the year a similar election led without difficulty to the same result in Ashton. Only Oldham therefore remained, but it held out much as Rochdale had done the year

[1] On Ashton, Oldham and Rochdale see: P.L.C., Twelfth Annual Report, *B.P.P.*, XIX, 17–18; MH 12.5413 Sept. 1844–Dec. 1845 correspondence.

before and not until the spring of 1846 were the Commissioners able, once again on the Rochdale pattern, to subdue it.

The Commissioners' determination in handling Rochdale, Oldham and Ashton was as extraordinary as the situation they had to contend with there. Essentially they had no choice but to intervene and bring these wholly anomalous Unions into line. On the other hand, where they did have a choice, the Commissioners almost always opted for conciliation and for normal routine administration rather than drama and conflict. Advance, in short, was effectively abandoned in favor of consolidation. By this time to be sure the Commissioners had something worth consolidating. Advances had been made. No Union was as independent as it had been two or more years before. All were subject to a few at least of the Commissioners' major regulations. It was perhaps legitimate after 1844 for the Commissioners to hope that a combination of constant inspection and above all, careful auditing, for which better provision was being made at just this time, would gradually bring the actual administration of relief into line with the letter of the regulations which had been issued to the northern Unions.[1] Even so, the situation in the North to which the Commissioners began in practice to resign themselves in 1844 fell very far short of even their minimum goals of a few years before. The discrepancy between theory and practice in such things as the administration of relief, the appointment of personnel and the management of workhouses might well be closed in time, but it was not likely to happen for years and, even if it did, the goal of regional let alone national uniformity remained and seemed likely to remain as far from realization as ever.

[1] The Poor Law Act of 1844 allowed the appointment of district auditors, P.L.C., Eleventh Annual Report, 13–14, 87. According to R. Boyson, *The History of Poor Law Administration in North-East Lancashire* (unpublished M.A. thesis Manchester 1960) it was through closer auditing primarily that greater control over the northern Boards of Guardians was eventually established.

XII Conclusion

The compromise or stalemate of 1844 was not quite the end of the story. In 1852, five years after it had replaced the Poor Law Commission, the Poor Law Board decided to complete the work abandoned in 1844 and issued a Labour Test Order to all of the Poor Law Unions in southern Lancashire and the central West Riding of Yorkshire.[1] Despite considerable opposition from the Guardians, the Poor Law Board persisted and by the end of 1852, almost exactly fifteen years after the Poor Law Commissioners had originally hoped to complete their work, the administration of relief to the able-bodied was at last subject to identical regulations throughout the textile districts. In theory this marked a considerable advance over the position of eight years before, but in practice the changes it made in the actual conduct of relief in the North and in the relations between the northern Boards of Guardians and the central authorities in London were small. The Poor Law Board's original order met with immediate opposition from most of the northern Boards of Guardians, which quickly set about composing memorials and petitions to the Poor Law Board, and, more often than not, continued to relieve the poor in deliberate defiance of the order. When, as expected, the Poor Law Board refused to compromise, the Oldham Guardians suggested that a protest and strategy meeting of delegates from all the Unions affected be held in Manchester late in October. The response was immediate and very nearly unanimous. Seventeen of the twenty-five Unions in the area as well as a number of Unions elsewhere in the North and Midlands sent delegates and the meeting voted without dissent to draw up a petition against the order, send a deputation to Somerset House and, should this fail, petition Parliament.

The Poor Law Board, faced with the most concerted opposition it or its predecessor had ever encountered, backed down. Restrictions on the percentage of relief that could be given in money to the ill, aged or widows were dropped, thus limiting the effects of the order to able-bodied males, and allowing the Boards of Guardians

[1] For the Labour Test Order and the controversy surrounding it see: *M.G.* 11 Sept.–22 Dec. 1852; Poor Law Board, Fifth Annual Report, *B.P.P.*, 1852–3, L, 15–6, 24–31.

complete discretion in dealing with other classes of paupers. The clauses prohibiting relief in aid of wages and requiring a labor test for all able-bodied male applicants were not dropped or altered but through the re-interpretation of these clauses and the re-writing of others they were significantly relaxed. For example, though it is highly unlikely that this is what it intended originally, the Poor Law Board assured the northern Guardians that the pro-hibition of relief in aid of wages was intended to apply only to those who sought relief on the grounds of inadequate wages and that relief given to a partially employed man to support him during that part of the week when he was unemployed would not be con-sidered a violation of the regulations. Similarly, while the require-ment of a labor test remained intact, the freedom of the Guardians to grant relief in direct violation of the order was broadened considerably. All such violations had to be reported to the Poor Law Board which could then allow or disallow them as it saw fit; but the deadline for reporting was extended from two to three weeks and the Poor Law Board gave up the right to ex post facto disallowance. This meant, in effect, that the northern Boards of Guardians would have a grace period of about a month in which they could grant relief virtually without restrictions, and even after that the re-interpretation of the prohibition of relief in aid of wages together with the usual exceptions made for sudden and urgent necessity, illness and so on provided enormous scope for local discretion. Far from being as tough or tougher than the Labour Test Orders issued nine or ten years before, which is certainly what the Poor Law Board had hoped for, the 1852 order was significantly less stringent.

The impact of the new Labour Test Order was limited in another respect as well. It involved no innovation in principle since a Labour Test Order was already in force in 20 per cent of the Poor Law Unions in the district. Nor did the Poor Law Board intend, as Mott and perhaps the Commissioners as well had intended a decade before, to use the introduction of the labor test as a means of opening the way to further advances. The Poor Law Board contented itself with completing the work begun in Keighley in 1842, entirely within the limits set by what had already been achieved. In so doing the Board more or less explicitly accepted what the Commissioners had implicitly acknowledged in 1844, that the North was a special area distinct from the rest of the country and that there were limits to what any central authority could hope to achieve there. That the stalemate of 1844 was in fact a turning point was a proposition that would have astonished the Poor Law Commissioners had anyone suggested it to them at the time. There is no reason to believe that they intended the existing relationship with the northern Boards of Guardians to define the outer limits of their future authority in the North, and why they relaxed their pressure at this time is therefore a difficult question to answer. Political and economic conditions in 1844 presented no obstacles and the Andover scandal, the first of the almost innumerable revelations about workhouse conditions to undermine the Commissioners' authority seriously, was not to break for another year. Not that Andover wasn't important, even in the North. By immobilizing and then destroying the Poor Law Commission the scandal there probably played an important role in transforming the stalemate of 1844 from a temporary into a permanent condition. It may simply be that the Commissioners, once the worst of the relief crisis was over, decided to reduce pressure in the North for a time in the hope that this would create a better climate for later advances, but that they were then overwhelmed by the Andover scandal before they could seize the initiative once again.[1]

In any case, whatever reasons the Commissioners may have had for accepting a compromise in 1844 and allowing it to continue thereafter, they are, in a wider context, of secondary importance. For, if a stalemate had not come then, it would have come a year or two or at most a few years later. At what point the Commissioners realized they would have to make some permanent concessions in the North was a matter of chance or choice, but that they would have to sooner or later was not. A compromise more or less along the lines of what emerged in 1844 was inevitable, possibly as early as 1837, certainly well before the Commissioners launched their second campaign in the North late in 1841. Both the Commissioners and the opponents of the New Poor Law were of course slow to recognize this. They continued to hope for victory long after any realistic prospect of it had vanished. The opposition's hopes were illusory from the very beginning. The failure to muster even a respectable number of votes against the passage of the New Poor Law precluded the possibility of wearing

[1] On the Andover scandal and its effects see: Webb, Poor Law History, Part II, Vol. I, 179–88; Reports and minutes of Evidence of the Select Committee on the Andover Union, B.P.P., 1846, V.

down the Poor Law Commissioners through constant attack from within the House of Commons, and, when popular resistance to the new law in rural England also failed to develop, the opposition rightly began to despair. The emergence of spontaneous resistance early in 1837 revived the opposition's hopes, but not their realistic prospects. Only something approaching a national movement with effective representation in Parliament would have been sufficient to check let alone reverse the progress of the Poor Law Commissioners, and there was never the slightest chance of these conditions being fulfilled. Once this had become clear beyond dispute, as it had by the spring of 1838, opposition to the Poor Law as a mass movement, the *raison d'être* of which was the promise of total victory, was bound to disintegrate and would have done so even had there been no growing Chartist movement to siphon off leadership and support.

This did not mean, however, that the popular resistance movement was pointless or that its importance lay solely in its legacy to northern Chartism. It failed only in terms of its own over-ambitious goals; judged by any less exacting standards it was a success. Without popular resistance the administrative machinery of the New Poor Law would have been introduced long before the end of 1837, the electoral and financial boycotts would have been limited to individual townships and therefore ineffectual, and the Commissioners would have felt free to compel compliance with the law rather than trying to win it through major concessions. As it was, though the Commissioners long refused to recognize this, the delays and concessions won by popular resistance permanently changed the conditions in which public welfare policy in urban areas was to develop. Relief policy, instead of being determined at the beginning along with the administrative structure of the Poor Law Unions, was left open, thereby becoming a subject for future negotiations. What is more, the discretion granted to the northern Boards of Guardians, together with the legal and practical limitations on the Commissioners' powers written into or implicit within the Poor Law Amendment Act, meant that the Guardians entered these negotiations with as much freedom of action and nearly as much leverage as the Commissioners possessed. To have returned from this to the sort of relationship the Commissioners had envisaged in 1837 would have been exceedingly difficult under any circumstances. During a major depression, when the Boards of Guardians had immediate and compelling reasons for holding on to their independence, it was impossible.

This, however, is only half the story. There is another and perhaps more important reason why a compromise more or less along the lines set out in 1844 was inevitable. Not only had both sides by this time implicitly accepted a stalemate, but there is every reason to believe that neither the Commissioners nor the northern opponents of the Poor Law any longer had a clear conception of how public welfare in industrial areas ought to be provided for. There can be little question that by this time the Commissioners were no longer committed to the implementation of the full rigors of the Poor Law Amendment Act in industrial areas. Doubts on this score dated back at least six or seven years, though their importance in the late 1830s can easily be exaggerated. Other factors, such as popular and Parliamentary opposition and the state of the economy, played an equally if not more important part in the Commissioners' decision to delay the introduction of many of their policies into the North. After 1842, however, there are clear indications that delays, which had been made initially largely for tactical reasons, were being extended because the Commissioners were no longer convinced of the relevance of some of their policies to northern conditions. This is exceedingly hard to pin down. The Commissioners no longer publicly explained or justified their actions as they always had in the years immediately following the passage of the New Poor Law. Nor, for that matter, did they admit to a change of tactics, let alone of policy. The change is evident more in what they did not do and say than in any positive words or actions.

First of all, the missionary zeal so characteristic of their early annual reports is entirely missing after about 1842. The decline of Edwin Chadwick was undoubtedly largely responsible for this, but not entirely. The tone and emphasis of the reports from Assistant Commissioners, who had always been Chadwick's staunchest allies, also began to change at this time. Long letters utilizing conditions in particular Unions as the occasion for extended essays on the applicability of the full rigors of the Law throughout industrial England, very common before 1843, gradually gave way thereafter to brief summary reports written on standard forms. In part, no doubt, this was simply one of the results of the effect of the passage of time in changing the New Poor Law from a cause into a matter of routine administration, but it also reflected a growing recognition of the complexity of the problems in the North and of the difficulties involved in applying many of the Commissioners' regulations to them. Thus, for example, the imposition of the workhouse test in the North was almost never mentioned after 1842, and the abandonment of Prohibitory Order in Nottingham and of the workhouses themselves in Todmorden in 1844 probably also marks the final abandonment of the concept of a workhouse test in industrial areas. If to this is added the manner in which the Commissioners backed away from the problems of rent payments and non-resident relief, the conclusion that they were suffering from a loss of self-confidence is inescapable.[1]

Yet, while the Commissioners by the middle 1840s were to a very large extent on the defensive, their opponents in the North were hardly in a position to take advantage of this. However often, and frequently with good reason, it complained that the Commissioners were essentially negative, that they were obsessed with restrictions and tests, that they were oblivious to the needs of the honest applicant for relief and that they failed to understand the peculiarities of the North, the opposition was no better off. It criticized the New Poor Law and demanded something more flexible, but it had no more idea than the Poor Law Commissioners did of how to cope with really severe distress. At no time did the major opponents in the North or elsewhere suggest a positive alternative.

In a way this is surprising, for a genuine alternative, social insurance, did exist and was at that time beginning to be put into practice on a large scale by the friendly societies.[2] The first decade of the New Poor Law in the North coincided with the first period of major growth of the most important of these societies, the Manchester Unity of Oddfellows. During those years its membership more than doubled and by the end of the period it was a truly national organization, though the bulk of its local affiliates and membership were still in the northern industrial districts where it had begun. The role which the friendly societies, even large ones like the Oddfellows or the somewhat later Foresters, could hope to play was, of course, relatively small. Few even attempted to go

---

[1] Compare the Commissioners' Annual Reports through 1842 with those from 1843 onwards, and also the correspondence of Mott and Power (MH 32.57, MH 32.63-4) with that of Austin and Clements (MH 32.7, MH 32.11).

[2] For the early growth of the Friendly Societies and their relationship with the state and the Poor Law Commissioners see: P. H. J. H. Gosden, *The Friendly Societies in England* (Manchester 1960).

beyond the provision of sickness benefits and burial expenses, and, since all contributions came from the members themselves, only the better-off workmen could afford to participate.

To overcome these deficiencies, to extend the functions of the friendly societies to include unemployment insurance or retirement benefits, and, above all, to make it possible for the great majority of the poor to participate, would have required a government-run or at least government-sponsored scheme, based very largely on public contributions. The creation of such a system was not as inconceivable in the early nineteenth century as might be imagined. The idea of state aid to the friendly societies had been fairly common a generation before and had even been incorporated to a limited extent in Pitt's abortive Poor Law reform proposals of 1796. Primitive and far from anything like a national insurance system as such proposals were, they did at least acknowledge the principle of public participation in a system of social insurance as a possible means of solving the problem of public welfare, if only for the working poor. What might have been built up on such a basis we do not know for in the generation after 1800 speculation along these lines was rapidly pushed aside by the growth of an alternative conception of the state and its role in public welfare, of which the Poor Law itself was the prime example.

The friendly societies were no longer looked to as models for a system of state aided public welfare but as examples of what could be achieved in the way of self help by the working classes. 'The rapid growth among the sound-hearted British populace of sick clubs and other Friendly Societies was the honourable substitute for the parish relief of the semi-slave by act of Parliament.'[1] These were the sentiments of the Grand Master of the Manchester Unity of Oddfellows and most other friendly society administrators would have endorsed them. So, too, would the Poor Law Commissioners, one of whose proudest claims, probably well founded, was that the tightening up of relief policy had driven many of the poor to seek economic independence and security through membership in the friendly societies.

What is strange is that the opponents of the New Poor Law, who dissented so strongly from the assumptions underlying such statements, never put forward the obvious alternative. At times they came frustratingly close. One pamphleteer declared metaphorically that 'the Poor Law is [the Labourer's] policy of insurance

[1] *Ibid.* 198.

and his labour . . . is the premium.' But neither he nor anyone else at this time took this argument to its logical conclusion and sought to transfer the metaphor into practice. The opposition merely opposed and, as long as they did nothing else, the Poor Law Commissioners, however inadequate their policies, had the advantage. The most that the anti-Poor Law movement could realistically hope to achieve was what had been achieved by 1844, delay, a demonstration of the inadequacy of the Law, and some modification of its rigors. Anything more substantial would have to wait until a positive alternative to the New Poor Law was put forward, and that was not to happen for more than half a century.

Appendix

(a) Statistics of Poor Law Unions in the textile districts of Lancashire, North Cheshire and the West Riding of Yorkshire

Name of Union	Counties in which situated	Pop. in 1,000s 1841	Area in 1,000 acres	No. of townships	No. of Guardians	Relief under B. of G.
Ashton	Ch., La.	102	41	13	20	1845
Blackburn	Lancs.	75	33	24	29	Oct. '37
Bolton	Lancs.	98	41	26	33	1839
Bradford	Yorks.	132	36	20	32	Dec. '37
Burnley	Lancs.	54	44	26	33	Sep. '38
Bury	Lancs.	77	33	12	25	1840
Chorley	Lancs.	39	38	25	27	Dec. '38
Chorlton	Lancs.	94	24	12	19	Sep. '37
Clitheroe	Yo., La.	23	130	33	35	Dec. '38
Dewsbury	Yorks.	61	24	11	23	Sep. '38
Halifax	Yorks.	109	52	19	31	Mar. '38
Haslingden	Lancs.	41	19	10	18	July '38
Huddersfield	Yorks.	107	69	34	41	Sep. '38
Keighley	Yorks.	36	36	6	16	Aug. '38
Leigh	Lancs.	29	15	8	18	Nov. '37
Manchester	Lancs.	192	12	12	24	1841
Oldham	Lancs.	72	16	8	21	1846
Preston	Lancs.	77	61	29	35	July '38
Rochdale	Lancs.	61	33	6	19	1845
Salford	Lancs.	70	5	4	18	Aug. '38
Stockport	Ch., La.	86	26	16	21	June '38
Todmorden	Yo., La.	32	22	6	18	Aug. '38
Wakefield	Yorks.	46	38	17	22	Dec. '37
Warrington	Lancs.	33	24	15	18	Sep. '37
Wigan	Lancs.	66	45	20	27	Aug. '38

Name of Union	New workhouse built	No. of workhouses 1846	Workhouse capacity	Labor test order issued	Relief costs in £100's for year ending March		
					1840	1843	1846
Ashton		1	145	1847	80	118	60
Blackburn		1	650		75	158	88
Bolton		2	412			247	120
Bradford		2	230	1843	174	285	195
Burnley		2	310		93	179	96
Bury		4	432			137	146
Chorley		2	370		60	100	65
Chorlton	1840	1	396		51	131	96
Clitheroe		2	180		87	104	61
Dewsbury		3	233			141	104
Halifax	1839	1	425	1843	138	199	169
Haslingden		2	190		39	77	46
Huddersfield		5	301		122	218	150
Keighley		2	101	1842	56	82	65
Leigh		2	238		46	68	49
Manchester	1842	1	1265			511	590
Oldham					68	147	95
Preston		4	791		124	235	125
Rochdale		5	262		62	115	95
Salford		1	350		79	103	93
Stockport	1841	1	690		106	236	99
Todmorden		0			44	90	61
Wakefield		1	150			146	124
Warrington		2	280	1843	64	94	77
Wigan		2	480		96	150	102

(b) The Northern Unions in comparison
with England and Wales as a whole

Population
Seventeen of the twenty-five unions in the area were among the fifty most populous in the country. The median population of the Poor Law Unions in the country as a whole was 18,500; in the textile districts it was 68,000.

Area
Area of unions in acres:

	Country	North
Largest	211,719	129,990
Median	48,000	34,000

Workhouses
The number of unions having:

	Country	North
1 workhouse	541	9
2 workhouses	46	10
3 workhouses	10	1
4 workhouses	4	2
5 workhouses	2	2

Relief Orders
The number of unions subject to:

	Country	North
Prohibitory order only	388	0
Prohibitory and labor test orders	79	0
Labor test order only	32	5
Ordinary restrictions on out-relief	25	0
None of the above	49	20

s

Bibliography

The titles of pamphlets in the Oastler Collection, Goldsmith's Library, Senate House, London, are followed by the word Oastler and the appropriate volume number in brackets. Among the unpublished official documents, the Ministry of Health and Home Office Papers are in the Public Records Office, London, and the Board of Guardians Minute Books are in the Lancashire County Record Office, Preston, Lancashire (except the Salford Minute Books which are in Salford Town Hall).

(1) Secondary sources

Aschrott, P. F., *The English Poor Law System Past and Present*. London, 1902.

Ashworth, T. Edwin, *An Account of the Todmorden Poor Law Riots*. n.p., 1901.

Beales, H. L., 'The Poor Law', *History*, XV (1931).

Beer, Max, *A History of British Socialism*, 2 vols. London, 1953.

Blaug, Mark, 'The Myth of the Old Poor Law and the Making of the New', *Journal of Economic History*, XXIII (1963).—'The Poor Law Report Re-examined', *Journal of Economic History*, XXIV (1964).

Bowley, Marian, *Nassau Senior and Classical Economics*. London, 1937.

Boyson, Rhodes, *The History of Poor Law Administration in North-East Lancashire*. Unpublished M.A. Thesis, Manchester, 1960.

Briggs, Asa, ed., *Chartist Studies*. London, 1959.

Clapham, J. H., *An Economic History of Modern Britain: The Early Railway Age 1820–1850*. Cambridge, 1930.

Cole, George Douglas Howard, *Chartist Portraits*. London, 1965.— *The Life of William Cobbett*. London, 1947.

Croft, W. R., *The History of the Factory Movement; or, Oastler and His Times*. Huddersfield, 1888.

Driver, Cecil, *Tory Radical: The Life of Richard Oastler*. New York, 1946.

Dyos, H. J., ed., *The Study of Urban History*. London, 1968.

Fay, C. R., *Life and Labour in the Nineteenth Century*. Cambridge, 1933.

Finer, S. E., *The Life and Times of Sir Edwin Chadwick*. London, 1952.

Fowle, T. W., *The Poor Law*. London, 1906.

Gammage, R. G., *History of the Chartist Movement 1837–1854*. London, 1894.

Gayer, Arthur, Rostow, W. W., and Schwartz, Anna Jacobson, *The Growth and Fluctuation of the British Economy 1790–1850*. 2 vols. Oxford, 1953.

Gill, J. C., *The Ten Hours Parson*. London, 1959.

Gosden, P. H. J. H., *The Friendly Societies in England 1815–1875*. Manchester, 1961.

Hammond, J. L. and Barbara, *The Age of the Chartists*. Hamden, Conn., 1962.

Hill, R. L., *Toryism and the People*. London, 1929.

Hobsbawm, Eric J., *Labouring Men*. London, 1964.

Holden, Joshua, *A Short History of Todmorden*. Manchester, 1912.

Holyoake, George Jacob, *Life of Joseph Rayner Stephens*. London, 1881.

Hovell, Mark, *The Chartist Movement*. Manchester, 1959.

Kydd, Samuel (Alfred), *The History of the Factory Movement*. London, 1857.

Maccoby, S., *English Radicalism 1832–1852*. London, 1935.

Mackay, Thomas, *A History of the English Poor Law from 1834 to the Present Time*. London, 1899.

Mather, F. C., *Public Order in the Age of the Chartists*. Manchester, 1959.

Matthews, R. C. O., *A Study in Trade Cycle History*. Cambridge, 1954.

McLachlan, H., *The Methodist Unitarian Movement*. Manchester, 1919.

Napier, W., *The Life and Opinions of General Sir Charles James Napier*, 4 vols. London, 1857.

Nicholls, George, *A History of the English Poor Law*, 2 vols. London, 1898.

Pearce, John, *Life and Teachings of Joseph Livesey*. London, 1886.

Read, Donald, *Press and People*, London, 1961.—*The English Provinces, c. 1760–1960. A Study in Influence*. London, 1964—and Glasgow, Eric, *Feargus O'Connor*. London, 1961.

Redford, Arthur, *Labour Migration in England 1800–1850*. Manchester, 1964.

Redlich, Josef, *The History of Local Government in England*. London, 1958.

Robbins, Lionel, *The Theory of Economic Policy in English Classical Political Economy*. London, 1952.

Rose, Michael E., 'The Anti-Poor Law Movement in the North of England', *Northern History*, I (1966).

Rosenblatt, Frank F., 'The Chartist Movement in its Social and Economic Aspects', *Columbia University Studies in History*, LXXIII (1916).

Rudé, George, *The Crowd in History 1730–1848*. New York, 1964.

Sykes, D. F. E., *The History of Huddersfield and Its Vicinity*. Huddersfield, 1898.

Ward, J.T., *The Factory Movement 1830–1855*. London, 1962.— 'Revolutionary Tory: The Life of Joseph Raynor Stephens', *Transactions of the Lancashire and Cheshire Antiquarian Society*, XLVIII (1959).—*Popular Movements, 1830–50*, London, 1970.

Webb, Sidney and Beatrice, *English Poor Law History; Part II: The*

Last 100 Years, 2 vols. London, 1963.—*English Poor Law Policy.* London, 1963.

West, Julius, *A History of the Chartist Movement*, 1920.

(2) Contemporary books and pamphlets

An Address to the English Nation Against the New Poor Law. London, 1839. [Oastler 13.]

An Address to the People of Nottingham on the New Poor Laws, by the Nottingham Workingmen's Association. London, 1838. [Oastler 16.]

Baxter, G. R. Wythen, *The Book of the Bastilles; or the History of the Working of the New Poor Law.* London, 1841.

Bentham, Jeremy, 'Tracts on Poor Laws and Pauper Management', *The Works of Jeremy Bentham*, Vol. VIII. Edinburgh, 1843.

Blakey, Robert, *Cottage Politics; or Letters on the New Poor Bill.* London, 1837.

Bligh, Richard, *Bellum Agrarium: A Foreview of the Winter of 1835.* London, 1834.

Bowen, John, *The New Poor Law: The Bridgewater Case.* London, 1839. [Oastler 12.]—*A Refutation of Some of the Charges Preferred Against the Poor.* London, 1837. [Oastler 11.]—*The Union Workhouse and Board of Guardians System.* London, 1842.

Brooker, Charles, *An Appeal to the British Nation.* Brighton, 1840.—*The Murder Den and Its Means of Destruction.* Brighton, 1842.—*The Rejoinder.* Brighton, 1841.

Brougham, Henry Peter, *Corrected Report of the Lord Chancellor's Speech . . . on the Poor Laws.* London, 1834.

Bull, George Stringer, *The New Poor Law Shewn to be Unconstitutional*, etc. London, 1838. [Oastler 12.]—*The Oppression of the Poor and the Poor Their Own Oppressors: A Sermon.* Bradford, 1839. [Oastler 13.] —*The Poor Law Act.* Bradford, 1834. [Oastler 8.]—*The Substance of a Lecture on the New Poor Law Act.* Bradford, 1835.

Butler, Rev. W. J., *A Friendly Letter Addressed to Richard Oastler* London, 1838. [Oastler 12.]

Chadwick, Edwin, *The Principles and Progress of the Poor Law Amendment Act.* London, 1837.

Cobbett, William, *Legacy to Labourers.* London, 1835.

Cookesley, W. G., *A Letter to the Ratepayers of Eton.* London, 1841.

Crewe, George, *A Word for the Poor and Against the Present Poor Law.* Derby, 1843.

Day, John, *A Few Practical Observations on the New Poor Law.* London, 1838.

Downing,—(anon.), *A Series of Letters on Rural Police and the Poor Law Amendment Act.* Ipswich, 1838.

Duncombe, Rev. Edward, *Gilbertise the New Poor Law.* York, 1841.

Edmonds, George, *Appeal to the Labourers of England.* London, 1835.

Fletcher, Matthew, *Migration of Agricultural Labourers*. Bury, n.d. [Oastler 15.]

Gaskell, P., *Prospects of Industry*. London, 1835.

Gower, S., *What Are the Poor Laws For?* London, 1837. [Oastler 15.]
—*A Word or Two to Mr. George Tinker*. Holmfirth, 1837. [Oastler 15.]

Great Meeting at the Crown and Anchor on the Inhuman Poor Law Act. London, 1838. [Oastler 16.]

Gurney, J. H., *The New Poor Law Explained and Vindicated*. London, 1841.

Hart, Rev. John, *The Cause of the Widow and Fatherless Child Defended*. Manchester, 1839. [Oastler 16.]

Higgins, William, *To the Labourers of England*. Royston, 1835.

James, Walter, *Thoughts Upon the Theory and Practice of the Poor Laws*. London, 1847.

Kersey, R., *A Letter to the Venerable Archdeacon Lyall . . . in Consequence of a Visit to Manchester*. Hadleigh, 1835.

Latey, John Lash (anon.), *Letters to the Working People on the New Poor Law, by a Working Man*. London, 1841.

Leslie, John, *Further Illustrations of the Principles Upon Which a Metropolitan Poor Rate is Administered*. London, 1836.—*A Letter to the Industrious Classes on the Operation of the Poor Law*. London, 1835. —*A Practical Illustration of the Principles Upon Which the Poor Law Amendment Act is Founded*. London, 1835.—*Remarks on the Present State of the Poor Law Question*. London, 1834.

Lewis, George Cornewall (anon.), *The English Poor Laws and Poor Law Commission in 1847*. London, 1847.

Lloyd, William Foster, *Two Lectures on the Poor Laws*. London, 1836.

Longfield, Montiford, *Four Lectures on the Poor Laws*. Dublin, 1834.

Maberly, Rev. F. H., *To the Poor and Their Friends*. London, 1836. [Oastler 14.]

Malthus, Thomas Robert, *An Essay on the Principle of Population*. London, 1803 (2nd edition).

Marshall, Rev. Henry Johnson, *On the Tendency of the New Poor Law Seriously to Impair the Morals and Condition of the Working Classes*. London, 1842.

Marsten, Thomas, *Reform and Workhouses*. Lynn, 1835.

McCulloch, J. R., *The Literature of Political Economy*. London, 1845.

Muggeridge, R. M. (anon.), *A Voice From the North of England On the New Poor Law*. London, 1837.

Nevile, Rev. Christopher, *The New Poor Law Justified*. London, 1838.

Nicholls, Robert, *Practical Remarks on the Severities of the New Poor Law*. London, 1837. [Oastler 15.]

Noakes, William, *Report of a Journey to Manchester*. Sandwich, 1836.

Oastler, Richard, *Brougham Versus Brougham on the New Poor Law*. London, 1847. [Oastler 10.]—*Damnation! Eternal Damnation to the*

Fiend Begotten, 'Coarser Food' New Poor Law. London, 1837. [Oastler 12.]—*Eight Letters to the Duke of Wellington.* London, 1835. [Oastler 8.]—*Letter to the Bishop of Exeter.* Manchester, 1838. [Oastler 16.]—*Letter to Nobility, Clergy, Farmers and Shopkeepers of the County of Nottingham.* n.p., 1839. [Oastler 13.]—*A Letter to Viscount Morpeth, MP.* London, 1837. [Oastler 15.]—*The New Poor Law Act.* Bradford, 1835. [Oastler 3.]—*The Right of the Poor Law to Liberty and Life.* London, 1838. [Oastler 12.]

Observations on the Poor Laws and the Effects of Their Administration on the Parish of Sunderland, by a Practical Man. Bishopwearmouth, 1840.

On the Possibility of Limiting Populousness, by Marcus. London, 1839. [Oastler 13.]

Osborne, Lord Sidney Godolphin (anon.), *The Prospects and Present Condition of the Labouring Classes, by a Beneficed Clergyman.* London, 1834?—*A Word or Two About the New Poor Law, by a Beneficed Clergyman.* London, 1834?

Palmer, William, *Principles of the Legal Provision for the Relief of the Poor.* London, 1844.

The Peers, the People and the Poor, by a Retired Tradesman. London, 1838. [Oastler 13.]

Poor Law Act: Public Meeting at Bradford. n.p., 1837.

The Poor Law Bill Exposed: Is It a Whig Measure? by a Friend to the Manufacturers. Huddersfield, 1837. [Oastler 11.]

The Poor Robbed and the Aristocracy Receivers of the Stolen Property, by an Englishman. London, 1836.

Porter, G. R., *Progress of the Nation.* London, 1851.

A Reply to a Letter to the Poor Law Commissioners, by a Guardian of the Basingstoke Union. Winchester, 1837.

Roberts, Samuel, *Lessons for Statesmen.* London, 1846.—*Lord Brougham and the New Poor Laws.* London, 1838. [Oastler 12.]

Roworth, W., *Observations on the Administration of the New Poor Law in Nottingham.* London, 1840.

Sandby, Rev. G., *Discretionary Power.* London, 1841.

Sclater, William, *A Letter to the Poor Law Commissioners for England and Wales on the Working of the New System.* Basingstoke, 1836.

Scrope, G. Poulett, *The Rights of Industry.* London, 1848.

Senior, Nassau, 'English Poor Laws', *Historical and Philosophical Essays,* 2 vols. London, 1865.—(anon.) *Remarks on the Opposition to the Poor Law Amendment Bill, by a Guardian.* London, 1841.

Spedding, Thomas Storey, *Letters on the Poor Laws,* London, 1847.

Spencer, Rev. Thomas, *The New Poor Law; Its Evils and Their Remedies.* London, 1841.—*Objections to the New Poor Law Answered.* London, 1841.—*The Outcry Against the New Poor Law.* London, 1841.—*The Successful Application of the New Poor Law to the Parish of Hinton Charterhouse*. London, 1836.—*The Want of Fidelity in Ministers of Religion Respecting the New Poor Law*. London, 1841.

Stanhope, Earl, *New Poor Law. Letter from Earl Stanhope to Mr. Richard Oastler*. London, 1837. [Oastler 11.]

Stephen, George, *A Letter to the Honourable Lord John Russell*. London, 1836.

Stephens, Joseph Rayner, *The Political Preacher: An Appeal From the Pulpit on Behalf of the Poor*. London, 1839. [Oastler 13.]—*Three Sermons Preached by the Rev. J. R. Stephens*. London, 1839. [Oastler 13.]

Taylor, W. Cooke, *Notes of a Tour in the Manufacturing Districts of Lancashire*. London, 1842.

Vincent, George Giles, *A Letter to John Bowen Exposing the Unprincipled Nature of the New Poor Law*. London, 1838. [Oastler 12.]

Wade, John, *Appendix to the Black Book*. London, 1835.—*History and Political Philosophy of the Middle and Working Classes*. Edinburgh, 1842.

Walter, John, *A Letter to the Electors of Berkshire*. London, 1834. [Oastler 10.]

Wilmot, —, *Disinherited*. London, 1835.

Wilson, Rev. William Carus, *Remarks on Certain Operations of the New Poor Laws*. Kirkby Lonsdale, 1838. [Oastler 12.]

Young, A. A., *The Poor Law: Is Any Alternative of it Necessary or Tolerably Practicable?* London, 1839.

(3) Published official documents
(a) Miscellaneous
Hansard, *Parliamentary Debates*, Third Series, 1834–42.
Lumley, William Golden, *A Collection of Statutes of General Use Relating to the Relief of the Poor*. London, 1843.
Poor Law Commissioners, *Official Circulars*, 6 vols. London 1840–6.

(b) British Parliamentary papers
Poor Law Commission Reports:
Report of H.M. Commission for Inquiring into the Administration and Practical Operation of the Poor Laws. 1834, XXVII (Report); XXVIII–XXX, XXXIV–IX (Appendices).
First Annual Report. 1835, XXV.
Second Annual Report. 1836, XXIX.
Third Annual Report. 1837, XXXI.
Fourth Annual Report. 1838, XXVIII.
Fifth Annual Report. 1839, XX.
Sixth Annual Report. 1840, XVII.
Report on the Continuation of the Poor Law Commission. 1840, XVII.
Seventh Annual Report. 1841, XI.

Eighth Annual Report. 1842, XIX.
Report of Commission for Inquiring into the State of the Population of Stockport. 1842, XXXV.
Returns Relating to the Keighley Union. 1842, XXXV.
Communications to the Home Office on Distress on Bolton. 1842, XXXV.
Report to the Poor Law Commissioners on the State of the Poor in Rochdale. 1842, XXXV.
Ninth Annual Report. 1843, XXI.
Tenth Annual Report. 1844, XIX.
Eleventh Annual Report. 1845, XXVII.
Twelfth Annual Report. 1846, XIX.
Copy of a Report Relative to the Bolton and Macclesfield Unions. 1846, XXXVI.
Thirteenth Annual Report. 1847, XXVIII.
Fourteenth Annual Report. 1848, XXXIII.

Miscellaneous
Report from the Select Committee on the Poor Law Amendment Act. 1837, XVII.
Report from the Select Committee on the Poor Law Amendment Act. 1838, XVIII.
Report of H.M. Commission on the Handloom Weavers. 1841, X (Report); 1839, XLII and 1840, XLIII–IV (Assistant Commissioners Reports).
Abstract of Answers and Returns Under the Population Act: Occupation Abstract. 1844, XXVII.
Report and Minutes of Evidence of the Select Committee on the Andover Union. 1846, V.

(4) Unpublished official documents
(a) Ministry of Health, Poor Law Union papers:
Bedfordshire:
    Ampthill MH 12.1
Berkshire:
    Hungerford MH 12.234
Buckinghamshire:
    Amersham MH 12.380
Cheshire:
    Macclesfield MH 12.968–9
    Stockport MH 12.1138–40
Cornwall:
    Camelford MH 12.1299
    Falmouth MH 12.1338
    Stratton MH 12.1516

Cumberland:
  Bootle MH 12.1565
Derbyshire:
  Glossop MH 12.2021
Devonshire:
  Barnstaple MH 12.2124
  Okehampton MH 12.2394
  South Molton MH 12.2493
  Torrington MH 12.2636
Durham:
  Easington MH 12.3052
  Sunderland MH 12.3268
Essex:
  Saffron Walden MH 12.3706
Hertfordshire:
  Bishop's Stortford MH 12.4536
  Royston MH 12.4639
Huntingdonshire:
  Huntingdon MH 12.4716
Kent:
  Faversham MH 12.5054
  Milton MH 12.5279
Lancashire:
  Ashton MH 12.5413–4
  Blackburn MH 12.5529–30
  Bolton MH 12.5593–7
  Burnley MH 12.5673–4
  Clitheroe MH 12.5752
  Haslingden MH 12.5840
  Lancaster MH 12.5889
  Leigh MH 12.5926
  Manchester MH 12.6039–40
  Todmorden MH 12.6272–3
Leicestershire:
  Leicester MH 12.6468–71
  Loughborough MH 12.6523–4
Norfolk:
  Docking MH 12.8249
  Loddon and Clavering MH 12.8455
Northumberland:
  Newcastle MH 12.9096
Nottinghamshire:
  Nottingham MH 12.9444–7
Staffordshire:
  Stoke-on-Trent MH 12.11458

T

Suffolk:
  Cosford MH 12.11793
  Hoxne MH 12.11837
  Ipswich MH 12.11855
  Plomesgate MH 12.11932
Sussex:
  Eastbourne MH 12.12854
  Uckfield MH 12.13157
Yorkshire (North and East Ridings):
  Bridlington MH 12.14256
  Helmsley MH 12.14483–4
  Northallerton MH 12.14560
  Pateley Bridge MH 12.15289
  Pocklington MH 12.14344–5
Yorkshire (West Riding):
  Bradford MH 12.14720–5
  Dewsbury MH 12.14830–2
  Ecclesall MH 12.14938–9
  Halifax MH 12.14974–6
  Huddersfield MH 12.15063–8
  Keighley MH 12.15158–9
  Leeds MH 12.15224
  Rotherham MH 12.15368
  Sedburgh MH 12.15419
  Sheffield MH 12.15465–6
  Skipton MH 12.15512
  Wakefield MH 12.15566–8
  Wortley MH 12.15655
Wales:
  Anglesey MH 12.15673
  Bangor and Beaumaris MH 12.15964–5
  Builth MH 12.15734
  Caernarvon MH 12.15998
  Conway MH 12.16023
  Corwen MH 12.16486
  Dolgelly MH 12.16503
  Lampeter MH 12.15845
  Llanfyllin MH 12.16543
  Llanrwst MH 12.16075
  Machynlleth MH 12.16564
  Merthyr Tydfil MH 12.16326
  Newtown and Llanidloes MH 12.16597
  Presteigne MH 12.16709
  Wrexham MH 12.16104

(b) Ministry of Health, Reports from Assistant Commissioners:
Alfred Austin MH 32.7
Charles Clements MH 32.11
Charles Mott MH 32.57
Alfred Power MH 32.63–4

(c) Home Office papers
Disturbances: Communications from the Provinces
HO 40.35, 37 and 38
Disturbances: Communications to the Provinces
HO 41.13
Information Received from the Poor Law Commissioners
HO 73.51–5

(d) Boards of Guardians Minute Books: Lancashire
Ashton PUA 1/1
Bury PUB 1/2–3
Chorley PUX 1/1–3
Preston PUT 1/3 and 8
Rochdale PUR 1/4
Salford 2 Vols.
Warrington PUV 1/1–2
Wigan PUW 1/1–2

(5) Newspapers and periodicals
Blackburn Gazette, Blackburn Standard
Bolton Chronicle, Bolton Free Press
Bradford Observer
Halifax Express, Halifax Guardian
Leeds Intelligencer, Leeds Mercury, Northern Star, Leeds Times
London: *The Times*
Manchester and Salford Advertiser, Manchester Courier, Manchester Guardian
Preston Chronicle, Preston Pilot
Wigan Gazette
Periodicals: *Edinburgh Review, Monthly Chronicle, Quarterly Review, Westminster Review*

General index

Index of places

Index of people

Althorp, (John Charles Spencer) Viscount, 11n
Alvanley, (William Arden) Baron, 11n
Ashworth, Henry, 51–2, 207
Austin, Alfred, 251, 260n

Baines, Edward, 46
Barnett, Absolem, 49–51, 201–2
Battye, 95
Bentham, Jeremy, 2, 6
Bower, Samuel, 62, 72, 73
Brougham, (Henry Peter) Baron, 11, 20–1, 177
Bull, George Stringer, background, 60–1; and resistance in Burnley, 81, 144; and resistance in Bradford, 109–10, 123; testifies before select committee, 138, and Tory–Radical alliance, 77, 177–9; retirement, 181–2, 188; mentioned, 63, 188
Buller, Edward, 11n
Burdett, Sir Francis, 15n
Bussey, Peter, background, 62; in Bradford, 109; opposes Tory–Radical alliance, 190; Chartist delegate, 185, 188

Chadwick, Edwin, influence on Poor Law Amendment Act, 2, 5–7; favors strict administration of P.L., 49, 70, 215; feud with P.L.C., 166, 195–8; in anti-Poor Law propaganda, 189; effects of decline of on P.L.C. policy, 205, 259
Clegg, William, 63, 123, 139
Clements, Charles, assigned to North, 213; reports on northern conditions, 213–16; and workhouse policy, 220–3; and labor test, 242–9; and non-resident relief, 252; on Oldham, Rochdale and Ashton, 253; mentioned, 260n
Cobbett, William, in Parliament, 12n, 15; view of Poor Law, 21, 60, 177–178; *Legacy to Labourers*, 22–4; *Political Register*, 25; influence on

others, 34, 59; influence on anti-Poor Law propaganda, 124, 137
Condy, George, 120
Crossley, 159

Day, William, 131
Doherty, John, 59

Eldon, (John Scott) Earl, 11, 124
Evans, George, 11n, 15n
Exeter, Bishop of, 14n

Ferrand, William Busfield, 241
Fielden, John, background, 58–9; and W. Clegg, 63; advocates class cooperation, 76, 82; advocates boycott of P.L., 79; and Oldham, 80; and Todmorden in 1837, 81; proposes Lancashire anti-Poor Law association, 119; and G. Condy, 120; leads petition drive, 126; repeal motion defeated, 127, 170; in Parliament, 137–8; advocates further petitioning, 139; leads Todmorden opposition, 144–9; advocates nonpayment of rates, 149; and overseers' resistance, 151–2; and Todmorden riots, 159–60; views on the relationship between opposition to the Poor Law and radical reform, 169, 170, 174, 180
Fletcher, Matthew, background, 61–62; harasses Alfred Power, 68; and middle class, 76; and dissenters, 77; leads Bury opposition, 82–3; during 1837–8 petitioning campaign, 123, 125; advocates a run on banks, 139; and Bury vestry, 150; on radicalism and the anti-Poor Law movement, 170, 185; Chartist delegate, 185, 188

Gilbert, William John, 37–8, 39, 196
Graham, Sir James, 241
Grote, George, 11n
Gulson, 49–51, 136

Harewood, (Henry) Earl, 113